Edmund Lewis, o
Massachusetts and some
of his Descendants

George Harlan Lewis

Alpha Editions

This edition published in 2020

ISBN : 9789354026034

Design and Setting By
Alpha Editions
email - alphaedis@gmail.com

Ranter's Wharf

By

Rosemary Noble

EDMUND LEWIS

OF

LYNN, MASSACHUSETTS

AND

SOME OF HIS DESCENDANTS

By GEORGE HARLAN LEWIS
of Los Angeles, California

[One hundred and twenty-five copies reprinted from the HISTORICAL COLLECTIONS OF THE ESSEX INSTITUTE, Volumes XLIII and XLIV.]

ESSEX INSTITUTE
SALEM, MASSACHUSETTS
1908

PREFACE.

The only excuse for the following records is the desire that they might be of use to others, and that the labor of gathering them be not wasted by no use being made of them.

I collected them in the search I made for my ancestry. In a few years many who gave me information will have passed over. There are errors I have no doubt. In some cases family and town records did not agree. Many people live and die who do not know when and where they were born, cannot tell the names of their grandparents or the maiden name of their mother or grandmothers. Few families think it of sufficient importance to keep a correct record made at the time events transpire, but trust to memory.

In preparing this work large quantities of land and probate court records were copied, and many items of interest that might have been printed in a subscription work are here omitted. I take pleasure in acknowledging the great assistance I received from Jacob Meek Lewis (574) and Mrs. Salome A. (Ward) Lewis (978) was particularly helpful by her interest and knowledge of family history, without whose aid much would not appear here.

I have received many inquiries as to my connection with this family. As my name does not appear elsewhere, I will state that I descend from William Lewis (1), mentioned on pages 1 and 3; John Lewis (2) and wife Hannah, of Lancaster and Dorchester, Mass.; John Lewis (3) of Dorchester, and Ann (Whiting) Eaton, daughter of Nathaniel and Hannah (Dwight) Whiting of Dedham, Mass.; Jonathan Lewis (4) of Dedham and Abigail

(Clapp) Everett, daughter of Thomas and Hannah (——) Clapp; Aaron Lewis (5) of Lyndeboro, N. H., and Sarah White, daughter of Benjamin and Mary (——) White of Stoughtonham, Mass.; Amasa Lewis (6) of New Boston, N. H., and Polly Dane, daughter of Daniel and Sarah (Goodhue) Dane of New Boston, N. H.; George Amasa Lewis (7) and Caroline Antoinette Cutter, daughter of Joshua and Sarah (Munt) Cutter of Cambridge, Mass.; George Harlan Lewis (8), born in Malden, Mass., Feb. 28, 1840; married (first), in Philadelphia, Pa., July 11, 1867, Frances Maria Whitney, daughter of William James and Mary Ann (Siver) Whitney of Albany, N. Y. She was born in Albany Nov. 5, 1845, and died in Brooklyn, N. Y., June 2, 1900, leaving three children. Married (second), in Brooklyn, N. Y., July 13, 1901, Augusta Wilkes Banta, daughter of William and Nancy Eliza (Thorpe-Mills) Banta of New York City. She was born in New York City Oct. 7, 1848, and died in Los Angeles, Calif., Dec. 22, 1908. Children now living: Harry Lincoln[9], born Jan. 17, 1869, in Chicago, Ill.; Edwin Whitney[9], born Oct. 2, 1870, in Chicago, Ill.; George Arthur[9], born Jan. 31, 1880, in Hackensack, N. J.

GEORGE HARLAN LEWIS.

EDMUND LEWIS OF LYNN, AND SOME OF HIS DESCENDANTS.

BY GEORGE HARLAN LEWIS OF LOS ANGELES, CAL.

Edmund Lewis, who came to this country and first settled in Watertown, is said to have come from Lynn Regis (King's Lynn), England, but there is no record of him or any of his family on the church registers there. Alonzo Lewis, in his history of Lynn (second edition), states that he was a brother of William Lewis, who was at Roxbury in 1630, and was a founder of Lancaster, Mass., in 1653, who descended from a good Welsh family, with a pedigree running back centuries. (Some Welsh pedigrees run back to Noah.) Where Lewis obtained his information is not at my command. I have searched the records of this colony and visited England and Wales, used the library of the British Museum, and consulted the records of Somerset House and Fetter Lane, London, without success. Alonzo Lewis has his pedigree upon his monument in the Western Burying Ground, Lynn, running from William, through Isaac, his son, who died childless. In point of fact, Alonzo Lewis was descended from Isaac, son of John, of Charlestown and Malden. If Alonzo Lewis had stated his Welsh pedigree, giving the name of the Welsh ancestor, or the place from which he emigrated, it might have been traced.

There is no authoritative connection of any of the Lewis immigrants to New England, during the 17th century, with any Welsh or English family. Without knowing his English home, it is impossible to trace a Welshman. It was not until the middle of the 16th century that the prominent families of Wales begun to adopt the surname as used by the English. They then took the name of the father, and William ap Lewis became William Lewis;

Lewis ap Edward became Lewis Edwards; Thomas ap Richard became Thomas Prichard or Richards; John ap Robert became John Probert or Roberts; John ab Owen became John Bowen; John ap Evan became Bevan or Evans; John ap Harry became Parry,—and so on through the whole list.

The name of Lewis was as popular in Wales as Washington and Franklin in this country. It was adopted as the English form for Llewellyn, who was the last ruling prince in Wales, and was killed in 1282, and whose head hung over the entrance to the Tower of London, after having been paraded through the streets as a warning to others who might rebel. Nearly every Welsh family had a son Lewis, and when the surname was adopted there were many Lewises.

But this did not take place universally at any given time, for at the beginning of the 19th century not half the people had surnames, and to-day in some of the northern parts of Wales the old ap or ab is used between father and child. Edmund might have been the first to adopt the surname, and his father may have been Lewis ap John, or some other name, therefore it is impossible to trace the ancestry in Wales without knowing the place of nativity and parents names, and even then it cannot be done with certainty.

All coats of arms are without authority for the same reasons. Ion Lewis, son of Alonzo, states in his biographical sketch of his father, that they descended from the family in Glamorgan. I have been to Cardiff and Greenmeadow, and inspected the family chart of Henry Lewis, M. P., who is the head of the family at this time, and find no connection. I have also consulted the printed records of the family and find none. The parish registers do not run back earlier than 1725, therefore all recorded connection is impossible. When a member of the family emigrated from England his record was discontinued, and no entry was made even if the family knew where the individual had gone.

That the Lewises came from a good family cannot be doubted. Thomas Lewis, who was the first, came to Saco in 1628, and was an educated man of means, or he could not have obtained the grant which he did. Philip Lewis of Greenland (Portsmouth), 1650, was a relative of —— Tucker, of Cleaves and Tucker. William Lewis of Roxbury was probably one of the young sons of a numerous family, where the eldest son inherited the estates, and the other sons had to look elsewhere. He was of an adventurous spirit, and came out when a mere youth, and returned to England where he may have interested his brothers in the colony, and possibly Edmund and John were brothers of his, as the similarity of names in the families will be noticed. After William's children were driven out of Lancaster (1675-6) by the Indians, Isaac is found fighting the Indians with John, the son of Edmund, and he received £3. 2. 0. from Lynn. (Bodge's Indian Wars, p. 371.) Later he is found in Malden, Chelsea, and Charlestown, where John's descendants are living.

There is no doubt but that Edmund was brought up by the sea. He had a good estate at Watertown, but it was away from the water, and he went to Lynn, where he found an ideal place, and bought forty acres directly upon the seashore. He may have been a sailor, as in his inventory appears a "cutlas," a weapon used in battle, at close quarters, on vessels. He may have bought his land of John Wood, as his lands are called "Wood end fields," and that end of the town was called "Wood end." In his will he mentions John and Thomas as having some property, and is solicitous for the welfare of the five youngest children, of whom only James and Nathaniel are recorded at Watertown, so the others were born in Lynn, and no record made. Whether he had five children younger than John, as Savage thinks, or five younger than Thomas, is uncertain. Of James I find no certain trace. Nathaniel, with his brother Joseph, sailed away to New London, Conn., in 1666.

It has been said that Benjamin Lewis of Stratford, Conn., who went from New Haven, Conn., in 1670, as one of the founders of Wallingford, and later sold out to Dr. John Hall and returned to Stratford, was a son of Edmund. Did he, like Nathaniel and Joseph, sail away, and not finding a place at New London, continue unt reached New Haven and Stratford? Did he later, Edmund, leave the inland town for the seashore? habits of youth are hard to eradicate. Another co: tion may be found in the fact that the names of his dren are almost identical with those of Edmund, and of John's, viz.: John, Mary, James, Edmund, Joseph, Hannah, Martha, Benjamin and Eunice. John had John, Hannah, and Benjamin. This is not positive proof, but is strong circumstantial evidence in support of the claim that Benjamin was the youngest child of Edmund. I do not include him, for want of absolute proof.

But with Joseph it is quite different, for I consider the written proof made over two hundred years ago identifying Nathaniel with Lynn, and Joseph with Nathaniel at Swansea, together with the presence there of their brother Thomas, as superior to the uninvestigated theory of Mr. Deane, who, in his History of Scituate, assumes that they were children of George Lewis of Barnstable. Other writers have repeated his statement, save Savage, who rejects it, and Amos Otis, who, in his Barnstable Families, throws it out entirely, and states that neither town, colony, or church records confirm the statement.

On April 10, 1634, Edmund Lewis, aged 33 years, his wife Mary, aged 32, son John, aged 3, and son Thomas, aged $\frac{3}{4}$ years, embarked in the Elizabeth, William Andrews, master, at Ipswich, England. He settled at Watertown, Mass., and shared in the first great division of lands. His homestead was on what is now the east side of Lexington street. He was granted land July 25, 1636, lot 26, 30 acres in the 1st division; Feb. 28, 1636-7, lot 82, 5 acres; June 16, 1637, lot 61, 5 acres; April 9, 1638, 6 acres. In the book of possessions he held in lands: (1) A Homestall of 6 acres. (2) One acre of meddow in Rockmeddow. (3) Thirty acres of upland being a great Divident in the 1st Division, the 25th Lott. (4) Five acres of Plowland in the further Plaine and the 91 lott. (5) Five acres of meddow in the remote meddows & the 61 lott. (6) A farme of hundred acres of upland. (7) One acre of remote meddow by estimation. He was admitted a freeman May 24, 1636, and was elected a selectman for the year 1638. Oct. 14, 1638, he was one of a committee chosen "To lay out the farmes as they were ordered, near the Dedham line." (Barker's Watertown, p. 4.) Alonzo Lewis' History of Lynn says he removed to Lynn in 1639. Bond's Genealogies of Watertown says he removed after 1642. He buried a child there Nov. 6, 1642; Savage says 1643. He had lived near the sea, and when he removed to Lynn he settled in the eastern part of the town, on what is now Lewis street. He died in January, 1650. His wife died Sept. 7, 1658.

In his will, made the 13, 11th month, 1650, he mentions five young children. The date of birth of two of them is not recorded, and the name of one of them is not known. His will, on file in Essex County Probate Records, Vol. 1, f. 119, is as follows:

"Line the 13th of the 11th mo. 1650. Memorandum that I Edmund Lewis beinge Sick & Weake, but of perfect remembrance, doe make & conferm this my last Will and testyment as followeth,

First. My Will is that my land att Watertown shall be soaled, & that my eldest son John Lewis shall have a double portyon & the rest of my children namely, the five youngest to have every one of them a licke portyon of my Estate.

Secondly. My deare & lovinge wife to have the third of all my whole Estate.

Thirdly. I desire that my wife may have a cow over & above towards bringinge upe of my youngest children.

Fourthly:—my desire is my wife to be my whole executor to dispose of my body & goods accordinge to my Will.

Fifthly:—my request to my son John is, to give his mother a Cow to helpe her towards the bringinge up of my youngest children.

Sixthly:—my request to my son Thomas Lewis is to give to his mother half of his Sheepe to help her as aforesaid.

Seventhly:—My desire and meaninge is that the Cow I

ask of John & the Sheepe I ask of Thomas is of them that they now have in their possession. Also my request is to Thomas Hastings to be my supervisor to assist my lovinge wife.

Witnesses — Edmund his X mark Lewis

John Deakin
Edward Burcham.

This will, with an inventory, was brought into court by Mary, widow of Edmund Lewis, on the 25th 12 mo 1650-1, and Edward Bureham swore to the truth of it, and the Court ordered "that the children shall have their several portyons paid them at the age of twentie & one years."

"The Inventory of the goods of Edmund Lewis of Line laite deceased, tacken by us whose names are heare under subscribed this 12th day of the 12th mo 1650-1

Imprimis: One payer of Oxen,	13	00	0
one payer of Oxen,	14	00	0
foure working steares,	24	00	0
one two year oulde heffer,	3	00	0
six shots at	3	00	0
one heffer at	2	00	0
too milch kine & a calfe,	9	00	0
three yearlings,	5	00	0
fouer wether sheepe,	2	16	0
fouer ewe sheepe,	6	00	0
three lames of this yeare,	1	06	0
hay £2 10s, too little harrowes 10s,	3	00	0
one plow with coulter & share,		06	0
one cheane,		2	6
one payer of old wheles,		10	0
A cart & draughts,	1	00	0
The Waine,	1	10	0
An old plow,		2	6
too yockes,		6	0
one bede with the furniter,	3	3	0
one bede with the furnituer,	1	1	0
Purse & aparell	2	0	0
Five pilar coverings & five napkins,		13	6
A table cloth,	0	2	0

A bedsteade,		5	0
A chiste,		3	4
Three wheeles & too littell chayers,		10	0
In yaren, flaxe & wooll,	1	17	0
In wheate 10 bushells,	2	10	0
In oats £5 7s a fan 3s 4d,	1	10	4
too sithes & fouer hooks,		9	0
three score bushells of Indyan Coren,	9	0	0
A sword belte & bandeleres,		12	0
too muskets & too rests,	1	16	0
A foulinge pece,	1	6	0
too small gunes,		16	0
A Cettell & too iern pots,		14	8
A gird ieren & a iern Kettell & a ould posnett,		6	0
Peuter 10s A frying pan & a hooke, 7s,		17	0
too trayes & a meale sive & other lumber,		11	0
three axes, too wedges & a drawing knife,			
three augers and a handsaw,		11	8
too drink barrels,		3	0
A bibell 8s A pece of lether, 6s,		14	0
a churn, a bottell, & a little tube,		5	0
too tubes, a brake & a crackell,		7	0
	122	7	6

John Deakin
James Arry
Edward Burcham
his
William X Tilton
mark
Appraisers."

Children :

2. JOHN, b. 1631, in England.
3. THOMAS, b. 1633, in England.
4. JAMES, b. 15, 11 mo, 1635-6, in Watertown.
5. NATHANIEL, born 25, 6mo, 1639, in Watertown.
5a. A CHILD, aged 20 days, was buried Nov. 6, 1642, in Watertown.
6. JOSEPH.

There is no record of the 6th and 7th children, who were alive at the time he made his will, and who must have been born after 1642, in Lynn.

2 **John Lewis**, yeoman, innholder, lieutenant, captain, and deacon, was born in England in 1631. He came into possession of his father's lands in Wood end fields, 40 acres fronting on the sea and through which Lewis street now passes. At that time the eastern end of Lynn was called "Wood end," and the western end, "Breed's end," and the locality back of where Samuel Graves settled was called "Graves end." For years these names appeared in the description of lands given in deeds.

On the 19, 5mo., 1669, John Lewis of Lynn, yeoman, and wife Hannah, sold to Ralph King for £23, four acres of upland in Lynn bounded on William King, said Lewis, and south by the sea. (Essex Deeds, Vol. 3, f. 95.) In 1699 he married for his second wife the widow of this Ralph King. Nov. 9, 1699, he deeded his lands to his two sons, John and Thomas, as follows:—John Lewis, sen. of Lynn, yeoman, for £160, to his two sons, John and Thomas, yeomen, in equal halves "all my housing and lands in Lynn, viz: a dwelling house where I formerly lived, a barn, with 40 acres tillage at Wood End fields, Also a parcel of Salt marsh in Rumney Marsh 12 acres." (Essex Deeds, Vol. 3. f. 191.) A division of the above was made, June 5, 1708, "the dividing line to begin at a flat rock about a pole & a half from the back side of John Lewis Jr. house and so running easterly on a straight line to a flat rock in the field where it has been formerly broke up, so from thence South East straight to a stake with a heap of stones, thence East to a stake with a heap of stones by the ditch that parts said lands formerly of Ezekiel Needham's, and all lands South of said line to be John's, and all lands North, with the house and barn, till it comes to the brook that runs from Collins' fresh meadow, to be Thomas, John to have all lands North of said brook, it to be the bound betwixt them in that place. As to the Marsh land, John to have the Easterly half, and Thomas to have Westerly half." (Essex Deeds, Vol. 21, f. 50.)

John Lewis was a lieutenant under Capt. Henchman in King Philip's War, and received £1. 14. 3. Aug. 20, 1675. He was granted land at Souhegan West, now Amherst, N. H., for his services, which his grandson, Edmund, secured in 1728. (Bodge's King Philip's War, p. 422.) He was paid £1. 16. 0. June 24, 1676, for services in Capt. Nick Manning's Co. (N. E. Hist. Gen. Register, Vol. 42, p. 95.) He was made a freeman, April 18, 1691, and was then called "lieutenant." (N. E. Hist. Gen. Register, Vol. 5, p. 352.) He was elected a deacon in the church at a town meeting held January 8, 1692:—"That Lieut. Lewis & Lieut. Fuller should sit at table." He kept a tavern in the eastern part of Saugus, known as the "Blue Anchor," probably being the successor of his father in law, Capt. Thomas Marshall, who died in 1683. This inn was later kept by his son Thomas (9) and grandson John (41), and is mentioned by travellers of that day.*

Madam Knight in her Diary also mentions this tavern.

He died in 1710, at the age of 79 years. His will† is as follows:—

I John Lewis Sr. of Lynn being of sound understanding & memory thro the goodness of God, considering the frailty of human nature in general and my own age in particular, not knowing how soon it may please God to take me out of this transitory life and, being desirous of making allotment of my outward estate and prevent any differences which might otherwise arise after my death between my wife and my children, do make this my last Will and Testament as followeth [commits his soul to God, and his body to the earth]. And as for that outward estate which God in his goodness hath lent unto me, I do dispose of it as hereafter is expressed. For as much as I have formerly done for my children what I judge meet, and sufficient and am now desirous according to my duty and ability to provide for y[e] comfortable livelyhood and subsistance of my now wife after my decease, if it be the pleasure of God that she outlive me, I do therefore give unto my said wife, Sarah Lewis, and my Will is that she shall receive, have and enjoy to her own absolute use and disposal, my whole Estate not formerly by me other-

*Samuel Sewall writing in his Diary regarding the funeral of his mother on Jany. 14, 1700-1, says, "Hired horses at Charlestown, set out about 10 o'clock in a great Fogg. Dined at Lewis' with Mr. Cushing of Salisbury. Sam and I kept on in Ipswich Rode."

†Essex Co. Probate, Vol. 310, f. 242.

wise disposed of, both reall and personal, whether in money or household stuff, or stock or cloathing, and also all debts & dues owing unto me from any and every person, whither by bill, bond or otherwayes, and I do constitute, ordain & appoint my sd loving wife Sarah Lewis to be my sole Executrix of this my last Will. Desiring and appointing my loving ffriends Mr. John Floyd of Rumney Marsh, & William Meriam of Lynn, to be my overseers, whom I pray to be assisting unto my loving wife, in ye execution of this my Will which I do hereby declare to be my last Will and Testament, nulling and making void all former or other Wills by me made or pretended to be made, so that this only shall be taken for my last Will & Testament. In confirmation whereof I doe Signe, Seal and publish the same this twenty fifth day of ffebruary, one thousand seven hundred six-seven.

Signed, sealed and published John Lewis [SEAL L]
in presence of
John ffloyd,
Samuel ffloyd,
Edmund Chamberlaine.

John Lewis married (Lynn records:—Jonathan), first, June 17th, 1659, Hannah, daughter of Capt. Thomas Marshall of Lynn. She died May 15, 1699. He married, second, Sept. 2, 1699, widow Elizabeth King, relict of Ralph King of Swampscott, and daughter of Capt. Richard and Jane (Talmage) Walker. (Essex Inst. Hist. Colls., Vol. 16, p. 77.) He married, third, Feb. 10, 1706-7, Mrs. Sarah Jenks, born Sept. 14, 1665, and died Jan. 4, 1740, widow of John Jenks, the son of Joseph and Elizabeth Jenks. She was the daughter of William and Elizabeth (Breed) Merriam of Lynn. At this time John Lewis was 75 years of age, and his wife was 41. He made his will fifteen days after this marriage. His land had been deeded to his two sons two months after his second marriage.

Children of John and Hannah:

7. JOHN, b. Mar. 30, 1660.
8. HANNAH, b. Feb. 25, 1661; m., May 12, 1686, Capt. Edward Fuller.

9. THOMAS, b. June 2, 1663.
10. MARY, b. Feb. 24, 1665; m., July 10, 1689, Thomas Baker.
11. BENJAMIN, b. Apr. 27, 1667; d. young.
12. NATHANIEL, b. Apr. 16, 1672; d. Nov. 25, 1692.
13. SAMUEL, b. July 25, 1675; d. Aug. 12, 1675.
14. ABIGAIL, b. May 16, 1679; d. May 30, 1706.
15. EBENEZER, b. July 16, 1681; not provided for by his father, or mentioned in his will.
16. REBECCA, d. Nov. 22, 1692.

Child of John and Sarah:

17. BENJAMIN, b. April 23, 1708.

3. Thomas Lewis, born in England in 1633, removed from Lynn to Northampton in 1661-1662, where he had a home lot of four acres, which he sold to Matthew Clesson in 1667. He was chosen to assist in building a mill, 27, 6 mo., 1666. He removed from there to Swansea, where, at a town meeting held Dec. 1, 1669, "Thomas Lewis was admitted inhabitant and member of this township, and to have a twelve acre lot where any two of the Com'te for admission of inhabitants shall approve of his settlement." At a town meeting held Feb. 9, 1670, it was ordered that all lots and divisions of land thereafter be granted according to the three-fold rank, by the selectmen. First rank, three acres; second rank, two acres; and third rank, one. Thomas Lewis was in the second rank. He was elected a selectman, May 21, 1672. He is mentioned at Bristol, R. I., as early as 1681, and was taxed at Mendon, Mass., in 1691, 1692 and 1693. He was elected a selectman, May 1, 1693, for the year, but declined to serve. The following is taken from the Annals of Mendon, p. 129, where it is used as a model for the peaceful settlement of a land dispute.

"Know all men by these Presents that I Thomas Lewis of Bristol, Doe Constitute and Appoint my well beloved Capt. Josiah Chapin of Mendon, In my Roome and Stead for to Joyne with sergent Abraham Staples of Mendon aforesaid to Devid A percell of medow that belonged to John Parris's Lot in Mendon, Now Eaqually belonging to me the said Lewis and ye Above sd Staples, and doe by these presents bind myself my heyers, Executors, administrators and Assigns, to stand to their Agreement about ye devision of sd medow, and after the decision is made to cause the same to be recorded, as Witness my hand this 9th of January, 1695-6. Thomas Lewis [Seal]."

In 1696, he was called of Mendon, with wife Hannah. In 1692, Thomas Lewis of Bristol, R. I., sold land to Capt. John Andrews. He also sold land there in 1701. In the Book of Possessions of Swansea his lands are recorded on page 9, and in the various proceedings of the town his name appears in regard to lands. On Dec. 23, 1704, he, with his wife Hannah, executed a deed of gift for good will and affection, of the "north part of my dwelling house in Bristol," to his daughter, Hepzebah Lewis. (Bristol Co. Deeds, Vol. 4, p. 319.)

The will of Thomas Lewis of Bristol, recorded in Bristol Co. Probate Records, Vol. 2, f. 257: "In the name of God, Amen, I Thomas Lewis of Bristol in ye County of Bristol in New England, being aged and very Infirm, and not knowing when or how soon I may be Removed out of a Chaingable world, to prevent Jarrs & Contentions after my Decease do make constitute and ordaine this to be my last Will & Testament in manner and form following; that is to say, I commend my Soul into ye hands of God and body to ye earth to be decently buried at the Discreſion of my friends, and as to my temporal estate which it hath pleased God of his mercy to lend me, I give bequeath and bestow in the following manner, Viz: After my ffuneral Charges and Just Debts are payed and sattisfyed by my Executrix hereafter mentioned, I give and bequeath unto my aged and beloved wife all my whole estate both Reall and personal after my decease During her natural Life with full power and Authority by Virtue of these presents to make sale of ye whole my Two acre lott in Bristol with the Dwelling house thereon except what I have before given by deed of Gift to my Daughter Hepzebath or any part or parsell of my said lott to such person or persons who shall appear to purchass the same hereby Impowering of my said wife Hannah Lewis to make, sign, seal and fully to Execute a good and sufficient Deed and Legall Convayance of the said two acre lott or any part or parcell thereof so sold as aforesaid for her necessary & Comfortable livelyhood During her natural life and after her Decease what shall be Remaining of my estate to be Devided to and among my Children in as Just and equal proportion as may be according to the direction of the law in such case made and provided, having a regard allwayes to what any of my Sons or Daughters have had formerly of my estate before my decease. And of this my Last Will & Testament I constitute and ordain my Beloved wife Hannah Lewis my sole Executrix Hereby making null & voydd all other and former Wills Legacies or Executors by me in any wise before this time named willed or bequeathed and in Testimony hereof I Thomas Lewis have hereunto sett my hand and fixed my seal the Eleventh day of August, A. D. 1708. Thomas Lewis [Seal]"

Proved July 6, 1709. Presented and sworn to by Hannah Lewis.

The widow Hannah Lewis sold, April 22, 1710, to Nath[l] Byfield, "one half of the two acre lot of land where ye dwelling house now stands being the eastern most half of those two acre lot with ye barn and house thereon" bounded East on High St, South on Queen St. West by land of said Thomas Lewis, being the other half, and northerly by land of Nath'l Byfield. (Bristol Co. Deeds, Vol. 6, f. 174.)

Thomas Lewis married, Nov. 11, 1659, Hannah, daughter of Edward and Joan Baker. They both died at Bristol, R. I., he dying April 26, 1709, aged about 76 years, and his widow following him in January, 1717.

Children of Thomas and Hannah:

18. Edward, b. July 28, 1660, at Lynn; d. July 15, 1662, at Northampton, Mass.

19. Hannah, m. Jan. 22, 1683, George Morey. Their children, born in Bristol, R. I., were: (1) John, b. Oct. 3, 1684, who m., about 1700, Margaret Linsford, b. in Braintree, Feb. 6, 1682-3, dau. of Edward and Hannah (Plumley) Linsford; (2) Mary, b. Mar. 24, 1687-8; (3) Sarah, b. Mar. 4, 1690-1; (4) Hannah, b. Mar. 18, 1693-4; d. Dec., 1717; (5) George, b. Aug. 31, 1696; (6) Martha, b. Mar. 12, 1698-9; (7) Abigail, b. Feb. 27, 1701-2; (8) Benjamin, b. Apr. 18, 1705; (9) Thomas, b. Jan. 1, 1708-9.

20. Mary, b. 1663; d. Mar. 26, 1666.

21. ESTHER, b. 1665; m., Jan. 7, 1684, Jeremiah Finney, at Bristol, R. I., where they had children born: (1) Mary, b. Mar. 26, 1686; (2) Hannah, b. Jan. 14, 1687-8; (3) Mehitable, b. May 8, 1689; (4) John, b. Aug. 3, and d. Oct. 23, 1690; (5) Rebecca, b. Feb. 24, 1691; (6) Esther, b. May 5, 1693; (7) John, b. April 13, 1696; (8) Abigail, b. April 17, 1697.
22. THOMAS, b. Sept. 28, 1666, at Northampton, Mass.; d. Jan. 11, 1666-7, at Northampton.
23. THOMAS, b. Apr. 29, 1668, at Lynn.
24. ELIZABETH, b. Dec. 7, 1669, at Swansea.
25. PERSITHE, b. June 15, 1671, at Swansea.
26. SAMUEL, b. Apr. 23, 1673, at Swansea.
27. HEPSEBAH, b. Nov. 15, 1674, at Swansea; m., Dec. 25, 1706, James Thurber, at Bristol, R. I. He died June 10, 1747. She died Nov. 11, 1753, at Bristol, R. I.
28. JOSEPH, b. May 13, 1677, at Swansea.
29. DEBORAH, b. Mar. 19, 1679, at Swansea.

5. **Nathaniel Lewis** was born at Watertown, 25th, 6 m., 1639. Caulkins' History of New London, p. 296, says, "Nathaniel and Joseph Lewis are names that appear on the rate list of 1667, as partners in estate. They were transient residents." They removed to Swansea and became inhabitants.

At a town meeting, Dec. 1, 1669, "Nathaniel Lewis is admitted townsman, and is to have a 12 acre lot where it may be Judged Convenient." He was of the 3d rank Feb. 7, 1670. In the Book of Possessions his lands are recorded on page 107, except his lot No. 85 in the sheep pasture, alias Towoset Neck, which is recorded by a mistake with his brother Joseph's lands on page 53. He married Mary ——, and died Oct. 13, 1683.

Children of Nathaniel and Mary:

30. NATHANIEL, b. July 17, 1673; d. Aug. 20, 1676.
31. MARY, b. Dec. 4, 1677, at Lynn; m., June 10, 1693, John Cole, jr., in Swansea, and had born there: (1) Lewis, b. Oct. 23, 1694; (2) Joanna, b. Feby. 20, 1696-7; (3) Nathan, b. Mar. 20, 1703.

6. **Joseph Lewis.** There is no record of his birth. His father died in 1650, and in 1658 his mother was taken away, and John, his eldest brother, did not marry until the next year (17 June, 1659), so that his childhood was not very propitious and early in life he had to start to build his own fortune. Being used to the water, with his brother

Nathaniel, he sailed along the coast, and was at New London, Conn., on Dec. 2, 1667, where they were transient residents and taxed £2. 3s. 9d. for the minister's rate. (New London, Ct., Records.) He removed to Swansea with his brothers, Thomas and Nathaniel, and became an inhabitant, and was granted land in the third rank, Feb. 7, 1670. At town meeting 9th, 12 mo., 1671, he was elected to assist the committee to "lay out the lands recently purchased at Metapoisett." His lands are recorded in the Book of Possessions on pages 53 and 54, and with them are recorded part of the lands of his brother Nathaniel (5) on page 53 by a mistake made at that time. The following certificate is self-explanatory.

Office of Town Clerk and Treasurer.

Swansea, Mass., Aug. 3, 1906.

"Nathaniel Lewis his land in the Sheep pasture alis Towoset Neck by a mistake were Recorded in page 53 with his Brother Joseph's Lands."

I hereby certify that the above is a true copy of the record as it appears on page 107 of the original "Proprietors Records" in the town of Swansea.

Henry O. Wood, Town Clerk.

[Seal of the Town of Swansea.]

There has been considerable discussion as to who were the parents of this Joseph Lewis. Mr. Deane's Scituate and Mr. Shepherd in the N. E. Hist. Gen. Register state that he was a son of George of Barnstable. There appears to be no foundation for such statement, as George had no son by that name, as is shown by Otis' Barnstable Families. There is ample evidence that Nathaniel was from Lynn, and the above is evidence that his brother Joseph was with him.

There is a tradition that Joseph Lewis was the first white man slain in King Philip's War. He was killed at Swansea, June 24, 1675. (Bodge's King Philip's War, p. 463.) A list of the slain reported by the clerk of the town at the time is: Joseph Lewis, Robert Jones, John Jones,* Nehemiah Allen, William Cohun, John Salisbury,

*The Joneses were relatives of Mrs. Joseph Lewis. The deaths probably occurred in the order named.

William Salisbury, John Hall. (Plymouth Colonial Records.)

"As the inhabitants of Swansea were returning from public worship, a number of Indians who lay in ambuscade, fired upon them, killed one of their company and wounded another. They next intercepted and killed two men, who were sent for a surgeon. The same night they entered the town of Swansea and murdered six men." (Hannah Adams' N. E. History, p. 120.)

"In the afternoon of June 24, 1675, being a fast day at Swansea, people were coming from Public Worship the Indians attacked them, killed one and wounded others, and killed two men who were going for a Surgeon, beset a house in another part of the town and murdered 6 more." (Hutchinson's History of Mass., Vol. 1, page 261.)

Joseph Lewis married Mary Jones, June 13, 1671. (Swansea Records.) She was the daughter of Robert and Anne (Bibble) Jones of Hull. Anne was the daughter of John and Sibyll Bibble of Malden. After the massacre Mary returned to Malden to live with her grandmother.* Mary, the widow of Joseph, married, Jan. 11, 1677, at Malden, Obadiah Jenkins. He died in 1720, and his sons Joel and Obadiah gave bond April 1, 1720, and were appointed administrators of his estate. His wife Mary must have died before that time, as she had no share in his estate. Their children were: (1) Joel, (2) Mary, (3) Annabel, (4) Lydia, (5) Sarah, m. —— Taylor; (6) Anna, m. Benj. Teal; (7) Obadiah, m. Mary Grover.

*The Will of John Bibble (N. E. Hist. Gen. Register, Vol. 9, p. 306-7) mentions son in law Robert Jones of Hull, daughter Annie and wife Sibyll, and calls himself "of Maldon being now of Hull," July 23, 1653. Ann Bibble was a petitioner for a minister to be settled at Malden, Oct. 28, 1651, so she must have married Robert Jones between that day and July 1, 1653, when her father made his will. Sybil Bibble, widow, married Miles Nutt, and on Oct. 30, 1674, became the wife of John Doolittle of Malden, where she lived and died Sept. 23, 1690, aged about 82 years. Her will, made at Malden, Dec. 25, 1683, proved in 1690, gives "to Obadiah Jenkins and Mary Jenkins his wife and their children, all my housing and lands in Malden, with all movables, he paying out of it to my grandchildren, Robert, Zachery, Benjamin and Rebeccah Jones £5, a piece when they become of age. * * * I make my grandson Obadiah Jenkins my Executor of this my last Will."

Sybil Doolittle [Seal.

Children of Joseph and Mary, born in Swansea:

32. JOSEPH, b. Aug. 6, 1672.
33. SYBIL, b. Mar. 18, 1674; m. in 1700, at Malden, Samuel Howard of Malden, and had: (1) Samuel, b. Apr. 25, 1701; m. July 12, 1727, Elizabeth Wayte; lived in Malden. (2) Joseph, b. Nov., 1702; d. May 18, 1725. (3) Mary, b. about 1708; m. Sept. 6, 1733, Thomas Mighills of Pomfret, Conn. (4) Sybill, b. about 1712; m. Dec. 27, 1738, Reuben Darbe of Pomfret, Conn. (5) Benjamin, b. in 1714; d. 1763; m. June 19, 1740, Abigail Walton of Reading. Settled at Malden, and removed to Holden, Mass., in 1749.

The following memorandum, filed in Middlesex County Probate, file 8876, is interesting proof of the relationship of all the parties thereto.

"Deacon Samuel Howard's mother was sister to the deceased* by his mother's side, i. e.: Obadiah's mother before she married his Father—married a Lewis & had 2 children. Viz:—Joseph and Sibilla, which Sibilla was mother to the said Samuel Howard, who claims Joseph was father to Benj[m] Lewis, who also claims Sibilla's children are Samuel and Sibella. Joseph's children are Benjamin, Joseph and Abigail."

The claims were allowed and settlement made as above.

7 John Lewis, born in Lynn, Mar. 30, 1660, was a lieutenant, and was made a freeman Apr. 18, 1691. In the division of his father's lands he had the south half next the sea. He died intestate about a year after his father, and his widow Elizabeth was appointed administratrix, June 27, 1711. The inventory of his estate, taken July 11, 1711, is as follows:

To an house, barn, & land adjoining to about twenty acres or more,	160	00	00
To 15 acre upland & meadow in same field,	60	00	00
To 7 acres Salt Marsh,	42	00	00
To Common Lotte,	42	00	00
To Forty sheep & two swine,	10	00	00
To Cow & Tools for husbandry,	4	07	00
To Wareing Cloth & Gun,	11	11	00

*Obadiah Jenkins.

To Fodder, beds & bedding, £8, & household stuff, £4 05,				12	05	00
To Cash,				4	10	00
Real Estate £304, Personal,	£67	13	0			
Debt due the estate,		12	0			
	£68	5	0			
Dr to sundry creditors,	83	9	8			
Allowance for youngest son until 6 years of age,	24	0	0			
Total,	£118	16	2			

John Lewis married Elizabeth Brewer, April 18, 1683, in Lynn.

Children of John and Elizabeth, born in Lynn:

34. ELIZABETH, b. April 7, 1684; m. Feb. 8, 1708-9, Samuel Graves, Jr., b. Aug. 2, 1684, in Lynn, son of Samuel and Sarah (Brewer) Graves, and had the following children born in Lynn: (1) Samuel, b. Jan. 19, 1710; (2) Sarah, b. Feb. 1, 1713; m. (int. Nov. 16, 1735), Job Collins.
35. HANNAH, b. Jan. 22, 1685-6; m. Nov. 13, 1711, Lieut. Samuel Stocker,* b. Nov. 29, 1684, son of Ebenezer and Sarah (Marshall) Stocker of Lynn. She died Dec. 16, 1760. Children, born in Lynn: (1) John, b. Feb. 15, 1711-12; m. 1st, Hannah Richards, m., 2nd, Ruth Breed; (2) Samuel, b. July 28, 1717, (twin); m., 1st, Elizabeth——, pub. Oct. 21, 1743; m., 2d, May 25, 1757, Priscilla Rhodes; (3) Joseph, b. July 28, 1717, (twin).
36. SARAH, b. April 5, 1688; d. young
37. JOHN, b. Sept. 23, 1690; d. young.
38. NATHANIEL, b. Jan. 18, 1692-3; d. young.
39. EDMUND, b. Dec. 8, 1695.
40. REBECCA, b. June 18, 1699; m. Feb. 17, 1725-6, Grover Pratt, son of Richard and Rebecca Pratt of Malden. He died Jan. 14, 1790. Had: (1) Richard, b. Nov. 27, 1728, in Lynn; d. Apr. 25, 1816; m. his cousin, Rebecca, dau. of Nathaniel, Jr. and Tabitha (Lewis) Ingalls, born Dec. 20, 1732. His "Common Place Book" has been published.
41. TABATHA, b. July 22, 1702; m. Jan. 1, 1722, at Lynn, Nathaniel Ingalls, Jr., b. Dec. 25, 1692, son of Nathaniel and Anne Ingalls. He d. Sept. 23, 1772.
42. THOMAS, b. May 10, 1708.

*Samuel Stocker's mother and his wife Hannah Lewis' grandmother, were sisters, both being daughters of Capt. Thomas Marshall.

9 **Thomas Lewis,** born June 2, 1663, in Lynn, married Mary Breed born in Lynn, Aug. 24, 1664, daughter of Allen jr. and Elizabeth (Ballard) Breed.

He was a yeoman and innholder, succeeding his father. He died Jan. 28, 1713-14, aged 50 years. She died Jan. 19, 1736-7, aged 74 years. His will made Jan. 27, 1713-14, the day before his death, follows: "I Thomas Lewis of Lynn in ye County of Essex in ye Province of ye Massachusetts Bay in New England being weak of Body yet God affording to me my Reason & perfect understanding...I will and bequeath as followeth. Imp—That all my honest & Just debts be truly & honestly payd. I give to my beloved wife Mary one third part of all my movable estate of what kind soever to give & dispose as she shall cause and my said wife to have ye best room in my Dwelling house at ye Wood end to dwell In so long as she remains my wife, and further my Will is y[t] my eldest son John Lewis shall provide corn, meat, firewood, and all things necessary for my Wife's comfortable subsistance so long as she remain my Widow. My said Wife accepting of all as above in Lieu or consideration of dower or thirds in my Estate. I give and bequeath to my eldest son John Lewis his heirs, all my housing, lands, both upland, salt, and pasture and woodland of what kind soever, over and above what I have given him allready by Deed of Gift, my said son providing for my above Wife, his Mother, all things as above described and he paying all my just and honest debts at his own cost and charge. I give and bequeath to my son Joseph Lewis and to my daughters Mary Mower, Abigail Lewis, Unice Lewis and Ruth Lewis all my movable Estate of what kind soever, to be equally divided between them, my said five children (excepting only so much of my said movable estate as I have, in this my Will already given to my Wife) said part to remain to her as aforesaid. My son Joseph shall be put out to a trade as my Wife shall judge best. I appoint my son John Lewis sole executor to this my last Will & Testament & for ye confirmation here of ye Thomas Lewis have hereunto affixed my hand & seale the day of date here of ye twenty seventh day of January, Anno Do. One thousand seven hundred thirteen, fourteen.

his
Thomas X Lewis.*
mark

Signed & sealed In y[e] presence of us

John Burrill
Mich[l] Bowden
Sarah Bowden.

On Jan. 13, 1713-14, 14 days before the execution of his will, he deeded to his eldest son John, of Lynn, "one half of all my dwelling house, barn & outhousing at Wood end and one half of all my lands, salt marsh, pasture & woodland of all kind."†

Inventory of the estate of Thomas Lewis made Feb. 8, 1713-14.‡

Wearing apparell,	21 - 16 - 0
Arms,	3 - 0 - 0
two beds & bedsteads & all the furniture, belonging to them in ye great chamber,	15 - 0 - 0
Three beds with bedsteads & all furniture, belonging to them in ye kitchen chamber,	23 - 0 - 0
one bedstead, bed & furniture in ye porch chamber,	7 - 0 - 0
two bedsteads & furniture in ye garrit,	8 - 0 - 0
nine pare sheets,	5 - 5 - 0
six pare pillowberes,	12 - 0
five dozen napkins,	2 - 0 - 0
six table clothes,	1 - 0 - 0
Powder,	6 - 0 - 0
Ironware in ye house,	8 - 0 - 0
one chest of Drawers 25s three old chests 20s	2 - 5 - 0
table forms & chears,	3 - 0 - 0
old barrils & lumber in ye house,	2 - 0 - 0
about 100 bushels of oats 2[s] a bushel,	10 - 0 - 0
weges, axes and tools,	2 - 5 - 0
plow, cart wheels, sleads, yoaks & chaines,	5 - 5 - 0

*Essex County Probate Records, Vol. 311, f. 104.
†Essex County Deeds, Vol. 26, f. 260—2.
‡Essex Court Probate Records, Vol. 311. f. 105.

nine cows, three pound ten apece & with other,	31 - 10 - 0
five oxen & two bulls,	24 - 0 - 0
two yearling steers,	3 - 10 - 0
forty sheep,	14 - 0 - 0
one horse, one young mare & two horse colts,	18 - 0 - 0
ten swine,	3 - 10 - 0
a hundred gallons of rum at 3s a gallon,	15 - 0 - 0
fifteen gallons Madare Wine 4s a gallon,	3 - 0 - 0
one pipe of green wine & fifteen barrels of cider	22 - 10 - 0
a smal lsloop with all appurtenances,	20 - 0 - 0
Saddle & pillians,	1 - 10 - 0
plate and money,	16 - 1 - 0
a negro man	30 - 0 - 0
	329 - 5 - 0

Out of the personal estate the widow was allowed best bed & furniture belonging to it	£13 - 0 - 0
One chest of drawers,	1 - 5 - 0
one pott & one kettel,	19 - 0
pewter & cheers,	1 - 15 - 0
one cow,	3 - 10 - 0
	£20 - 9 - 0

	£	s.	d.
To house & homestead & land adjoining,	131	5	0
To a Lott in the general field,	8	5	0
To common Lott £58, To salt marsh £24,	82	0	0
	£221	10	0
By ye Personal Estate			
To Inventory on file in Quick Stock	£329	05	0
	£550	15	0

To the said Estate Dr.

	£	s.	d.
Sundry Creditors as per list on file,	435	02	0
Allowing ye Widow necessary,	20	9	0
Allowing Admr. Extra trouble,	15	0	0
Expenses Admr. &c.	21	10	9
	£492	1	9

Children of Thomas and Mary, born in Lynn:

43. JOHN, b. Aug. 2, 1687.
44. THOMAS, b. Dec. 2, 1689; d. young.
45. MARY, b. Aug. 4, 1691; m., Nov. 13, 1711, Thomas Mower. Adm. on the est. of Thomas Mower, late of Lynn, deceased, was granted to his wid., Mary Mower, on 8 March, 1730-31. Youngest child was then 2 yrs. old.
46. REBECCA, b. Mar. 18, 1693-4; d. June 11, 1694.
47. BENJAMIN, b. June 26, 1695; d. young.
48. ABIGAIL, b. Oct. 14, 1696; m. (int. Sept. 30, 1716), John Stocker, b. Nov. 13, 1693, son of Ebenezer and Sarah (Marshall) Stocker of Lynn. He was a shipwright, and resided in Boston, where several children were born. Had: (1) Thomas, b. Mar. 25, 1715. (2) John, b. Oct. 1, 1717. (3) Thomas, b. Mar. 25, 1719. (4) Abigail, b. Mar. 29, 1721. (5) Sarah, b. Dec. 1, 1723. (6) William, b. July 30, 1726.
49. JOSEPH, b. April 28, 1699; cooper; d. Nov. 23, 1726.
50. EUNICE, b. Nov. 18, 1701; m., Mar. 26, 1720, Thomas Pearson, a cooper, of Boston.
51. BENJAMIN, b. Jan. 16, 1703; d. young.
52. RUTH, b. Jan. 18, 1705; m., April 12, 1725, Thomas Copp of Boston, who d. soon after.

23 Thomas Lewis, born April 29, 1668, at Lynn. He bought land of the Trustees of the Province of Massachusetts Bay, in the northeastern corner of Swansea, 5 Sept., 1715 (Bristol County Deeds, Vol. 9, f. 478). He also bought land of Zachariah Eddy, of Peletiah Mason, and Thomas Brooks. He bought a farm in Rehoboth of Ephraim Pearce on July 5, 1717; 20 acres in Metapoiset of Thomas Bowen, on Mar. 28, 1718; and 27 acres in Rehoboth of John Martin, on Oct. 21, 1718. He is called a weaver. His will, dated 12 Aug., 1717, probated Nov. 4, 1717, is as follows:

Imprimis:—I give and Bequeath to Elizabeth my Dearly Beloved Wife The one halfe of my household goods to be at her dispose allso I give to my said wife the one third part of the use or profit of both my ffarms, the one in Swansea and the other in Rehoboth and the use of the best room in each house on said ffarms During her being my widow, but if she marry again to Dismiss her Right to housing and lands to my two sons hereafter named, they paying to her the sum of three pounds in money yearly during her natural life.

It. I give and bequeath unto my eldest son James Lewis all that my ffarm situate in Swansea containing about seven score acres as it is butted and bounded with . . . improvements and all appurtenances belonging to him his heirs and assigns forever, he allowing to his mother that abovesaid.

It. I give and bequeath to my son Timothy Lewis the one half of my ffarm situate in Rehoboth with the Dwelling house being the South end of said ffarm that I bought of Ephraim Peirce with the appurtenances belonging to the said South halfe part of said ffarm, to him and his heirs and assigns forever, he allowing to his mother as aforesaid:—

It. I give and bequeath to my son Samuel Lewis the other half of my said ffarm situate in Rehoboth being the north end of said ffarm when he come to Twenty one years of age, to his heirs and assigns forever.

It. I give and bequeath to my daughter Mary the sum of fifty pounds, to be payed to her in money or Goods when she comes to age, or time of marriage.

It. I give and bequeath to my daughter Debora the sum of fifty pounds and also to daughter Tabitha and daughter Lydia on the same terms. Also I ordain constitute my well beloved wife Executrix and my sons James and my son Timothy Executors of this my last Will and testament, And all the rest of my lands I give to my said Executors to pay my Debts and Legacies Also my movables. Thos Luis*

Inventory of his property shows £1604,19.0.

Extract from the will of Elizabeth Lewis, widow of Thomas Lewis, made 8th Nov., 1731. I Elizabeth Lewis of Swansea, widow, and lately wife of Thomas Lewis of Swansea, deceased, being sick, etc. To daughter Mary, wife of Isaac Carter, my best and biggest bible, & to her two daughters Elizabeth & Sarah Carter. To daughter Deborah, wife of Samuel Eddy, to her daughter Abigail Eddy. To daughter Experience Mason and her two sons

*Bristol County Probate Records, Vol. 3, f. 36.

Nathan and Benjamin Mason. Equally. To daughter Tabitha Martin, wife of Daniel Martin, Hannah & Lydia Martin. To daughter Lydia, Sons Samuel & Timothy and James Lewis sole Executors; appointed 29 Nov., 1731.*

Thomas Lewis married in Swansea, Apr. 10, 1689, Elizabeth, daughter of Timothy Brooks of Swansea, formerly of Billerica.

Children born in Swansea, except Abigail:

53. NATHANIEL, b. Dec. 14, 1690.
54. ABIGAIL, b. Jan. 8, 1691, born in Bristol, R. I.
55. MARY, b. Jany. 2, 1694, m. Isaac Carte .
56. JAMES, b. Nov. 14, 1695.
57. TIMOTHY, b. Feb. 23, 1697-8.
58. DEBORAH, b. Mar. 4, 1699-1700; m. Samuel Eddy.
59. SAMUEL, b. Apr. 16, 1702.
60. EXPERIENCE, b. Apr. 27, 1704; m. Jan. 26, 1723, in Swansea, Samuel Mason, b. Feb. 24, 1700, in Swansea, son of Isaac and Hannah Mason. She was appointed admx. of his estate, Oct. 25, 1731, and married, 2d, Mar. 28, 1734, Ebenezer Martin. Children born in Swansea: (1) Nathaniel Mason, b. Oct. 9, 1724. (2) Nathan Mason, b. Nov. 12, 1726. (3) Hannah Mason, b. Feb. 4, 1728. (4) Benjamin Mason, b. Dec. 14, 1730.
61. TABITHA, b. May 8, 1706; m. Daniel Martin.
62. LYDIA, b. Mar. 2, 1708-9.

26 Samuel Lewis, born April 23, 1673, in Swansea, married Susannah Jones, Sept. 29, 1698, at Woodbridge, N. J.

Children of Samuel and Susannah:

63. SAMUEL, b. Jan. 1, 1702.
64. LEVI, b. Apr. 15, 1706.

28 Joseph Lewis, born in Swansea, May 13, 1677, removed to Haddam, Conn., where he died May 27, 1742. He married Elizabeth, daughter of John and Sarah Birge of Bristol, R. I. In the cemetery at Bristol, R. I., are two gravestones inscribed Mr. John Birge, died Sept. 5, 1733, in his 85th year. Sarah, wife of John Birge, died Jan. 25, 1716-17, in her 63rd year.

*Bristol County Probate Records, Vol. 7, f. 266—267.

Children of Joseph and Elizabeth:

65. SARAH, b. 1703-4; m., Nov. 16, 1725, Thomas Beckwith of Lyme, Conn., born there July 1, 1702, son of Capt. Joseph and Marah (Lee) Beckwith.
66. ELIZABETH, b. 1705-6; m., Nov. 24, 1027, Hezekiah Shailer of Haddam, Conn.
67. REBECCA, m., June 24, 1730, Joseph Lee of Guilford, Conn.
68. HANNAH, m., Mar. 6, 1734-5, Simon Arnold of Haddam, Conn.
69. DEBORAH, b. April 16, 1721, at Haddam; m. Daniel Clark of Haddam, Conn.
70. JOHN, b. April 14, 1723, at Haddam.

32 Joseph Lewis, born in Swansea, June 6, 1672, was brought up with the family of his stepfather, Obadiah Jenkins, in Malden. After his marriage, in 1700, to Hannah Jones of Malden, he settled in Woburn, in that part which was set off to Wilmington, Sept. 25, 1730, on or near the Billerica line. In 1733 he was of Wilmington. He disposed of his father's lands in Swansea, for £6, to Thomas Lewis (23) of Swansea (Bristol Co. Deeds, Vol. 14, f. 34). He also sold to John Luther of Swansea, land at Mattapoisett (Middlesex Co. Deeds, Vol. 99, f. 668). These deeds identify him with his father Joseph (6). His sister Sybil was an heir to her grandmother, and they both were heirs of Obadiah Jenkins, Jr., a half-brother. Joseph Lewis died in Wilmington, July 25, 1755, and his will, made July 1, 1751, gives to his wife Hannah £7 lawful money, with all my provisions and live stock to improve and dispose of during her life, the dwelling house and barn, and all household goods of all sorts. Thomas Pearson, a son-in-law, is made executor, and ordered to fence lands, get in hay, make cider, and put it in the cellar, care for cows, winter and summer, drive and fetch them, provide a horse for meetings, etc.; also 20 bushels of meal (12 indian, 8 rye), 140 pounds of meat (100 pork, 40 beef), one bushel of malt, and firewood. Care for the widow tenderly in sickness, and bury her decently after death. To son Benjamin £20, also a £50 bond he owes his father is his portion. To son Joseph, 20 shillings. To son John, 20 shillings. To daughter Abigail, and to her husband Thomas Pearson, all lands and meadows of all sorts, homestead and outlands. To 4 grandchildren, children of daughter Hannah Durant, £7. All wearing apparel to Benjamin, Joseph and John.

The will of the widow, Hannah Lewis of Wilmington, made June 13, 1757, and probated May 25, 1761, gives to son Benjamin Lewis £10, who is appointed executor. To son Joseph Lewis £10. To daughter Abigail Pierson £10. To son John Lewis, if living, £50. In case of his death, to his two children, John Lewis and Susannah Lewis. To children of son Joseph Lewis, " which he hath by his first wife Lydia Lewis," remaining estate.

She died Nov. 6, 1760, in Wilmington.

Children of Joseph and Hannah, born in Woburn:

71. HANNAH, b. Oct. 13, 1700; m. —— Durant.
72. MARY, b. Feb. 22, 1702.
73. BENJAMIN, b. June 5, 1705.
74. JOSEPH, b. Jan. 1, 1707.
75. ABIGAIL, b. April 11, 1710; m. Thomas Pearson.
76. JOHN, b. June 9, 1713.

39 Edmund Lewis, born in Lynn, Dec. 8, 1695, was a yeoman. He came into possession of his father's lands by purchase of the rights of the other heirs. He also obtained possession of most of his uncle Thomas' land by purchase from his son John (43). Nov. 10, 1736, he also bought of John Lewis (43), tanner, for £600, a certain messuage, or tenement, consisting of upland and meadow, with one dwelling house and barn, situate in Lynn, bounded northerly on land of Nathaniel Ingalls, easterly on land of Edmund Lewis (39), and partly on Bassett's land, southerly on said Edmund Lewis' land, and westerly on Lynn commons, containing about 20 acres (Essex Co. Deeds, Vol. 73, f. 179). This was the house and barn of Edmund (1) which John (43) inherited from his father Thomas (9), who inherited it from John, Sen (2).

Edmund Lewis re-conveyed this property to his brother Thomas, the following month, for £250. Together with Hannah, his newly married wife, he conveyed to his eldest son John, for £19. 18s., "the east end of my Dwelling House, and one half my barn, and one half my salt marsh, wood and upland," on Dec. 8, 1756 (Essex County Deeds, Vol. 178, f. 172). He died intestate, and Sept. 29, 1777, Samuel Ingalls was appointed administrator (Essex Co. Prob. Rec., file 16,745). The widow's dower was set off to her by the court on May 4, 1779, viz.: The west end of the dwelling house, the line running through the centre of the chimney, with a privilege to use the front and back doors, entry and stairs. The east end of the barn containing two Bays, and is 20 feet in length. 100 poles of land, on part of which the dwelling house stands, the east line running through the centre of the chimney. One acre, 96 poles of land in the field by the house. Seven acres, 136 poles of land, part tillage, and part fresh meadow. Four acres of pasture land near the house. Four acres of woodland laid out to John Lewis on town common, it being part of a ten acre lot, the total being appraised at £870. 6. 8.

John Lewis, eldest son of said intestate, having received as advancement of his father certain real estate fully equal to a single share, his heirs desired that only one share be set off to them. The estate was divided into seven lots, and apportioned to Jonathan Blaney Lewis (148), representative of Nathaniel Lewis, deceased, to Lydia Ingalls, Elizabeth Ingalls, Joseph Lewis, Edmund Lewis, Sarah Newhall, and to the legal representatives of John, the eldest son, deceased. The portions were each valued at £248. 13s. 4d.

Edmund Lewis married, Jan. 8, 1723-4, Hepsebah, daughter of Allen, 3d, and Elizabeth (Ballard) Breed of Lynn. She was born June 19, 1697, and was buried Mar. 15, 1756. He married, second, Nov. 25, 1756, Mrs. Hannah (Prince) Fuller, widow of Capt. John Fuller* of Lynn, son of Hannah (8) (Lewis) Fuller. She died in 1795.

Children of Edmund and Hepsebah, born in Lynn:

77. JOHN, b. Oct. 16, 1724. Called "Junior."
78. SARAH, b. Oct. 25, 1726; m., April 10, 1746, John Newhall, son of John and Lydia (Scarlett) Newhall of Lynn. He was b. May 12, 1721, and d. Jan., 1810. She d. about 1793. (See Newhall genealogy, No. 338.)
79. LYDIA, b. Aug. 7, 1729; m. Samuel Ingalls, son of Samuel and Sarah (Ingalls) Ingalls, born in Lynn in 1720. He was a cordwainer. His will was dated July 10, 1794.
80. NATHANIEL, b. Oct. 30, 1731.
81. JOSEPH, b. March 15, 1733-4.
82. ELIZABETH, b. July 8, 1736; m., Nov. 27. 1758, Eleazer Collins Ingalls, born 1731, in Lynn, son of Joseph and Rebecca (Collins) Ingalls. He was a shipwright, and lived in Lynn.

Child of Edmund and Hannah, born in Lynn:

83. EDMUND, b. June 20, 1757.

42 Thomas Lewis, born in Lynn, May 10, 1708. He was the first of the family to learn the trade of shoemaking. He lived in the old Edmund (1) Lewis house, which he bought of his brother Edmund on Dec. 23, 1736 (Essex Co. Deeds, Vol. 73, f. 179.), until he sold it to John Ingalls on Jan. 26, 1758. Afterwards he lived in East Saugus on land bought of the Stockers, and others. His will made Nov. 5, 1774 and probated Jan. 2, 1775, is as follows:

Item—I give and bequeath unto my beloved Wife Elizabeth Lewis the whole use and Impovment of the one half of my Estate both real and personal so long as she shall remain my Widow and all my Household Furniture, to her own Disposal, her Improvement in the House to be the Westerly end & one half of the barn.

I give and bequeath unto my son Amos Lewis and unto his Heirs & Assigns forever the Easterly end of my

*Capt. John Fuller, m., Sept. 15, 1746, Hannah Prince, and had two children, born in Lynn: Millicent, b. Sept. 7, 1748; James, b. June 7, 1752.

Dwelling House & half an acre of land lying on the northerly side of sd Dwelling house also one half my Barn.

I give unto my three sons, Amos Lewis, Thomas Lewis & Nathaniel Lewis and unto their Heirs and Assigns forever the other half of my Estate both real and personal in equal Proportion.

I give and bequeath unto my daughter Elizabeth Johnson, the wife of Timothy Johnson, twenty four shillings yearly & every year to be paid her by my Executors out of my Estate so long as my Wife's Improvement continueth and at the end of my Wife's Improvement I Will, give & bequeath unto her children forty pounds to be paid unto her, if living, or her children if Providence so do order that she dieth before my Wife.

After the Improvement of my Wife is ended, I give unto my sons Thomas & Nathaniel the west end of my House.

I give and bequeath unto my three sons Amos, Thomas & Nathaniel the whole remaining part of my Estate both real and personal unto them, their Heirs and Assigns forever, to be equally divided betwixt them.

Constitutes wife Elizabeth and son Amos as executors.

Dec. 10, 1779, Amos Lewis (85), cordwainer, of Lynn, Elizabeth Lewis, widow, of Lynn, and Thomas Lewis (87) of Boston, cordwainer, for £12,750 (depreciated currency) conveyed to Jacob Newhall of Lynn, a farm of 120 acres in Lynn, also two lots of salt marsh, 7 acres, and 2 lots of woodland, 5 acres. (Essex Co. Deeds, Vol. 138, f. 51.)

May 16, 1777, Ephraim Rhodes and wife Mary, conveyed to Thomas (87) and Nathaniel Lewis (88) of Plymouth and Amos Lewis (85) of Lynn, 5 acres land in Lynn. (Essex Co. Deeds, Vol. 123, f. 278.) On July 19, 1777, John Batt of Lynn for £186 conveyed to Amos Lewis (85) of Lynn, and Thomas (87) and Nathaniel Lewis (88) of Plymouth, 80 acres land in Lynn, bounded on Amos, Thomas and Nathaniel Lewis and Thomas Stocker. (Essex Co. Deeds, Vol. 123, f. 278.)

Thomas Lewis married Dec. 8, 1741, in Lynn, Elizabeth Carder. He was buried in Lynn, Nov. 12, 1774.

Children of Thomas and Elizabeth, born in Lynn:

84. ELIZABETH, b. May 6, 1744; m. Nov. 27, 1766, Timothy Johnson. 3rd church records say m. Jan. 12, 1767. Had: Nathaniel Lewis, b. Oct. 18, 1774.
85. AMOS, b. Sept. 26, 1746.
86. THOMAS, b. Sept. 14, 1748; d. Jan., 1749.
87. THOMAS, b. Nov. 1, 1750.
88. NATHANIEL, b. Nov. 14, 1751.

43 John Lewis, born in Lynn, Aug. 2, 1687. He was an innholder succeeding his father and grandfather. Later he became a tanner and owned a tannery on the Boston road. He was elected deacon for life in the 3d church in 1757. He owned about the last slave, owned in Lynn, and to whom he gave his freedom. The slave was brought from Africa when a boy. John Lewis died in 1778 at the ripe age of 91 years. Alonzo Lewis says he died 1775, aged 92 years, whereas, he was alive in 1778. (History of Lynn, 2d Edition, p. 215.) In 1720 he kept the grammar school. (History of Lynn, 2d Ed. p. 196.) The next year he opened a tannery, for Dec. 21, 1721, Theophilus Burrill of Lynn, tanner, conveys to John Lewis "my tan house and tan yard and 26 poles of land near said Lewis' dwelling house, beam house, mill stone, horse, cart, 2 sleds, 1/3 of Malt house given me by my Father." (Essex Co. Deeds, Vol. 38, f. 278.) He bought considerable land that had formerly belonged to his wife's father Samuel Burrill, and her grandfather John Burrill, and about 1747 he retired from the tannery business, as May 12, 1747 he is "John Lewis, Gentleman," in a deed to John Lewis, jr., schoolmaster (his son) of a dwelling house, barn, several out buildings, and one-half acre of land in the body of Lynn, late in the possession of Joshua and Lydia Ward of Salem, and conveyed by them to John Lewis (Essex Deeds, Vol. 44 f. 49), late enjoyed by Col. Burrill deceased and conveyed to said Lydia, by said Burrill in his will. (Essex Co. Deeds, Vol. 101, f. 89.) There are over 30 deeds on record bearing his name. His father Thomas gave him one-half his house, barn, outhousing and lands, two weeks before his death, and left him the other half if he would pay his debts, care for his widow, etc.; which he declined, but the

Judge of Probate appointed him Administrator of the Estate, and he worked it out of debt, and paid the other heirs £30 each. His will probated Oct. 5, 1778, contains the following items:

Constitutes his son-in-law, Revd. Mr. John Carnes, executor.

Item. I give and bequeath to my daughter Lydia Henchman, widow of the late Rev. Nathaniel Henchman, the sum of ten shillings she being entitled to her proportion of that part of my Estate that came of her Mother, and having my note of hand for a sum to make her equal to my other daughters, as to her fitting out at the time of marriage, and her circumstances in several respects being so much better than those of my other heirs. But I dont do this for want of affection for my dear daughter, for whom I bear a great regard. Item I will, give & bequeath to my daughter Mary Carnes, and to her heirs and assigns, forever, one just and equal third part, in all regards of my remaining Estate, which with what I have already given to and done for her is her full portion in my Estate.

Item: I will, give and bequeath to my three grandchildren, Samuel Lewis, Sarah Lewis and Mary Lewis, children of my deceased son John Lewis, two just and equal third parts of my remaining Estate as aforesaid, that is to say, to the said Samuel, Sarah and Mary Lewis in just and equal parts, or shares, being one third part of the said two thirds of my said Estate to each of them, and their respective heirs and assigns forever, and my will and pleasure is that my said Grandson Samuel Lewis have my Tan house and Tan yard with all the appurtenances & utensils for the Tanning Business belonging, if the said Samuel shall choose the same, and receive them in part of his interest in my Estate aforesaid, which with what I have already given to and done for their deceased Father in his lifetime is their portion in my Estate.

Item: I will and order that the division of my said Estate between my said daughter and grand children be made according to the appraisal & Inventory of my said Estate.

His second wife's estate was settled by Joseph Ballard in 1790, and among the charges was one for nursing since 1778.

The inventory of his estate amounted to £1508. 8s. old tenor. The inventory of the estate of his wife Mary, amounted to £612. 10. old tenor. In the division of her estate, to John and Mary Carnes was set off one-half of the homestead, viz. house and barn, and a third of the old malt house, with other small buildings, together with land. To Samuel Lewis was set off the tan house and yard. To Sarah Newhall and the heirs of Mary Newhall, the whole of the brick yards. Deeds were given by the heirs Sept. 19, 1782.

John Lewis married, first, Nov. 10, 1715, Mary Burrill, born Aug. 24, 1698, the daughter of Samuel and Margaret (Ruck) Burrill. She died Aug. 31, 1754. He was published, second, in Boston, Apr. 25, 1756, with Jane (Ballard) Hunting, widow of Joseph Hunting of Boston, the daughter of John Ballard. They were married in June, 1756. She died about 1790. Administration was granted on her estate July 15, 1790.

Children of John and Mary, born in Lynn :

89. LYDIA, b. Aug. 20, 1716, became the 2d wife of Rev. Nathaniel Henchman, b. Nov. 22, 1700, and d. Dec. 23, 1761. She m. 2d, Russell Trevett, a merchant of Marblehead, and d. before Mar. 26, 1799, when her will was proved. Had: (1) Anna, b. Feb. 25, 1735-6 ; d. Sept. 6, 1736. (2) Lydia, b. Apr. 20, 1740; d. Sept. 19, 1761. (3) Anna, b. May 18, 1742; m. Humphrey Devereaux, jr. of Marblehead.

90. SARAH, b. Jan. 5, 1717-18; m. Mar. 20, 1748-9, Dr. Jonathan Fuller. She died July 1, 1751 and he m. 2d, Apr. 15, 1755, Mary Wyman.

91. MARY, b. Apr. 19, 1720; d. June 15, 1798; m., July 16, 1747, Rev. John Carnes, b. in Boston July 11, 1723, and d. in Lynn Oct. 23, 1802, son of John and Sarah (Baker) Carnes of Boston. John Carnes, sen., was a Colonel in the English army, commanding artillery in Boston in 1748. Rev. John Carnes graduated at Harvard College in 1742, was pastor at Stoneham from 1746 to 1757, at Rehoboth from 1759 to 1764, and lived in Boston during the seige of 1775, corresponded

with General Washington, was suspected by General Gage, had his house and papers searched, and was ordered to leave, which he did. Was chaplain in the army during the Revolution; Justice of the Peace; Representative in the Massachusetts Legislature, 1784 to 1790, 1794, 1795; and delegate to ratify the constitution of the U. S. in 1788. He lived on the John Lewis place, Boston street, Lynn. Children: (1) Dorothy, b. Apr. 25, 1749, in Stoneham; m. Jonas Walsh. (2) John, b. July 17, 1751, in Stoneham. (3) Lewis, b. Oct. 31, 1753, in Stoneham; d. Aug. 1, 1799, in Demarara, W. I. (4) Thomas, b. July 12, 1755, in Stoneham; d. Aug. 5, 1755, in Stoneham. (5) Thomas, b. Oct. 11, 1756, in Stoneham. (6) Burrill, b. July 24, 1761, in Rehoboth. (7) Edward, b. Feb. 12, 1765, in Rehoboth. (8) Joseph. (9) Mary; m. Rev. Benj. Wadsworth, b. in Milton, July 29, 1750 (second wife). He d. Jan. 28, 1826. Her will was recorded in Suffolk County, May 6, 1845.

92. LOIS, b. July 17, 1722; d. Nov. 7, 1750; m. May 7, 1750, in Boston, Capt. Richard Mower, jr. He d. before March 1, 1761. Their daughter Sarah died Oct. 30, 1750, aged 7 days (g. s.), a premature birth, that probably caused the mother's death. See Henchman tomb in Western Burying Ground.

93. JOHN, b. Nov. 7, 1724.

56 James Lewis, born Nov. 14, 1695, at Swansea; received by his father's will the farm in Swansea, consisting of about 140 acres. On May 8, 1723, he conveyed to his brother Samuel 60 acres in Metapoiset (Bristol County Deeds, Vol. 16, f. 336), and on June 25, 1725, he conveyed to his brother Timothy, a house, barn, outhousing, and 80 acres of land in Swansea (Bristol County Deeds, Vol. 16, f. 337). He was executor of his mother's will, Nov. 29, 1731, and was then of Rehoboth. On June 7, 1742, Hannah Lewis of Greenwich, Providence Co., R. I., widow of James Lewis, for £1000, conveyed to Nathan Pierce of Warwick, 100 acres of Oak swamp in Rehoboth (Bristol County Deeds, Vol. 31, f. 74).

57 Timothy Lewis, was born in Swansea, Feb. 23, 1697-8. He received by his father's will one-half of his farm, with the dwelling house, it being the southern end of the farm formerly purchased of Ephraim Pearce, and June 25, 1725, he bought of his brother James 80 acres of land in Swansea, with the buildings thereon.

Administration on his estate was granted to Anne Lewis, his widow, Feb. 18, 1754.

Children of Timothy and Anne, born in Swansea:

94. THOMAS, b. Mar. 22. 1726; m. Jan. 14, 1753, Hannah Martin. Lived in Rehoboth.
95. ELIZABETH, b. Nov. 20, 1728; m., Jan. 22, 1756, Benjamin Mason. Lived in Swansea.
96. ANNE, b. Jan. 11, 1730; d. 1806.
97. HEPZABETH, b. Feb. 14, 1732; m. July 18, 1751, Gideon Cornell.
98. ABIGAIL, b. Feb. 3, 1734; m., 1766, Elisha Cornell; lived in Swansea; and d. Dec. 2, 1769.
99. DEBORAH, b. Feb. 23, 1736; m., Nov. 4, 1787, Richard Hale.
100. MARCY, b. Nov. 6, 1739; d. 1811; will proved Mar. 5, 1811.

59 Samuel Lewis, born April 16, 1702, in Swansea, received by his father's will the northern half of his farm in Rehoboth. He married Hannah ——, and died in 1763.

His will, made March 13, 1762, and proved Oct. 10, 1763, appointed Hannah, his wife, executrix, and gave to her the improvement and profit of all the farm, house and buildings during her life, together with all the stock and household goods. His son Benjamin received the housing and land in Diton (Dighton). This he afterwards sold and gave him the money, as appears by a codicil dated Sept. 16, 1763. His son Joseph received all the land that laid south of what he had sold him, he paying his mother £12 yearly during her widowhood. Samuel received 50 acres on the north end of the home field, he allowing his mother firewood and timber for rails for use on the place during her widowhood.

His sons Benjamin, Joseph and Samuel received his wearing apparel, arms, all his tools and tackling. His daughter, Betty Cornell, one cow and £20. His daughters, Tabitha, Mary, Hannah and Phebe, "all the land between the land I have given to Samuel and to Joseph after their mother's death divided equally." To the daughters that remained single at their mother's death all the household goods and stock that remained after her death, and use of two lowermost rooms so long as they remained single, then all buildings to go to Joseph.

The inventory, filed Oct. 5, 1763, amounted to £128. 11. 6.

Children of Samuel and Hannah, born in Swansea:

101. BETTY, b. Mar. 29, 1729; m. April 13, 1752, Elisha Cornell, and d. Dec. 28, 1765.
102. TABITHA (twin), b. Dec. 21, 1733(?); m., Sept. 24, 1764, William Baker.
103. BENJAMIN (twin), b. Dec. 21, 1733(?); m., Aug. 22, 1754, Ruth Norton.
104. SAMUEL, b. June 20, 1734(?); m., Jan. 12, 1758, Mary Martin.
105. JOSEPH, b. April 2, 1736; m. Patience Pierce.
106. MARY, b. Aug. 7, 1741; m. Joseph Fisk.
107. HANNAH (twin), b. Dec. 29, 1744.
108. PHEBE (twin), b. Dec. 29, 1744.

63 Samuel Lewis, born in Woodbridge, N. J., Jan. 1, 1702; married there Effie Davenport.

Children of Samuel and Effie:

109. JOHN, b. Oct. 16, 1727.
110. SUSANNAH, m. John Stout.
111. DOROTHY, m. Jeffrey Cooper.
112. SARAH, m. John Dow.

70 John Lewis, born April 14, 1723, at Haddam, Conn.; married there, June 21, 1744, Deborah ———, who died Feb. 1, 1813, in her 90th year. He died at Saybrook, Conn., Aug. 9, 1801.

Children of John and Deborah, the first eight born at Haddam, the last two born at Saybrook:

113. JOSEPH, b. Mar. 24, 1744-5.
114. JOHN, b. June 27, 1746; d. before 1765.
115. SIMON, b. 1749; d. Oct. 3, 1791, æ. 42 yrs. (Bible record)
116. SAMUEL, b. 1752-3; d. Sept. 10, 1780, æ. 27 y. (g. s.)
117. MARY, b. Aug. 16, 1758.
118. ANDREW, bapt. Oct., 1759.
119. ANDREW, b. Sept. 12, 1761.
120. SARAH, b. 1760-1762; d. June 29, 1806, æ. 45 y.; m., first, —— Barker; second, —— Jones.
121. JOHN, b. Mar. 23, 1764; d. Mar. 25, 1786.
122. ABNER, b. July 25, 1766.

73 Benjamin Lewis, born in Woburn, June 5, 1705, settled in that part that was set off to Wilmington Sept. 25, 1730. He was a yeoman and member of the church at Wilmington in 1735. He was of Billerica in 1744 and was a selectman in 1753-4 and 9. He was on the tax list Dec. 1776, for £2. 2. 5. as in the "Andover district near Salem Road." He was executor of his mother's will, and also was heir to a part of the estate of Obadiah Jenkins, a half-brother to his father.

Benjamin Lewis died Sept. 23, 1777. His will made Jan. 31, 1771, proved Nov. 10, 1777, gives to his wife Elizabeth the use of all household furniture during her natural life, a good cow, and three sheep to keep for her use during life, firewood, 8 bushels corn meal, 6 bushels rye, 120 weight good pork, 60 pounds beef, sufficient cider and molasses, and so much sauce as she needs, also the interest on £26. 13. 4. lawful money, to be paid her yearly. One half by the executor, and other half by son Benjamin. Also use of a horse to ride to meeting and when needed, all the use of such parts of the house as she chooses and all the conveniences during her life. "Sons Benjamin, Jonathan, John, Reuben and Samuel, each of them have received of me their full portions out of my real estate as will appear by their discharges." To son Ebenezer, £40 to be paid him in 3 months by executor, after decease of the widow.

All money, bonds, notes of hand, apparel, live stock, husbandry tools, to be equally divided between sons then surviving, except money, bonds, notes of hand, which shall be divided after wife's death. To daughter Elizabeth and daughter Esther, all that he gave his wife, also to Esther 40 shillings. "I have given to Elizabeth (125) her full portion out of my real estate." To son James Lewis all lands and buildings in Billerica and in Tewksbury, he to be executor.

Inventory filed Nov. 27, 1777, amounts to £317. 13. 2.

He was of medium height, thick set, inclined to corpulency, weight 180-200 pounds, of great humor and joviality of disposition. (Charles Lewis)

He married, June 5, 1728, in Woburn, Elizabeth Jaquith,

daughter of Abraham and Sarah (Jones) Jaquith of Woburn. She was born June 5, 1708 and died Oct. 1, 1777.

Children of Benjamin and Elizabeth:

123. BENJAMIN, b. Sept. 28, 1729, in Woburn.
124. JONATHAN, b. Apr. 10, 1731, in Woburn. (Family Bible, May 10, 1731.)
125. ELIZABETH, b. Jan. 8, 1733, in Woburn; m. Jan. 29, 1760, Jacob Baldwin of Townsend, Mass.
126. JAMES, b. Sept. 25, 1735, in Wilmington.
127. JOHN, b. Aug. 5, 1737, in Wilmington.
128. REUBEN, b. Sept. 25, 1739, in Wilmington.
129. MARY, b. Nov. 13, 1741, in Wilmington; d. June 6, 1749.
130. ESTHER, b. May 28, 1744, in Wilmington; m. Mar. 22, 1764, Abijah Wood.
131. SAMUEL, b. June 10, 1746, in Billerica; m. June 3, 1773, Betty Parker. He was then of Chelmsford.
132. SARAH, b. June 30, 1748, in Billerica; d. June 8, 1749.
133. EBENEZER, b. Dec. 4, 1750, in Billerica. (Church record, Nov. 4.)

74 Joseph Lewis, born in Woburn, Jan. 1, 1707, received 20 shillings by his father's will and was an heir to Obadiah Jenkins, jr. receiving part of his father's share.

He received £10 old tenor from his mother's will made June 13, 1757. She left all her residuary estate equally to his "children by his first wife, Lydia." He and his wife were members of the church at Wilmington in 1742.

He married in Wilmington, Oct. 22, 1731, Lydia Pearson, probably daughter of Deacon Kendall Pearson.

Children of Joseph and Lydia, born in Wilmington:

134. LYDIA, b. July 17, 1731; m. Oct. 15, 1751, Samuel Buck, jr. of Wilmington.
135. JOSEPH, b. Oct. 17, 1733.
136. TIMOTHY, b. May 24, 1736.*

76 John Lewis, born in Woburn, June 9, 1713, was in the army as Sergeant in Capt. Jonathan Butterfield's

*There may have been other children and another wife. His mother's will mentions the children of his first wife Lydia, from which it may be inferred that he had another wife in 1757 when the will was made.

company on the expedition against Crown Point in 1756 and was reported lost with Hodges.

His mother's will reads, viz: "If he shall be living and shall continue until time of payment [after her death] £50 old tenor, in case of death, his two children John and Susannah to enjoy it equally."

His wife was a member of the church at Wilmington in 1742, as were Benjamin Lewis (73) and wife, Joseph Lewis (74), and Thomas Pearson and wife (75). John Lewis died before Mar. 14, 1757 when Thomas Pearson was appointed administrator of his estate. Inventory was filed Feb. 22, 1760 amounting to £22. 18. 8. with debts of £29. 18. 2.

He married, first, Susannah, by whom he had John, born May 16, 1739 and died young. He married, second, Mar. 14, 1744-5, in Billerica, Phebe Walker, born May 5, 1723, daughter of Jacob and Hannah Walker of Billerica.

Children of John and Phebe:

137. SUSANNAH, b. Apr. 9, 1746; m. Apr. 7, 1768, Philip Peters.
137*a*. PHEBE, b. Nov. 14, 1747; probably d. in infancy.
138. JOHN, b. 1748, who chose his Uncle Benjamin (73) as guardian, Dec. 31, 1763, then in his 15th year.

77 John Lewis, born in Lynn, Oct. 16, 1724, was called junior, John (43) being senior. He was a yeoman and resided on the east half of his father's farm which had been given to him by his father, Dec. 8, 1756, a few days after his father's second marriage.

He added to his inheritance and was quite a land owner at the time of his death, which must have occurred but a few days after his father's, for the administrator of his estate was appointed Sept. 29, 1777 and the administrator of John, jr.'s estate on Oct. 7, 1777.

The inventory of his estate filed March 3, 1778, shows real estate valued at £1664. 9. 8.

Nov. 3, 1778 the same committee that divided his father's estate was appointed to appraise John, junior's and after setting off the widow's dower to Mrs Elizabeth Lewis, the remaining two-thirds were divided into 9 parts, the eldest son, John Lewis, receiving a double portion.

The other children were named as follows: Edmund, Hepzibah, Joseph, Elizabeth Ingalls, Martha Ingalls, Nathaniel, Benjamin.*

John was appointed guardian for his brother Benjamin, and Jacob Ingalls was appointed guardian for Joseph and Nathaniel, on March 3, 1778.

John Lewis, junior, married, Nov. 22, 1748, in Lynn, Elizabeth, born July 24, 1728, daughter of Joseph and Elizabeth (Potter) Newhall of Lynn.

Children of John and Elizabeth, born in Lynn:

139. MARTHA, b. Sept. 22, 1749; m. June 4, 1772, Jacob Ingalls, b. in Lynn, July 1, 1747, and d. Jan. 19, 1823, son of Jacob and Mary (Tucker) Ingalls of Lynn.
140. JOHN, b. Oct. 15, 1751.
141. EDMUND, b. Feb. 10, 1754.
142. HEPZEBAH, b. June 10, 1756; m. June 17, 1783, Ephraim Alley, who d. May 2, 1821. She died Feb. 4, 1828. Children: b. in Lynn: (1) Joseph (twin), b. May 6, 1784; (2) Benjamin (twin), b. May 6, 1784, d. May 23, 1821; (3) Lewis, b. Sept. 5, 1786; (4) Nathaniel, b. Mar. 24, 1789; (5) Mehitabel, b. Dec. 14, 1791; (6) Hepsibah, b. July 13, 1794, m. — Cheever; (7) Lydia, b. Mar. 27, 1797, m. — Batchellar.
143. ELIZABETH, b. Nov. 4, 1758; m. Oct. 8, 1778, her cousin Daniel Ingalls, b. 1760, son of Samuel and Lydia (Lewis) Ingalls. He was a cordwainer and lived in Lynn.
144. BENJAMIN, b. Jan. 31, 1761.
145. SARAH, b. Jan. 25, 1763; d. Aug. 12, 1765.
146. JOSEPH, b. Feb. 4, 1765.
147. NATHANIEL, b. 1768.

80 Nathaniel Lewis, born in Lynn, Oct. 30, 1731, was a cordwainer and lived in Lynn where he died May 23, 1767. (g. s.) He married, Sept. 22, 1757, Abigail, daughter of Jonathan and Hannah (Grey) Blaney of Lynn. After his death his widow married, second, Jan. 13, 1774, Capt. Joseph Felt of Salem, and had a daughter Molly Felt, b. June 6, 1779, who married John Lewis (152). Capt. Felt died and she married, third, Nov. 25, 1790, John Watts of Lynn, and died his widow about 1800.

*Essex County Probate, Vol. 354, f. 70-73.

Children of Nathaniel and Abigail, born in Lynn:

147*a*. A child, d. in infancy.

147*b*. A child, d. in infancy.

148. JONATHAN BLANEY, b. 1760; d. 1780. In the settlement of the estate of Edmund (39) he drew his father's share. His uncle John was appointed his guardian, Jan. 4, 1774 and administration on his estate was granted July 12, 1780 to his mother, Abigail Felt.

81 Joseph Lewis, was born in Lynn, Mar. 15, 1733-4. By his marriage, he came into possession of the old Edmund (1) Lewis house, John Ingalls having bought it from Thomas Lewis (42) on Jan. 26, 1758. Joseph Lewis was a cordwainer and died between Sept. 12, 1799, when he made a deed, and 1805, when his widow's dower was divided. He married Dec. 19, 1765, Mrs. Sarah (Alley) Ingalls, widow of John Ingalls who was drowned in "ye Pines River" Sept. 30, 1762.

Children of Joseph and Sarah, born in Lynn:

149. JAMES, b. 1766.

150. NATHANIEL, b. 1768.

151. WILLIAM.

152. JOHN.

83 Edmund Lewis, born in Lynn, June 20, 1757, was a private in Capt. Wm. Farrington's Co. which marched from Lynn to Concord on the alarm of April 19, 1775. He married Nov. 25, 1779, Rebecca, born Sept. 7, 1760, daughter of Robert and Mary (Newhall) Mansfield of Lynn. He died in 1789, and his wife's brother, Robert Mansfield, was appointed guardian of his two sons, April 6, 1795. After his death his widow married, second, Nov. 29, 1792, his nephew Benjamin Lewis (144). Her sister Martha, married John Lewis (140).

Children of Edmund and Rebecca, born in Lynn:

153. JAMES FULLER, b. Feb. 20, 1781.

154. EDMUND, b. Feb. 8, 1784.

85 Amos Lewis, born in Lynn, Sept. 26, 1746, was a cordwainer and executor of his father's will. He removed to Boston and resided on Sun Court street leading into North Square. He applied for a license as a retailer at a town meeting held Aug. 11, 1786. On the 14 March, 1796, he was elected constable for the year and from 1803 to 1810 inclusive. He died July 23, 1812, aged 66 years (Boston Records). His will made May 29, 1812; proved Aug. 10, 1812, appoints his wife Lydia, executrix, and mentions his children: Sally, wife of Joshua Ellis, cordwainer, of Boston, Amos, John's two children, Lydia, Betsey, Sukey, Asa, Joshua and Charlotte. He married Dec. 25, 1768, Lydia Newhall, born in Lynn, Sept. 11, 1750, died in Boston, May 24, 1837, (Copps Hill Epitaphs) daughter of Moses and Susanna (Bowden) Newhall of Lynn.

Children of Amos and Lydia:

155. SALLY, m. in Boston, Dec. 25, 1791, Joshua Ellis. He was a cordwainer with a dwelling house on North Square, Boston, which was burned in March, 1812. He was b. in Sandwich, May 4, 1769 and d. July 29, 1829.
156. AMOS, b. 1771; d. of fits, July 13, 1816, æ. 45 y. (Boston Records) He was licensed as an auctioneer in Boston in 1805 and 1808.
157. JOHN, b. 1773; d. Apr. 7, 1811, æ. 38 y. (Boston Records) leaving two children.
158. LYDIA.
159. BETSEY.
160. SUKEY.
161. ASA.
162. JOSHUA.
163. CHARLOTTE.

87 Thomas Lewis, born in Lynn, Nov. 1, 1750, was a wharfinger in Boston, and held wharf property near the foot of Fish, now North street. At that time the water of the bay or harbor came up to Fish street, and it was some time later when the improvement was made of filling in the harbor and building Quincy Hall market. He lived on Fish street, near North square, at that time a residential part of the town. He had large interests in that quarter. After his death there was litigation over his affairs, and his children did not agree.

In addition to his Boston property he owned a farm in the south part of Malden, now Everett. He died May 9, 1813.

Administration on his estate was granted to his wife Sarah, on July 12, 1813. Inventory:—

Household furniture,	$618.30
Malden, farming utensils and stock,	217.75
Pew in New Brick Meeting house,	200.00
	$1,036.05

Real Estate:

Lewis Long Wharf (so called) in North end of Boston, incumbered by two mortgages, one to Samuel Dexter, and the other to Jno. Merry,	$60,000.00
Lewis Short Wharf,	7,700.00
Mansion house and land,	6,000.00
Brick house at corner, incumbered by a mortgage to Jonathan Merry,	5,000.00
Brick block on land in Fish St. adjoining mansion house, undivided half, incumbered,	7,000.00
One piece of flats, south side Lewis Wharf, incumbered,	13,000.00
Farm in Malden, incumbered,	2,800.00
One-half Lewis & Watts Wharf, incumbered,	4,000.00
Land and house in Hallowell, Me.,	800.00
9 shares in 100 of Lewis & Dexter's Wharf,	963.00
Total,	$107,263.00

List of Debts:

Thomas Lewis, claim,	$57,376.40
Abiel Smith's claim,	19,200.00
John and Samuel Willis, Samuel Spear & Abiel Wood, Jr.,	17,944.50
Isaac Warren,	1,700.00
Dr. John Warren,	150.00
Elijah Nickerson,	867.00
John Lewis,	12,551.11
W. A. Fales, as trustee of Polly Lewis,	1,155.86
Jonathan Merry,	131.40
Others,	519.35
	$111,595.62

Thomas Lewis married, April 19, 1770, in Lynn, Sarah Merry, born in Lynn Nov. 19, 1750, daughter of Ralph and Sarah (Noah) Merry. She died in Boston, May 22, 1835.

Children of Thomas and Sarah, born in Boston:

164. THOMAS, b. ——, 1771.
165. DAVID, b. June 18, 1776. He was a portrait painter, and d., unm., Dec. 6, 1807.
166. JOHN, b. Aug. 27, 1779. (g. s.)

88 Nathaniel Lewis, born in Lynn, Nov. 14, 1751, was a cordwainer, and removed to Plymouth, Mass. He was lieutenant in Capt. Abraham Hammett's company, which marched on the alarm of April 19, 1775; also a subaltern in Capt. Thos. Mahew's company, in Col. Cotton's regiment, stationed at Roxbury; also lieutenant in the same company and regiment on a muster roll dated Aug. 1, 1775; also in Capt. Lathrop's company, Col. Freeman's regiment, probably in 1778, guarding prisoners belonging to the (British) ship Somerset. The will of Lucy Lewis, his widow, made Dec. 9, 1852, mentions, Mary Elizabeth Edmunds, wife of J. Lincoln Edmunds; Georgianna Shaw, wife of George Shattuck Shaw; and Cornelia and Grace Henshaw, children of her daughter Mary Ann Henshaw, wife of John Henshaw, deceased.

John Andrew Henshaw, son of her daughter Mary Ann Henshaw, also received a legacy. To her daughter-in-law, Mary C. Lewis, wife of her son Charles H. Lewis, is given the miniature likeness of her sons, Charles H. and George A. Lewis, which are set in one frame. All the rest of her property to her children, Hannah Lewis, wife of John Lewis; Lucy S. Danforth, wife of Joseph Danforth; Edmund H., Samuel S., Charles H., and George A. Lewis (Middlesex County Probate, file 28,984). She was a pensioner of the United States, at the rate of $106.66 a year.

Nathaniel Lewis married, first, Hannah Drew, born 1752, and died May 29, 1790, in her 38th year (Plymouth Epitaphs), daughter of James and Mary (Churchill) Drew. He married, second, Sept., 1791, Lucy Shaw, born in Plymouth, June 2, 1773, and died in Malden, June 2,

1859, daughter of Ichabod and Priscilla (Atwood) Shaw, of Plymouth. He died Feb. 25, 1818 (Boston records).

Children of Nathaniel and Lucy, the first six born at Plymouth:

167. HANNAH, b. Oct. 12, 1792; m. John Lewis (166).
168. LUCY SHAW, b. Sept. 8, 1794; m., Oct. 22, 1815, Joseph Danforth of Louisville, Ky. Had: (1) Joseph Lewis, b. April 19, 1822; (2) Julia.
169. EDMUND HUTCHINSON, b. Nov. 22, 1796.
170. SAMUEL SHAW, b. June 19, 1799.
170a. INFANT, b. and d. Dec., 1801.
170b. INFANT, b. and d. Feb., 1803.
171. CHARLES HENRY, b. June 26, 1804.
172. MARY ANN, b. July 29, 1806, at Hallowell, Me.
173. GEORGE ATWOOD, b. Mar. 8, 1809; d., unm., at Louisville, Ky.
174. NATHANIEL, b. Aug. 10, 1811; d. June 3, 1813.

93 John Lewis, born in Lynn, Nov. 7, 1724; graduated from Harvard College in 1744, and was a practicing physician. His father called him schoolmaster in a deed dated May 12, 1747. He died Oct. 21, 1754.

In the inventory of his estate, taken Nov. 4, 1754, is listed 1 small fish house, 1-2 shed by brick yard, 1-2 small schooner, 1-4 of a lighter, 1 old horse, 1-2 a Gundalo, 1-2 a boat, 1 pump in brick yard, gun & swords, books valued at £10. 5. 1., dwelling house, barn and several small buildings, 2 acres land. Total, £630. 18. On April 16, 1755, his widow and administratrix, far £150, current lawful silver, conveyed to Zaccheus Norwood, innholder, a dwelling house, barn, and several other buildings in the body of Lynn, and about two acres of land (Essex County Deeds, Vol. 102, f. 56). This was the same property conveyed to him by his father, May 12, 1747, and is now situated on the corner of Boston and North Federal streets, formerly Hart's Lane (Essex County Deeds, Vol. 101, f. 89).

He married, in Woburn, July 2, 1751, Abigail, born Oct. 2, 1729, the daughter of Timothy and Abigail (Wyman) Brooks of Woburn. She removed to Woburn, Oct. 17,1757, and married, second, Dec. 15, 1757, Samuel Belknap of Woburn, and there she died, Oct. 16, 1761.

Children of John and Abigail, born in Lynn:

175. SAMUEL, b. June 6, 1752.
176. SARAH, b. Nov. 15, 1753; m. Dec. 3, 1772, Thomas Newhall, son of Joseph and Elizabeth (Hodgman) Newhall of Salem and Danvers. She d., and he m., second, Nov. 27, 1806, Sally Hudson.
177. MARY, or POLLY, b. Mar. 6, 1755 (posthumous): m. Dec. 12, 1776, Charles Newhall, son of Allen and Love (Breed) Newhall. She d. Mar. 27, 1780, and he m., second, Mar. 15, 1781, Lois, daughter of James and Lois (Burrill) Newhall of Lynn, and d. Oct. 11, 1817, æ. 65 y. Had: (1) Polly (Martin), b. Oct. 17, 1777; d. Oct. 11, 1800; (2) Charles Newhall, b. Dec. 27, 1779. Child by second marriage: James Newhall, b. Feb. 16, 1782.

94 Thomas Lewis, born in Swansea, Mar. 22, 1726, received by his father's will 19 acres of land and half the house. His sister, Marcy or Mercy (100), left part of her property to his son Thomas, on condition that he provide and care for his parents during life. Jan. 4, 1763, he sold to Benjamin Lewis (103) of Dighton, 44 acres of land in Swansea, lying westerly on land of Abigail Lewis (Bristol County Deeds, Vol. 57, f. 102). He married, Jan. 14, 1753, Hannah Martin, in Swansea.

Children of Thomas and Hannah, born in Swansea:

178. TIMOTHY, b. Oct. 21, 1753; m. Dec. 17, 1778, in Swansea, Elinor White.
179. NATHANIEL, b. Aug. 18, 1755; m. Jan. 9, 1783, in Swansea, Candace Peirce.
180. ELIZABETH, b. July 12, 1757.
181. DANIEL, b. Aug. 1, 1760.
182. THOMAS.

103 Benjamin Lewis was born in Swansea, Dec. 21, 1733(?). He received money from his father for his portion of the estate. He bought, Jan. 4, 1763, 44 acres, 144 rods of land, from Thomas (94) (Bristol County Deeds, Vol. 57, f. 102). He married, Aug. 22, 1754, Ruth Norton. His will, made April 9, 1767, proved April 27, 1767, contains the following bequests: "Being sick," etc. To beloved wife, two cows and all household goods and movables, income and profit of all estate that remains after debts and funeral charges, so long as she remains his widow, to enable her to bring up children. To five sons: James, Aaron, Benjamin, Timothy and Reuben, all real estate equally after their mother's decease, they paying £4 each to their sister Betty. To daughter Betty £20. Appoints wife and brother Joseph Lewis (105), executors.

Feb. 6, 1792, Timothy Lewis of Swansea, yeoman, Aaron Lewis of Rehoboth, yeoman, Reuben Lewis of Rehoboth, cordwainer, Nathan Goff, yeoman, and Betsey, his wife, of Rehoboth, for £30, paid by Benjamin Lewis of Rehoboth, cordwainer, convey all right, title and interest "we have or ought to have in 28 acres 144 rods in Swansea, and buildings thereon, being ye dwelling house whereof our honored father, Benjamin Lewis, deceased, dwelt, and is all the Real Estate our father died seized of, except 12 acres sold by his Executor, bounded as may appear from deed of Thomas Lewis (94) to our father, that is all ye right we had to said house and land by our sd father's Will and as Heirs to ye share that did belong to our brother James Lewis" (Bristol County Deeds, Vol. 72, f. 5).

Children of Benjamin and Ruth, born in Dighton:

183. JAMES, d. between Apr. 9, 1767, and 1792.
184. AARON.
185. BENJAMIN, b. Feb. 16, 1761.
186. TIMOTHY.
187. REUBEN.
188. BETTY, m. at Rehoboth, April 9, 1782, Nathan Goff of Rehoboth.

105 Joseph Lewis was born in Swansea, April 2, 1736. He was a private in Capt. Peleg Peck's company, Col. Thomas Carter's regiment, Aug. 3 to Aug. 9, 1780; also named twice for warrant for pay, dated July 7, 1784; marched to Tiverton, R. I.; also again on roll of same date (Mass. Rev. Rolls). He was a cordwainer and yeoman, and married Patience Pearse in 1770. His will, made 16 Nov., 1798, and proved Apr. 2, 1799, contains the following bequests:

I give and bequeath to Patience Lewis, my beloved wife, the use and improvement of all my real estate, except what I shall hereafter mention, until my son Joseph Lewis shall arrive at lawful age, and afterwards the use and improvement of one-half of my Real Estate as long as she remains my widow and no longer. I also give to my wife all my household goods and indoor movables, except what I shall otherwise dispose of . . . as long as she is my widow. Also all the Provisions that I have by me at my death. What I have herein given to my said wife is in lieu of Rights or Thirds. If my wife Patience shall marry then I only give her one feather bed furniture, one riding horse, one cow, one set of copper plate, curtains, and my brass kettle.

Item. I give to my son Joseph Lewis all my Real Estate except what I shall herein otherwise dispose of after the use & Improvement for the term that I have herein disposed of to my wife.

Item. I give to my daughter Sarah Pearse in addition to what I have already given to her, one cow at my death and £20 in 3 years.

Item. I give to my daughter Mary Lewis one cow at lawful age or marriage day and household goods and indoor movables to be equal to what I have given my daughter Sarah and £20 in 6 years, and use of my great chamber while single.

Item. I give to my two daughters Sarah Pearse and Mary Lewis a lot of land equally, a lot I bought of mother Hannah Lewis late of Swansea deceased.

Item. I give to my son Joseph Lewis my saddle and bridle, desk and all my wearing apparel, with all farming tools and utensils. Finally, I give my said wife all my living stock that I haven't given away to enable her to pay the legacies, debts and charges, and lastly constitute and ordain my wife Patience Lewis my sole Executrix.

Children of Joseph and Patience:

189. Sarah, m. May 15, 1784, Preserved Pearse.
190. Mary.
191. Joseph.

109 John Lewis, born in Woodbridge, N. J., Oct. 16, 1727; died in 1773, in London, Eng. He married, in 1751, Mary Gifford.

Children of John and Mary:

192. WILLIAM, b. 1752; d. 1774.
193. SAMUEL, b. Sept. 29, 1754, in New York, N. Y.

122 Abner Lewis, born July 25, 1766, in Saybrook, Conn.; married, June 19, 1794, Lois, b. June 5, 1772, daughter of Daniel and Jemima Kelsey of Killingworth, Conn. A family Bible in the possession of Mrs. Daniel Levan of Middleport, N. Y., contains a record of the birth of eleven children, of which six were born at Saybrook, Conn., two at Chester, Conn., two at Homer, N. Y., and the last child at Solon, N. Y.

Children of Abner and Lois:

194. JOHN, b. July 26, 1795.
195. REBECCA, b. Dec. 30, 1796; m. July 3, 1823, Zimri Augur, and d. at Mt. Auburn, Ill.
196. LOIS KELSEY, b. June 9, 1798; m., 1825, at Cambria, N. Y., Samuel Boynton Crosby, b. Aug. 30, 1795, at Andover, Mass., son of John and Hannah (Boynton) Crosby. She d. at Cambria, N. Y., Jan. 16, 1837, and he m., 2d, her sister Achsah.
197. NANCY, b. Feb. 11, 1800; m. Orsemus Braman; d. at Rome, Wis.
198. DAN KELSEY, b. Oct. 15, 1801.
199. ELECTRA, b. Aug. 19, 1803; m. Amos Jones; lived at Medina, N. Y.
200. ORPHA, b. Feb. 1, 1805; m. Herman Fox; lived at Homer, N. Y.
201. WARNER, b. Jan. 15, 1807; m. Achsia Bradley of Solon, N. Y.
202. ACHSAH, b. Oct. 16, 1808; m., 1st, Allen Skinner; m., 2d, Samuel B. Crosby.
203. RICHARD, b. July 27, 1810.
204. TRUMAN, b. Nov. 15, 1812.

123 Benjamin Lewis, born in Woburn, Sept. 28, 1729; was taxed in Billerica in 1755, and was a soldier in the public service between 1745 and 1762. He was an early settler at Duxbury School Farm, later called Milford, N. H., where he had a farm on the north side of the Soughegan river, near the Wilton line (History of Milford, N. H.). He removed to Lyndeboro, N. H., where he and his wife were members of the church in 1780. He, his brother James, and his son Benjamin, jr., were taxed there in 1786. A large slate stone marks his resting place in the old cemetery, and is inscribed, "died Jany. 13, 1796, aged 67 years." His wife died and was buried at Milford, N. H., her gravestone having the inscription, "died Oct. 24, 1777, in her 46th year." He married, April 9, 1752, Mary Brown, born in Billerica, Dec. 9, 1731, daughter of Samuel and Mary (Davis-French) Brown of Billerica.

Children of Benjamin and Mary, born in Billerica:

205. BENJAMIN, b. May 6, 1753.

206. MARY, b. Jan. 19, 1755; m., Nov. 20, 1779, Amos Boardman of Reading, b. 1775, son of Amos and Elizabeth (Smith) Boardman of South Reading. They had a large family.

207. ASA, b. Oct. 22, 1756. He was one of the first who enlisted for three years in the Revolutionary war. His head was shot off by a cannon ball at the battle of Bennington, Aug. 16, 1777.

208. SARAH, b. June 14, 1758; m., 1st, Dec. 23, 1784, Zebadiah Holt of Andover, b. July 28, 1759, and d. Mar. 15, 1817; m., 2d, Jotham Blanchard. Mr. Holt was in the Revolutionary war from the Concord fight, April 19, 1775, until Dec. 20, 1783, when he was discharged at headquarters in New York, with the rank of sergeant major. He often remarked that he did not receive to the value of fifty dollars in silver for his ser-

vices. Children of Zebadiah and Sarah: (1) Amasa, b. Dec. 30, 1785; d. at Lynn. (2) Zebadiah, b. Apr. 25, 1787. (3) Sally Lewis, b. April 5, 1789; d., unm., Oct. 19, 1837. (4) Asa Lewis, b. June 1, 1791. (5) Jonathan, b. June 17, 1793. (6) Elizabeth Gould, b. June 13, 1795. (7) Charles, b. April 30, 1797.

209. HANNAH, b. Jan. 12, 1761; d. April 10, 1844; m. Elias Boardman of Reading, who d. May 16, 1844, æ. 89 y.

210. PATTY, b. March 3, 1763; m. Jonathan Holt of Boscawen, N. H.

211. KEZIAH, b. June 22, 1766; m. —— Hinckley.

212. MOSES, b. April 17, 1770.

213. BETSEY, m. —— Gould.

124 Jonathan Lewis, born in Woburn, April 10, 1731 (also recorded at Wilmington), was taxed at Billerica in 1755, and was a soldier in the public service during the period between 1745 and 1762. He removed to Pepperell, where he died Nov. 10, 1776. He was a yeoman, and married, April 3, 1755, Persis Crosby, born Aug. 9, 1733, daughter of Lieut. Simon and Abigail (Kidder) Crosby. After his death, she married, second, John Green of Pepperell, and had a son Benjamin.

Children of Jonathan and Persis, the first six born in Billerica:

214. PERSIS, b. Dec. 15, 1755; m. Benjamin Hatch.

215. JONATHAN, b. Mar. 20, 1758.

216. MARY, b. Apr. 3, 1761; m. Sept. 16, 1784, Elijah Noyes, b. Oct., 1758, at Chockermouth, son of Deacon Enoch and Elizabeth Noyes (Hollis, N. H., records).

217. RHODA, b. Oct. 17, 1763; m. Nathan Nutting.

218. ISAAC, b. Feb. 4, 1766; m. Elizabeth Cram.

219. DAVID, b. May 7, 1768; m. Mary Boynton.

220. ANNA, b. July 17, 1770; unm.

221. ABIGAIL, b. Oct. 2, 1773; m. Nov. 13, 1793, Samuel Perley, of Harrison, Me., son of Samuel and Hepzibah (Fowler) Perley of Gray, Me. (Fowler Genealogy, p. 113).

126 Capt. James Lewis, born in Wilmington, Sept. 25, 1735, was an officer in the militia during the whole of the Revolutionary War, and also was at Concord bridge on the 19 April 1775. His name is on the tax list at Billerica, Dec., 1776, for £2 15^{s} 1^{d}, as of the Andover district near Salem road. He was a selectman in 1781 and 1785 and from 1787 to 1790. He removed from Billerica to Groton on May 24, 1796, where he was highly respected and died lamented June 12, 1810. (See obituary in Groton Historical Series.) He married Jan. 3, 1760, Rebecca Brown, born Feb. 18, 1738-9, daughter of Samuel and Mary (Davis-French) Brown, who died Jan. 1, 1814, æ. 75 years (g.s.)

Children of James and Rebecca, born in Billerica:

222. JAMES, b. Jan. 26, 1761.
223. REBECCA, b. July 15, 1762; d. June 21, 1809.
224. SETH, b. Jan. 1, 1764; d. Jan. 3, 1764.
225. RIZPAH, b. Mar. 13, 1765; d. Mar. 17, 1765.
226. SETH, b. Sept. 22, 1766.
227. RIZPAH, b. May 6, 1768; d. Jan. 9, 1776.
228. AARON, b. June 27, 1770; d. Jan. 12, 1776.

127 John Lewis, born in Wilmington, Aug. 5, 1737, was on the tax list in Billerica, Dec., 1776, for 13^{s} 9^{d}. He was at Bunker Hill, Cambridge, Lexington, and at the siege of Boston. He was 2nd Lieutenant in Capt. Stickney's Co. Col. Bridge's regiment, and was also Ensign in Capt. Stickney's Company, and Lieutenant in Capt. Solomon Pollard's Co., Col. Samuel Denny's Regt. and marched to Claverack in 1779. There is no record of his marriage.

Children of John, born in Billerica:

229. HENRY, bpt. July 16, 1769.
230. MOLLY, bpt. July 12, 1772.
231. SARAH, bpt. Apr. 9, 1775.
232. BENJAMIN, bpt. June 21, 1778.
233. JOHN, bpt. Aug. 11, 1782.

128 Reuben Lewis, born in Wilmington, Sept. 25, 1739, was a corporal in Capt. L. Butterfield's Co., Col. Ebenezer Bridges' regiment, on Apr. 19, 1775. He was also a Lieutenant in the Continental Army, and served under Gen. Washington in his campaigns, and was at White Plains, N. Y., and at Valley Forge. He was a prayerful man, a Christian, a philanthropist and a patriot. He was one of the proprietors of Groton Academy. He sold his farm in Dracut, Mass., taking Continental money for pay, which became worthless, making him a poor man with a large family to support. He possessed an independent spirit. A powder horn with his initials upon it was presented by his son Reuben to the Groton Historical Society. He married, May 17, 1770, Abigail Shed, born Feb. 13, 1748, oldest child of Daniel and Abigail (Patten) Shed, and died in Groton, May 4, 1804, where she also died Oct. 20, 1817.

Children of Reuben and Abigail:

234. ABI, b. July 9, 1771; d. Apr. 21, 1863. For over 30 years she was a governess in the family of Hon. Josiah Quincy, the mayor of Boston.
235. REUBEN, b. Nov. 13, 1772; d. Sept. 29, 1773.
236. REUBEN, b. Aug. 6, 1774; d. Sept., 1777.
237. ZILPAH, b. Mar. 22, 1776; d. Sept. 25, 1777.
238. ZILPAH, b. June 17, 1778; m. John Vose, b. Nov. 5, 1780, in Boston, and d. there Sept. 3, 1824; she d. in Charlestown, Jan. 29, 1865. Had: (1) John Henry, b. June 16, 1811; d. in Walpole, Mar. 17, 1897. (2) Susan Ann, b. Aug. 22, 1813; m. 1st, Richard P. Cory; m. 2d, Geo. W. Palmer and d. Mar. 18, 1898 in Charlestown. (3) Thomas Charles, b. Aug. 8, 1818; m. June 22, 1845, Harriet Sophia Dayton; d. in Walpole, April 15, 1891.
239. BETSEY, b. July 18, 1780; m. David Torrey.
240. ANNA, b. Feb. 19, 1783.
241. AARON, b. Oct. 21, 1785; m. Ruth W. Dix who d. Jan. 5, 1823. No children. He was instantly killed Oct. 16, 1821, by falling out of a chestnut tree.
242. OLIVER PRESCOTT, b. July 10, 1787; d. July 29, 1820, leaving no children. He served in the War of 1812.
243. ASA SHEDD, b. June 25, 1790.
244. SUKEY HAMBLETT, b. Feb. 22, 1793; d. Mar. 4, 1793.

131 Samuel Lewis, born June 10, 1746, married June 3, 1773, Betty Parker. He was then of Chelmsford, Mass. The following record was furnished in 1898 by his granddaughter Mrs. Nancy C. Robinson of Townsend, Mass.

Children of Samuel and Betty (not in the order of birth):

244*a*. SAMUEL, b. Aug. 24, 1779.
244*b*. JOHN, b. 1781 at Washington, N. H.; m. 1806, Rhoda Baldwin.
244*c*. ISAAC, m. Mary or Polly Holt.
244*d*. SALLY, m. Samuel Currier of Concord, N. H., and had 8 children.
244*e*. HANNAH, m. Fred Reed and lived in Peterboro, N. H., had 2 children, a son and a dau.
244*f*. NANCY, d. at Henniker, N. H., of spotted fever when a young woman.
244*g*. DAVID, went to sea in the War of 1812; was wounded in the foot and had a sword cut. Swam the St. Lawrence river and never came home.
244*h*. DANIEL, a half brother to John, lived in Medford, Mass., was bitten by a mad dog and died.

133 Ebenezer Lewis, born in Billerica, Dec.4, 1750. (Nov. 4. family and church record), was married by Wm. Stickney, Esq. Sept. 29, 1772, to Ruth, born July 3, 1752, daughter of Benjamin and Mary (Corey) Parker. She was the first person buried in the new cemetery at Windham, N. H. He died 3 Oct., 1825 (Groton Records).

Children of Ebenezer and Ruth, born in Groton, now Ayer:

245. MARY, b. Sept. 20, 1774; m. Sullivan Davis.
246. JULIA, b. Jan. 8, 1777; m. Washington Davis.
247. ASA, b. July 19, 1778.
248. RISPAH, b. Sept. 7, 1781; d. Aug., 1800.
249. JOHN, b. Apr. 7, 1784; m. Nancy Childs; d. Mar., 1818.
250. SALLY, b. Apr. 3, 1786; d. Nov. 1808.
251. HENRY, b. July 5, 1788; m. Hannah Allen; d. June 18, 1832.
252. EBENEZER, b. July 25, 1790; m. Mary Hamblett ; d. Nov. 12, 1869.
253. BENJAMIN, b. Feb. 1, 1793 ; d. unm. Nov. 1823.
254. LUTHER, b. Nov. 12, 1795.
255. LUCY, b. Nov. 12, 1795; m. June 5, 1814, Lewis Putnam of Cambridge.
256. ELIZABETH, m. Wm. H. Wait, b. Dec. 19, 1807, son of Phineas and Ruth (Bicknell) Wait of Shirley, Mass. (Groton Hist. Series, v. 13, p. 55.)

140 John Lewis was born in Lynn, Oct. 15, 1751. He was cordwainer and received parts 6 and 7 of his father's estate including one-half of a small dwelling house situated near the Friend's Meeting House which had been owned in common by John Lewis (2) and his son John Lewis (7). He died intestate Apr. 16, 1813, and his son Robert Lewis was appointed administrator and guardian for John, Henry Amos and George, minor children.

He married Feb. 4, 1773, Martha, daughter of Robert and Mary (Newhall) Mansfield of Lynn. She died April 16, 1839.

Children of John and Martha, born in Lynn:

257. SARAH, b. Mar. 22, 1773; d. Mar. 3, 1793.
258. ROBERT, b. Apr. 3, 1774.
259. MARTHA, b. Mar. 25, 1777; d. Feb. 20, 1796.
260. JOHN, b. Feb. 15, 1779.
261. BLANEY, b. Oct. 7, 1780.
262. ELIZABETH, b. Oct. 7, 1780; d. Apr. 3, 1781.
263. NATHANIEL, b. Jan. 22, 1783.
264. HENRY, b. Jan. 20, 1785.
265. ELIZABETH, b. Sept. 7, 1787; d. Feb. 21, 1810; m. Nov. 15, 1807, Jacob Phillips. Had: (1) Walter, b. Aug. 15, 1808; (2) John L., b. Feb. 11, 1810. Mr. Phillips, m. 2d, Rebecca Farrington and 3d, Mrs. Martha (Ingalls) Atwell, daughter of Jacob and Martha (Lewis) Ingalls (139). She was the widow of Major John D. Atwell.
266. MARY, b. Sept. 4, 1789; d. Nov. 17, 1792.
267. ASA, b. Jan. 4, 1792; d. 1812.
268. AMOS, b. Oct. 17, 1794.
269. GEORGE, b. May 31, 1800.

141 Edmund Lewis, born in Lynn Feb. 10, 1754, was a cordwainer and lived in Lynn. He marched on the Alarm of April 19, 1775 He married Nov. 4, 1784 his cousin Hepzibah, daughter of John (338 Newhall Gen.) and Sarah (Lewis) (79) Newhall. He died Oct. 16, 1815, and she died Jan. 19, 1837. All his children died without heirs except Sarah, whose daughter Elizabeth Cloutman lived with her grandmother Hepzibah Lewis and deeded land with her as sole heir.

Children of Edmund and Hepzibah, born in Lynn:

270. SALLY, b. May 4, 1785; m. Sept. 25, 1805, Nathaniel Cloutman of Salem. Had: Elizabeth Cloutman (see 278).
271. ELIZABETH, b. Mar. 24, 1787.

272. HEPHSIBETH, b. Sept. 10, 1789.
273. ANNA, b. Mar. 30, 1792.
274. BENJAMIN, b. Apr. 9, 1795; d. June 9, 1813.

144 Benjamin Lewis, born in Lynn, Jan. 31, 1761, was a yeoman and cordwainer and lived in Lynn. He married, Nov. 29, 1792, Mrs. Rebecca (Mansfield) Lewis, widow of his Uncle Edmund Lewis (83). She died in 1794 and he married, second, Apr. 14, 1796, Mrs. Hannah (Richards) Lewis, widow of his brother Joseph (146). She died Oct. 14, 1813, and he died July 19, 1839.

Children of Benjamin and Hannah, born in Lynn:

275. BENJAMIN, b. Nov. 3. 1796.
276. LYDIA R., b. Apr. 9, 1798; m. Dec. 11, 1823, Joseph Lewis (307).
277. HANNAH, b. Feb. 15, 1800; m. June 19, 1843, William Watts, b. Nov. 29, 1810, son of William and Sally (Parrott) Watts.
278. BETSEY, b. May 20, 1802; d. May 18, 1836; m. Dec. 26, 1822, John M. Coombs and lived in Lynn. Had: (1) Eliza Jane, b. Aug. 14, 1823; d. Sept. 11, 1824. (2) Eliza Jane, b. Aug. 30, 1825; (3) Hannah, b. Aug. 17, 1827; (4) George, b. Aug. 10, 1829; (5) John M., b. June 25, 1832. John M. Coombs, sen. m. 2nd. Mar. 28, 1837, Elizabeth, daughter of Nathaniel and Sally (Lewis) Cloutman.
279. JOHN RICHARDS, b. June 20, 1804.
280. FRANCES B., b. May 20, 1807; m. July 30, 1837, Oliver Hall, and had (1) William Oliver, b. Mar. 17, 1844; (2) Mary Frances, m. Albert Lewis, b. in East Boston, Jan. 10, 1843, son of Oliver and Lydia (Bodge) Lewis of Reading. She d. Aug. 28, 1889.

146 Joseph Lewis, born Feb. 4, 1765, in Lynn, married April 13, 1786, Hannah Richards. After his death his widow married, April 14, 1796, his brother Benjamin Lewis (144). She died Oct. 14, 1813.

Children of Joseph and Hannah:

281. JOSEPH, b. Oct. 6. 1790. Was brought up in his uncle's family and often called his son.
281*a*. A daughter, d. in infancy.

147 Nathaniel Lewis, born in Lynn, in 1768, was a shoemaker and lived in Lynn, where he died Jan. 24, 1824. He married Mar. 13, 1791, Rebecca Richards, who died Aug. 7, 1821.

Children of Nathaniel and Rebecca, born in Lynn:

282. RICHARD, b. Sept. 26, 1791; d. July 15, 1792.
283. BENJAMIN RICHARD, b. May 26, 1793.
284. BETSEY, b. May 9, 1795; m. Sept. 5, 1816, Frederick Newhall, b. Aug. 1, 1795, son of William and Martha (Mansfield) Newhall. Lived in Lynn. Had: (1) Eliza, b. July 18, 1817; (2) Frederick Augustus, b. Sept. 13, 1818; (3) Nathaniel Cyrus, b. July 19, 1822; (4) Hester Ann, b. Mar. 31, 1826; d. Sept. 10, 1826.
285. REBECCA, b. Mar. 29, 1797; m. Edmund Lewis (154).
286. NATHANIEL, b. May 29, 1799; d. Dec. 30, 1822.
287. THOMAS, b. Jan. 7, 1801.
288. RICHARD, b. Nov. 6, 1802.
289. HEPZABETH, b. Sept. 16, 1804; m. in Malden, Nov. 8, 1827, Denison Gage of Malden, and d. June 20, 1885.
290. JOHN, b. June 6, 1806; d. Jan. 20, 1808.
291. LUCY ANN, b. Mar. 4, 1808; m. in Lynn, Apr. 28, 1830, Joseph A. Proctor, and d. Mar. 23, 1888. Lived in Lynn. Had: (1) Mary Elizabeth, b. June 5, 1831. (2) Joseph Warren, b. about 1836; d. young; (3) Joseph Warren b. Feb. 16, 1840.
292. JOHN, b. Sept. 5, 1812; m. June 21, 1835, Mary Jane Todd of Malden. Went to California and never heard from. 4 chn.

149 James Lewis, born in 1766, was a yeoman and lived in Lynn. He was married four times. He used to say he wore the same coat at each wedding and it was still a good coat. He married, first, Dec. 7, 1791, Elizabeth Newhall. He married, second, Aug. 1, 1797, Elizabeth Thomas, who died Aug. 9, 1812. He married, third, Dec. 27, 1813, Betsey, daughter of Nathaniel and Abigail Tarbox, who was born in Lynn, July 9, 1787, and died April 22, 1825. No children. He married, fourth, Mar. 2, 1826, Hepzibah Tarbox, sister of Betsey, born in Lynn Oct. 11, 1781 and died Dec. 1, 1835. He died Oct. 28, 1840, aged 74 years (g. s. in Western Burying ground).

Children of ames and Elizabeth, born in Lynn:

293. SALLY, b. Dec. 20, 1791; m. Aug. 20, 1812, Joshua Bacheller, who d. Oct. 21, 1840. Children, born in Lynn: (1) Hannah, b. Mar. 25, 1815; (2) Joshua Warren, b. Mar. 27, 1817; (3) Sally Ann, b. Aug. 12, 1819; d. Sept. 17, 1820; (4) Sarah Ann, b. July 4, 1821; (5) George Augustus, b. Oct. 3, 1823.
294. STEPHEN, b. Jan. 4, 1794.

Children of James and Elizabeth, born in Lynn:

295. POLLY or Mary, b. Aug. 1, 1800; m. Sept. 24, 1818, in Lynn, Ephraim G. Taylor and d. Oct. 31, 1822. Had: (1) Sally, b. June 25, 1819; (2) Benjamin I., b. June 21, 1821.

296. NANCY, b. June 1, 1802.

297. BETSEY, b. Jan. 22, 1808; pub. Apr. 17, 1828, Nicholas Mailey. Children, born in Lynn; (1) Mary Jane, b. Sept. 18, 1828; (2) Nicholas James, b. Nov. 1, 1830; (3) Georgiana, d. Aug. 15, 1857; ae. 5 y. 2 m.; interred in Eastern Burying Ground.

150 Nathaniel Lewis, born in Lynn about 1768, was called "Junior" in deeds and birth records of his children. He was a laborer and lived in Lynn and was familiarly called "Turtle." He married, in Lynn, May 25, 1790, Rebecca Clark, probably born Apr. 2, 1771; daughter of Edmund and Elizabeth Clark of Lynn. She died Apr. 2, 1852, aged 81 years. (Lynn Records.) He died June 11, 1843, aged 75 years. (g. s.)

Children of Nathaniel and Rebecca, born in Lynn:

298. MARY, b. Sept. 29, 1790; m. in Lynn, May 5, 1811, Samuel Ashton, Jr., son of Samuel and Sarah Ashton. He was a shoemaker and lived in Lynn. She d. Nov. 29, 1841. Children, born in Lynn: (1) Otis B., b. Oct. 10, 1811; d. Oct. 2, 1817; (2) Warren, b. Oct. 17, 1813; (3) Mary Lewis, b. Oct. 13, 1817; (4) Hannah Phillips, b. Mar. 3, 1820; (5) Ann Jane, b. Feb. 19, 1822, m. Wm. D. Thompson; (6) Benjamin Franklin, b. May 9, 1827; d. Mar. 18, 1845, æ. 17 y. 10 m. (g.s.); (7) William Alden, b. Oct. 10, 1829; (8) Sarah Elizabeth, b. July 16, 1831.

299. HANNAH, b. May 25, 1793; m. Dec. 13, 1812, in Lynn, James Phillips, Jr., b. in Lynn, Mar. 5, 1790; son of Zacheus and Sarah (Ingalls) Phillips, shoe manufacturer; resided in Lynn. Had: (1) Eliza Jackson, b. Jan. 19, 1817, m. Thomas Collyer; (2) Sally Ann, b. July 25, 1822; (3) William Badger, b. Feb. 28, 1825; (4) Hannah Maria, b. Jan. 9, 1828.

300. EDMUND CLARK, b. Apr. 17, 1795; d. June 11, 1824.

301. REBECCA, b. Feb. 25, 1797; m. Dec. 25, 1817, Samuel G. Ashton. He d. Sept. 2, 1848, æ. 58 yrs. 10 mos. (g. s.) Painter; lived in Lynn. Had: (1) Samuel Gale, b. Apr. 21, 1819; (2) Benjamin Franklin, b. Nov. 5, 1820;(3) Elizabeth, b. Oct. 14, 1823; (4) James, b. Sept. 28, 1827; d. Oct. 19, 1828; (5) Sally Maria, b. Mar, 29, 1829.

302. NATHANIEL, b. Feb. 28, 1799.

303. PAMELIA, b. May 27, 1802; m. in Lynn, Dec. 12, 1822, Samue Haskell, Jr. of Gloucester. He d. May 9, 1868, æ. 68 y. 7 m. (g. s.) She d. Jan. 11, 1881. (g. s.) Shoemaker; lived in Lynn; Had: (1) Abigail Dennison, b. May 29, 1824; (2) Eliza Ann, b. Dec. 16, 1826; (3) Pamelia Augusta, b. Nov. 10, 1828; d. Apr. 1, 1832; (4) Hannah Maria, b. Jan. 3, 1831; (5) Samuel George, b. July 3, 1838.

304. SUSAN, b. Sept. 4, 1804; m. Oct. 10, 1824, Allen S. Rich, Jr.

305. MERANNE, b. Jan. 3, 1807.

306. BETSY MANSFIELD, b. Dec. 24, 1810; m. June 4, 1829, Samuel V. Spear of Philadelphia, Pa.

151 William Lewis, was a laborer and lived in Lynn. He married Nov. 23, 1794, Ann, daughter of Eleazer Collins and Elizabeth (Lewis) Ingalls. He died Sept. 12, 1836. She died Nov. 4, 1856, æ. 82 years (g. s.).

Children of William and Ann, born in Lynn:

307. JOSEPH, b. Mar. 21, 1796.

308. BETSEY BLANEY INGALLS, b. Apr. 13, 1805; m. in Lynn, May 29, 1822, Thomas Chapman. He d. Nov. 19, 1878, æ. 74 yrs. (g. s.), and she d. May 5, 1890. Children born in Lynn: (1) William Ashton, b. Sept. 7, 1822; (2) Alanson Burrill, b. Aug. 28, 1825; d. Jan. 16, 1850.

309. ANN OR NANCY, b. Oct. 7, 1812. In the will of her grandfather, Eleazer Collins Ingalls, she is called Ann but she signed her name Nancy. She m. Mar. 13, 1831 (as Nancy), Archibald Selman and had one child and possibly more, born in Lynn. (1) Nancy Ellen, b. May 20, 1831.

152 John Lewis, called "Junior," was a cordwainer and resided in Lynn. He married in Lynn, April 9, 1797, Molly, daughter of Capt. Joseph and Abigail (Blaney-Lewis) Felt of Salem (see No. 80). In the Eastern Burial Ground her grave stone says she died Sept. 6, 1870, aged 91 years. He died in Lynn, Feb. 9, 1817.

Children of John and Molly, born in Lynn:

310. SARAH, b. Feb. 2, 1798; m. in Lynn, Dec. 3, 1815, John Seger. (His father and mother were of Marblehead.) He d. July 31, 1852, æ. 60 yrs. and was interred in Swampscott cemetery. He was 64 years of age according to an old Bible record. His widow d. Dec. 13, 1879. Children, born in Lynn: (1)

John L., b. Oct. 5, 1819; (2) John Lewis, b. Oct. 10, 1823; (3) William, b. Nov. 1, 1826; m. Mary Standley and d. Feb. 6, 1899. (4) Henry, b. Nov. 2, 1829; m. 1st, Clara Standley, and d. 1896.

NOTE. The Standley sisters were daus. of Thomas and Sarah (Phillips) Standley of Swampscott.

311. JONATHAN BLANEY, b. Nov. 22, 1799.

312. ABIGAIL, b. May 22, 1802; m. in Lynn, Nov. 21, 1819, Samuel Atkins, fisherman; who died Mar. 19, 1864, æ. 70 years. Children, born in Lynn: (1) William, b. July 19, 1820; d. unm. (2) Caroline, b. Oct. 22, 1821; m. Rufus Questrom. (3) Warren, b. Dec. 10, 1823; (4) Samuel, b. Feb. 1, 1827; (5) Mary Jane, b. May 16, 1831; m. Apr. 16, 1848, Joseph Standley.

313. JOSEPH FELT, b. Sept. 2, 1804.

314. MARY, b. Aug. 30, 1806; m. in Lynn, Sept. 22, 1823, Abraham Perkins, son of Jonathan and Margaret Perkins of Lynn. Was a cordwainer. Children born in Lynn: (1) Shipley Wilson, b. Oct. 6, 1823; (2) Foster, b. Oct. 26, 1824; (3) Theodore, b. Sept. 16, 1826; (4) Margaret Maria, b. Mar. 1, 1828; (5) John, b. Sept. 7, 1829; d. July 31, 1830; (6) John, b. June 1, 1831; (7) Abraham, b. Oct. 6, 1837; (8) Hannah Maria, b. July 1, 1839; (9) Edward Augustus, b. Sept. 10, 1842; (10) Sylvester, b. Aug. 12, 1844; (11) Waldo, b. Sept. 26, 1846.

315. HANNAH (F.?), b. Jan. 22, 1809; m. Edward H. Lewis; his 2d wife. No children.

316. PERMELIA MERRIAM, b. Mar. 13, 1812.

317. HARRIET, b. Dec. 2, 1812?; the record of birth was filed after the death of her father, and may not be correct. She m. in Lynn, Mar. 5, 1834, Charles Harradon, who d. Nov. 5, 1843, æ. 31 yrs. Children born in Lynn: (1) Charles Oscar, b. Sept. 22, 1837; d. Feb., 1902; (2) Harriet Emily, b. Apr. 16, 1841; d. Aug. 23, 1853.

153 James Fuller Lewis, born in Lynn, Feb. 20, 1781, was a shoemaker and resided in that part of Lynn called Gravesend. He died Jan. 3, 1842. He married in Marblehead, Oct. 27, 1801, Abigail Humphreys, born Sept. 27, 1781, daughter of Benjamin and Jemima (Gale) Humphreys of Marblehead, who died in Lynn, June 27, 1852.

Children of James Fuller and Abigail, born in Lynn:

318. JAMES, b. Feb. 11, 1802.

319. REBECCA, b. Oct. 26, 1804 (Oct. 24. Family Rd.); m. May 29, 1830 (May 9, 1829. Family Rd.), George Hobby, b. in Charlestown, son of William Hobby. She d. June 22, 1838. Children, born in Lynn: (1) George Henry, b. Mar. 8, 1831; d. Nov. 2, 1898; (2) Mary Ann, b. July 2, 1833; (3) Rebecca Ellen, b. Feb. 23, 1835; (4) Abby Green, b. May 6, 1837; d. Sept. 23, 1837.

320. SAMUEL HUMPHREYS, b. Jan. 26, 1807; m. July 5, 1833, in Lynn, Sally Parrott; d. July 26, 1873.

321. WILLIAM, b. June 8, 1809; d. Sept. 26, 1832; m. Nov. 20, 1831, in Lynn, Mary Newman. No children.

322. RUTHE, b. Feb. 17, 1812; d. Mar. 6, 1815.

323. NABBY, b. Nov. 8, 1813; d. Nov. 1, 1892; m. as Abigail, Dec. 15, 1836, in Lynn, Abner Silsbee, b. in Lynn, Sept. 11, 1812 and d. Aug., 1890, son of Henry and Mary (Chase) Silsbee. Farmer. Children, born in Lynn: (1) William Lewis, b. Sept. 12, 1837; (2) James Albert, b. Nov. 11, 1839; d. Apr. 17, 1848; (3) Abbie Maria, b. Mar. 6, 1841; d. Sept., 1883; (4) Alden Burrill, b. Aug. 15, 1845; d. Mar. 22, 1849; (5) Sylvester, b. Jan. 24, 1848; d. Apr. 13, 1849; (6) Charles Albert, b. May 5, 1850.

324. RUTH VICKARY, b. Mar. 19, 1816; d. Sept. 21, 1843; m. in Lynn, May 15, 1839, James Grover Brown, b. in Danvers, Oct. 9, 1812, and d. in Lynn, Oct., 1879. Children, born in Lynn: (1) James Otis, b. Feb. 7, 1840; (2) Melinda Ann, b. Mar. 2, 1842; d. Nov. 2, 1842; (3) Emeline Ruth, b. Sept. 12, 1843.

325. EMELINE, b. Nov. 24, 1818, Family Rds. (Nov. 29. Lynn Rds.); m. in Lynn, Apr. 29, 1841, George Hobby, and died Aug. 30, 1842; he d. April 7, 1879. Had: Lewis, b. May 6, 1842; d. Oct. 21, 1842.

326. THOMAS VICKARY, b. Sept. 3, 1820.

327. HORACE FULLER, b. July 23, 1827; d. Mar. 24, 1885. He m. 1st, Nov. 30, 1848, Mary Angeline, dau. of Benjamin and Martha (Putnam) Ireson, b. July 16, 1830; and d. Sept. 12, 1849, in Lynn. He m. 2nd, July 17, 1853; Martha Ann Ireson, sister of his first wife, b. May 29, 1827, Lynn Rds. (May 30, 1827. Family Rds.); and d. Dec. 3, 1891, in Lynn.

154 Edmund Lewis, born in Lynn, Feb. 8, 1784, was a shoemaker, lived on Lewis street, Lynn, and died Oct. 8, 1870. He married in Lynn, Nov. 10, 1816, Rebecca Lewis (285), who died Dec. 18, 1861, æ. 64 years, 9 months.

Children of Edmund and Rebecca, born in Lynn:

328. EDMUND, b. July 20, 1817; farmer; removed to Rockford, Ill.; d. there, unm., May 5, 1878. Interred in Eastern Burial Ground, Lynn.
329. REBECCA, b. Dec. 26, 1818; d. Oct. 1, 1842; m., in Lynn, May 28, 1838, Jesse Smith Punchard, b. in Salem, Feb. 6, 1813, and d. Feb. 12, 1864. Had: (1) Mary Lewis, b. May 15, 1839; m., 1st, Feb. 22, 1872, at Salem, Robert Henry Wilson of Peabody; m., 2d, Charles H. Whipple of Peabody; (2) Rebecca Pickworth, b. Sept. 25, 1842; m., Feb. 20. 1865, William B. Cressy of Rowley, who d. July 21, 1873.
330. NATHANIEL, b. June 24, 1821; d. Sept. 1, 1821.
331. EDITH HANSON, b. Aug. 14, 1822; m. in Lynn, May 7, 1843, George Whippen, b. Oct. 6, 1819, son of Joseph and Patience Whippen. Had: (1) Eliza Jane, b. May 16, 1844, in Lynn; (2) George Edmond, b. Feb. 1, 1846, in Lynn; (3) Louis Ivers, b. June 15, 1848, in N. J.
332. OLIVE SAUNDERS, b. Mar. 8, 1825; d. Aug. 12, 1854; m. in Lynn, Jan. 21, 1844, Jesse Smith Punchard. Had: (1) Olive Delina, b. Mar. 21, 1845; d. April 15, 1845; (2) Olive Delina, b. May 31, 1846; d. young; (3) Emma Maria, b. June 30, 1849; m., in Salem, Jan. 26, 1871, George H. Symonds of Salem; (4) Eliza Ellen, b. Aug. 29, 1853; d. Mar. 9, 1906; m., Apr. 3, 1873, George P. Woodbury of Salem, who d. Sept. 28, 1893.
333. BRIDGET, b. Apr. 13, 1828; d. June 18, 1856, unm. Death recorded as Hannah B.
334. CLARINDA, b. Oct. 13, 1830; d. Feb. 15, 1899; m. as Elizabeth C., in Lynn, Oct. 15, 1853, Ephraim G. Ricker of Boston, æ. 25 y. Removed to Rockford, Ill.
335. HEPZIBAH MARIA, b. June 1, 1833; m. in Lynn, June 3, 1868, Charles H. Carling, æ. 41 yrs., b. in England, son of Charles H. and Elizabeth Carling, a glass blower, who d. in 1893.
336. LUCY ABBA, b. May 1, 1837; m. in Lynn, May 17, 1860, Edward A. Dickerson, b. in Lynn, Oct. 15, 1835; son of Edward and Mary Dickerson. He d. in 1889.

164 Thomas Lewis, born in 1674, married, first, in Boston, Jan. 1, 1794, Elizabeth Carpenter. He married, second, in Boston, Jan. 6, 1806, Priscilla Nye. She died in childbed, Sept., 1810, aged 29 years, and he married, third, in Boston, Nov. 25, 1813, Polly Clapp, born in Scituate Jan. 23, 1780, daughter of William and Priscilla

(Otis) Clapp. She died in Framingham, Mass., Dec. 19, 1865. He was thrown from a carriage, his skull fractured and he died Aug. 18, 1824.

Children of Thomas and Elizabeth:

337. SARAH, bp. Mar. 22, 1795; m. Benjamin Scott; d. childless.
338. ELIZA, bp. Dec. 25, 1796; m. Edmund Hutchinson Lewis (169).
339. CATHERINE L., bp. July 27, 1799, in Boston; m. Mar. 28, 1821, Jonathan Pratt Robinson of Roxbury. Had: (1) Henry Ware, b. Jan. 31, 1822 in Fredericksburg, Va.; d. Nov. 28, 1890; m. July 22, 1846, Sarah W. Ware; (2) Thomas Lewis, b. Sept. 26, 1823; d. Aug. 26, 1887, in Brighton, Eng.; m., Nov. 15, 1848, in Fall River, Hannah Valentine Durfee, b. Jan. 25, 1828; (3) Robert Lambert, b. May 7, 1827 in Boston; d. Aug. 23, 1866 in St. Louis, Mo.; (4) Catharine Augusta, b. Feb. 4, 1830, in Boston; d. Dec. 18, 1850, in Roxbury; (5) Hannah Hortense, b. Aug. 20, 1839, in Roxbury; m. Jules G. Tournade; d. Jan. 12, 1885, in Brooklyn; (6) Francis Kettell, m. Etta Stevens.
340. HANNAH BRACKETT, bp. Dec. 21, 1800; m. Samuel Shaw Lewis (170).

Children of Thomas and Priscilla:

341. THOMAS, b. May 24, 1808.
342. JOSEPH.
343. PRISCILLA NYE, bp. Nov. 25, 1810; d. in Boston, May 31, 1812.

Children of Thomas and Polly:

344. ABIEL SMITH, b. July 15, 1814.
345. WILLIAM GUSTAVUS, b. Aug. 21, 1816.
346. FRANCES MARY PRISCILLA, b. Nov. 5, 1819; m. John Littlejohn Wilson of Charleston, S. C. Living in 1907.

166 John Lewis, born Aug. 27, 1779 (g. s.), resided in Boston and Malden. He married, first, in Boston, Nov. 22, 1807, Mary Ann Ouvre (marriage intention Oliver), born in Guadeloupe, W. I. She d. June 30, 1814, æ 28 y. He married, second, in Boston, July 30, 1815, Hannah Lewis (167). She died in Malden, Jan. 16, 1862 (g. s.). He died in Malden, March 27, 1871, aged 91 years, 7 months (g. s.).

Children of John and Mary Ann:

347. MARY ANN, m., in 1832, David N. Badger, b. in Boston, July 16, 1799; d. in Malden, Dec. 4, 1878. Had: (1) David N.; (2) Mary Ann; (3) Sarah; (4) Elmer.

348. SARAH ELOISE, d. July 5, 1812, æ. 2 y. (Boston Rds.).

Children of John and Hannah:

349. JOHN, b. Apr. 29, 1816, in Boston; d. Apr. 30, 1816.

350. JOHN, b. Mar. 3, 1817, in Boston; d. Jan. 24, 1818.

351. JOHN, b. Jan. 21, 1819, in Boston.

352. HANNAH AUGUSTA, b. July 20, 1820, in Boston; d. Oct. 10, 1821.

353. CHARLES HENRY, b. Nov. 1, 1821, in Boston, d. in Malden, Jan. 12, 1877; m. Dec. 10, 1843, Almira Tufts, dau. of Joseph Tufts of Malden. No issue.

354. HANNAH AUGUSTA, b. Feb. 15, 1823, in Boston; m. in Boston, Aug. 18, 1843, Wm. Wilkes, b. Jan. 27, 1820, in Fredonia, Ind., s. of Henry and —— (Ballard) Wilkes. He lived in Louisville, Ky., and was of the firm of Lewis & Wilkes, wholesale hardware dealers. Later he removed to Alton, Ind., and engaged in agriculture. Was county commissioner of Crawford county, about 16 yrs.; and d. Aug. 3, 1891. She d. Aug. 27, 1893. Children, all but the first, b. in Alton, Ind.: (1) George, b. Oct. 7, 1844, in Louisville, Ky.; d. July 6, 1860; (2) Hannah A., b. July 24, 1846; m. John Birkla; res. at Alton, Ind.; (3) Alice G., b. Mar. 1, 1848; d., July 31, 1860, in Louisville, Ky.; (4) Louis, b. June 12, 1849; m. Cornelia M. Ridge; res. at Alton, Ind.; (5) John F., b. Jan. 16, 1851; m. Elizabeth Goad; (6) Thomas, b. Sept. 15, 1854; m. Eunice Carberry; res. at Alton,; Ind. (7) Benjamin, b. Sept. 23, 1858; m. Sarah E. Kemp; res. at Alton, Ind.; (8) William, b. Sept. 11, 1860; m. Amanda Culver; res. at Alton, Ind.; (9) Isabel, b. April 21, 1863; m. John Grubbs; res. at Skurry, Kaufman county, Texas; (10) Perry W., b. Nov. 10, 1865; m. Sally A. Pearson; res. at Alton, Ind.

355. LUCY DANFORTH, b. Sept. 5, 1824, in Malden; m. June 27, 1850, Paschal Paoli Pope Ware, b. in Wrentham, June 12, 1820; d. in Everett, Oct. 20, 1882. Children, b. in Malden: (1) Lucy Elizabeth, b. Nov. 15, 1855; m., Oct. 28, 1880, Theodore H. Pierce; (2) Paschal P. P., b. May 27, 1760; m., May 13, 1890, Lora D. Ward.

356. SARAH, b. Jan. 21, 1826, in Malden; m. Francis B. Wallis of Boston, and d. Nov. 8, 1894, in Everett. Children: (1) Arthur D.; (2) Mina.

357. NATHANIEL, b. Sept. 21, 1827, in Malden.
358. THOMAS, b. July 21, 1829, in Boston.
359. DAVID, b. Jan. 15, 1831; d. Jan. 18, 1831, in Boston.
360. GEORGE A., b. July 21, 1832, in Boston; d. May 8, 1843, in Malden.

169 Edmund Hutchinson Lewis, born in Plymouth, Mass., Nov. 22, 1796; married Sept. 5, 1819, Eliza Lewis (338). He resided in Louisville, Ky.

Child of Edmund and Eliza:

371. HENRY EDMUND, m. Margaret Clark. Had: Eliza, who d. childless.

171 Samuel Shaw Lewis, born in Plymouth, June 19, 1799; married in Boston, Nov. 3, 1824; Hannah Bracket Lewis (340).

He was a member of the Ancient and Honorable Artillery Co., 1845-1849. He was agent of the Cunard Steamship Co. and also various railroads, and originator of the project for filling in what is now Commercial Street, Boston. He was one of the principal promotors of the Grand Junction R. R.

His wife died June 4, 1859, and he died in 1869, in Boston.

Children of Samuel Shaw and Hannah:

362. FRANKLIN HENSHAW, b. July 20, 1825, in Boston.
363. LUCY ELIZABETH, d. Mar. 19, 1832; æ. 4 y. 4 m. (Boston Rds.)
364. CATHERINE AUGUSTA, d. Jan. 20, 1830, æ. 8 mos.
365. SAMUEL SHAW, d. Nov. 30, 1831, æ. 8 mos.
366. ANNA RICHMOND, b. 1833; unm., res. at 38 Norfolk Road, Brighton, Eng.
367. JOSEPHINE, b. 1835; m. Dec. 24, 1856, George Lyman Perry, and had one son, Lyman Lewis Perry.
368. FRANCES WILSON, b. 1837; d. 1885, unm. at Brighton, Eng.
369. SAMUEL SHAW, b. 1838; d. unm. in 1880 at London, Eng.
370. CAROLINE SUSAN, b. 1840; d. 1878; m. Frederick Smith, U. S. Navy, of Charleston, S. C., and had Rachel Gertrude, unm., who resides in Washington, D. C.
371. GERTRUDE MACIVOR. b. 1842; d. unm. Apr. 17, 1899, at Brighton, Eng.

171 Charles Henry Lewis, born in Plymouth, June 26, 1804; married in Cincinnati, Ohio, June 19, 1838, Mary Clark Anderson, born in Pittsburgh, Pa., daughter of Paul and Mary (Clark) Anderson of Pittsburgh, Pa. Resided at Louisville, Ky.

Children of Charles Henry and Mary Clark:

372. B. FRANKLIN.
373. CHARLES ANDERSON.
374. FANNIE CALDWELL, m. William Henry Kaye. Resides in Louisville, Ky. Had: William Henry, m. Mary E. Griffith and had one son, Lewis Griffith.
375. KATE CALDWELL.
376. MARY PAUL, m. David Edgar Park of Pittsburgh, Pa. and had one son, Lewis Anderson.

175 Samuel Lewis, born in Lynn, June 6, 1752, was a Mattross in Capt. Winthrop Gray's Co., Col. Craft's artillery regiment. His pay abstract, sworn to in Boston June 8, 1776, has his autograph signature. He received a tannery by will of his grandfather. He married in Lynn, Nov. 29, 1770, Susannah Meachum, born in Lynn, June 29, 1754, daughter of Isaac and Ruth Meachum of Lynn. She died Feb. 14, 1815 (g. s.). He died Apr. 25, 1806.

Children of Samuel and Susannah, born in Lynn:

377. JOHN, b. Feb. 15, 1772.
378. SUSANNAH, b. Mar. 24, 1774.
379. THOMAS, b. Sept. 29, 1776.
380. HENRY, b. Nov. 3, 1782.
381. ISAAC, b. Apr. 12, 1785.
382. SALLY, b. July 12, 1787.
383. SAMUEL, b. Nov. 3, 1789.
384. JESSE L., b. Apr. 16, 1792.

179 Nathaniel Lewis, born in Swansea, Aug. 18, 1755, was a private in Capt. Jonathan Danforth's Co., Col. D. Brewer's regiment, from May 7, 1775 to Oct., 1775; also in Capt. Peleg Peck's Co., Col. Carpenter's regiment, Sept., 1777, and again in Aug., 1780. He married in Swansea, Jan., 9, 1783, Candace Peirce.

Children of Nathaniel and Candace, born in Swansea:

385. ANNE, b. Aug. 26, 1785.
386. CANDACE, b. June 21, 1787.
387. MARCY, b. Apr. 14, 1789.
388. NATHANIEL, b. Feb. 16, 1791.
389. HIPSEY, b. Dec. 12, 1792.
390. AMOS, b. Jan. 14, 1795.
391. MASON, b. Dec. 21, 1796.
392. JESSE, b. Oct. 20, 1798.
393. POLLE, b. Aug. 4, 1800.
394. LEDIA, b. July 4, 1804.

184 Aaron Lewis, was a private in Capt. Peleg Peck's Co., Col. John Daggett's regiment, on the alarm at Rhode Island, Jan. 14, 1778, and was in the same company in the following August. On Nov. 6, 1820, the selectmen of Dighton complained that he was spending his fortune in drink and on Nov. 10, Ebenezer Talbot was appointed as guardian. He married Apr. 4, 1779, Mary, daughter of Noah Davis of Providence, R. I., who died May 13, 1814.

Children of Aaron and Mary:

395. JOHN, b. 1780.
396. JOSEPH, b. Dec. 17, 1793.
397. MARY.
398. BETSEY, m. Henry Harrison.

185 Benjamin Lewis born in Dighton, Feb. 16, 1761, married, first, by Elder Jacob Hix, at Rehoboth, Nov. 23, 1783, Lydia Bosworth, born Oct. 11, 1756, and died July 29, 1795, the daughter of John and Lydia (Capron) Bosworth. He married, second, by Elder Hix, Mar. 27, 1796, Hannah, daughter of Joseph and Hannah Rounds of Rehoboth, born Mar. 12, 1777, and died June 29, 1853. He died Feb. 16, 1849, on his 88th birthday. Of his remarkable family of eighteen children, thirteen reached the age of 66 years or upwards and possessed a marked degree of individuality. Most of the men were masons, and they ably carved out their way to success in life.

Children of Benjamin and Lydia, born in Dighton:

399. BENJAMIN, b. Feb. 14, 1785.
400. JAMES, b. Sept. 10, 1787.
401. LYDIA, b. Oct. 5, 1789; m. in Providence, in 1822, Benjamin Pidge, a widr. who d. Oct. 13, 1839, æ. 63 y. She d. May 1, 1867, in Providence, R. I. Had: (1) Charles W., b. May 11, 1823; (2) Sophia E., b. 1825? (3) Frances H., b. 1827? (4) Samuel J., b. Oct., 1832; (5) Henry C., b. Apr. 25, 1834; d. Oct. 7, 1835; (6) Henry P., b. May 7, 1835; d. Mar. 29, 1840.
402. A CHILD, buried at Swansea.
403. A CHILD, buried at Swansea.

Children of Benjamin and Hannah, born in Dighton :

404. SAMUEL, b. Mar. 24, 1797; m. 1st, Lydia R. West, daughter of Capt. John West, who d. June 10, 1859, æ 57 yrs.; m. 2d, Jan. 27, 1873, in Providence, R. I., Mary Ann, dau. of William and Ann Creswell of England. He endowed her with $700.00 a year during her life. He died Sept. 26, 1873, and she returned to England and m. again. He was a mason by trade and resided at Providence, R. I. where he accumulated quite a fortune.
405. CHACE, b. Nov. 1, 1798.
406. BOWERS, b. Mar. 13, 1801.
407. LEVI, b. May 24, 1803.
408. HANNAH, b. June 20, 1805; d. in Providence R. I., June 4, 1892; m. Charles Williams, b. July 4, 1804 and d. Nov. 8, 1877. Had: (1) Charles A., b. Oct. 8, 1828; d. Mar. 27, 1867; (2) Benjamin F., b. Sept. 22, 1831; unm; (3) Hannah E., b. May 29, 1835; d. Sept. 27, 1836; (4) Virgil C., b. Dec. 30, 1837; d. Apr. 7, 1862; (5) Hannah V., b. July 30, 1839; (6) Archelus A., b. Feb. 19, 1843; d. Feb. 6, 1856; (7) Alanson A., b. Feb. 19, 1843.
409. JEREMIAH, b. Dec. 2, 1806.
410. ALMIRA, b. Mar. 2, 1808; d. unm. June 12, 1876.
411. ALFRED, b. Feb. 28, 1810.
412. SYLVESTER, b. May 2, 1812.
413. CAROLINE, b. Nov. 26, 1813; d. Nov. 8, 1814.
414. CALEB MASON, Nov. 28, 1814; d. Jan. 29, 1815.
415. ANGELINE, b. Nov. 25, 1816; d. May 3, 1831.
416. ORIN JUDSON, b. Mar. 25, 1818; d. Sept. 15, 1883, in Dayville, Conn.; m. Hannah R. Sears. No issue. He was a hardware merchant and manufacturer of belts at Dayville, Conn.

186 Timothy Lewis, married May 9, 1788, Submit Bullock who died May 1, 1844. He died Nov. 22, 1821.

Children of Timothy and Submit, last six born at Dighton:

417. POLLY, b. Jan. 7, 1789; d. Aug., 1865.
418. BETSEY, b. Feb. 7, 1791; d. Oct. 12, 1854.
419. WILLIAM, b. Aug. 11, 1793.
420. RUTH, b. Nov. 3, 1794.
421. TIMOTHY, b. Dec. 18, 1795; d. Apr. 29, 1839.
422. SALLY, b. May 3, 1798; d. Feb. 21, 1865.
423. SUBMIT, b. June 18, 1800; d. 1887.
424. LEONARD, Dec. 31, 1802; d. Apr. 2, 1842, while serving in the Indian War.
425. NANCY VOCE, b. Nov. 27, 1804; d. Mar. 26, 1880, in Providence, R. I.; m. Apr. 7, 1826, Increase Sumner, b. Jan. 3, 1801, at Woodstock, Conn., d. Apr. 25, 1866. Had: (1) George Lowell, b. July 4, 1827 , in Providence, R. I.; d. July 21, 1827; (2) Eliza Ann West, b. Oct. 5, 1828, in Providence, R. I.; m. May 21, 1849, Edwin Blake Larchar, resides in N. Y. City; (3) Sarah Maria, b. Nov. 27, 1830; m. Aug. 25, 1855, Noble Warren DeMunn, in Providence, R. I.; (4) Timothy Increase b. Oct. 7, 1832; d. Mar. 17, 1849; (5) Nancy Lewis, b. June 24, 1835, in Providence, R. I.; d. Feb. 27, 1896, in Boston; m. Sept. 12, 1859, Charles Henry Crump; (6) Lydia Rand, b. Apr. 12, 1838; (7) Mary May, b. May 3, 1841; d. Jan. 27, 1893; m. Aug. 13, 1873, Wm. Woodward; (8) Julia DeEtt, b. Aug. 10, 1844; d. Aug. 2, 1848; (9) Julia DeEtt, b. June 1, 1848.
426. ISAAC, b. Dec. 5, 1807; d. July 10, 1872; m. 1st, Asea Ann Goff, who d. Jan. 13, 1863; m. 2d, May 22, 1864, Betsey J. West of Rehoboth, Mass.

187 Reuben Lewis, married by Elder Russell Mason, on Mar. 31, 1793, at Rehoboth, Luraney Brown of Swansea.

Child of Reuben and Luraney:

427. REUBEN, b. abt. 1797; m. in Providence, R. I., Sarah Borden of Fall River, Mass, and d. by suicide, in Providence, R. I. May 4. 1858, æ. 61 yrs.

193 Samuel Lewis, born Sept. 29, 1754, in New York city; married, in 1778, Elizabeth Godfrey, and died Sept. 30, 1822.

Children of Samuel and Elizabeth:

428. SAMUEL J. N., b. Aug. 22, 1799; d. 1849.
429. MARYANA, b. Mar. 4, 1782; d. 1861.
430. FREDERICK, b. Nov. 22, 1784; d. 1786.
431. SARAH, b. Aug. 19, 1786; m. James Johnston.
432. HENRY, b. Oct. 4, 1788; d. 1822.
433. ELIZABETH, b. July 4, 1790; d. 1791.
434. JAMES, b. Mar. 29, 1792.
435. EDWARD SIMMONS, b. Nov. 26, 1794; d. 1829.
436. GEORGE, b. Aug. 27, 1798; d. 1883.
437. HARRIET, b. Feb. 26, 1800.
438. CHARLES, b. Feb. 27, 1803; d. 1863.
439. WILLIAM GIFFORD, b. Mar. 24, 1807; d. 1851.

194 John Lewis, born at Saybrook, Conn., July 26, 1795; married Emily Symonds, and died at Cambria, N. Y. Another report states that he died in Michigan.

Children of John and Emily:

440. JOHN.
441. LYMAN.
442. WILLIAM.
443. GERALDINE.

198 Dan Kelsey Lewis, born at Saybrook, Conn., Oct. 15, 1801; married at Hinsdale, N. Y., Nov. 2, 1828, Catherine, born Aug. 16, 1809, at Geneva, N. Y., daughter of John and Catherine (Foot) Conrad. He died Dec. 2, 1886, at Fontanelle, Neb., where his widow and family reside.

Children of Dan Kelsey and Catherine:

444. LOIS, b. Mar. 8, 1830, at Hinsdale, N. Y.
445. AUGUSTUS, b. Jan. 30, 1832, at Hinsdale, N. Y.
446. AUGUSTA, b. Jan. 30, 1832, at Hinsdale, N. Y.; d. Jan. 17, 1846, at Burlington, Iowa.
447. JOHN CONRAD, b. April 29, 1834, at Portville, N. Y.
448. CATHERINE, b. July 11, 1837, at Hinsdale, N. Y.; d. July 19, 1851, at Burlington, Iowa.
449. OSCAR, b. Oct. 25, 1840, at Portville, N. Y.

450. OSMAR, b. Oct. 25, 1840.
451. HELEN, b. July 24, 1849, at Burlington, Iowa; m., Nov. 28, 1873, Frank W. Gibson, at Burlington, Iowa. Live at Lakeport, Calif. Had: (1) Birdie Amelia, b. Dec. 5, 1874; (2) Cora Helen, b. Aug. 8, 1878; (3) Osmar, b. June 27, 1881; d. June 23, 1884.
452. AMELIA JANE, b. Dec. 27, 1852, at Burlington, Iowa; m., Nov. 28, 1876, Adrian Green, at Fontanelle, Neb.; reside at Middletown, Iowa. Had: (1) Lewis A., b. Oct. 14, 1879; (2) Paul A., b. Dec. 11, 1881; (3) Roy W., b. Dec. 13, 1883; d. Oct. 31, 1894; (4) Bessie Helen, b. Jan. 20, 1885; (5) Inda Lois, b. July 6, 1889; (6) Eunice Amelia, b. May 6, 1892.

203 Richard Lewis, born July 27, 1810, at Homer, N. Y.; married, Dec. 18, 1844, at Lockport, N. Y., Harriet Augusta, born May 31, 1818, at Darien, N. Y., daughter of George and Ruth (Clark) Hawley. He died at Minneapolis, Minn., Oct. 5, 1886.

Children of Richard and Harriet Augusta, born at Lockport, N. Y.:

453. LOUISA JANE, b. May 23, 1846.
454. GEORGE HAWLEY, b. July 23, 1847.
455. SOPHIE JANE, b. May 4, 1849.
456. CHARLES HINMAN, b. April 6, 1851.
457. RUTH CLARK, b. July 26, 1852.
458. JAMES RICHARDS, b. June 28 or July 5, 1855.
459. HARRIET AUGUSTA, b. May 23, 1861; m., Dec. 12, 1887, at Minneapolis, Minn., Frederick Earle Dunn, b. March 6, 1859, at Shelby, Ontario, son of William and Adeline Olivia (Earle) Dunn. Had: (1) Lewis Earle, b. Dec. 4, 1888; (2) Helen, b. May 11, 1892.

204 Truman Lewis, born Nov. 15, 1812, at Solon, N. Y.; married, March 11, 1838, at Pendleton, N. Y., Theresa, daughter of Benjamin and Naomi Simonds of Homer, N. Y. He died Sept. 14, 1884, at Pendleton, N. Y.

Children of Truman and Theresa:

460. PRUDENCE AMELIA, b. Aug. 25, 1840, at Cambria, N. Y.
461. EDGAR DAVID, b. Nov. 15, 1842, at Lewiston, N. Y.
462. RANSOM, b. Dec. 25, 1844, at Lewiston, N. Y.
463. EMMA SOPHIA, b. June 19, 1849, at Pendleton, N. Y.

205 Benjamin Lewis, born May 6, 1753, in Billerica, Mass.; was a farmer at Duxbury School Farm, now Milford, N. H., on the north side of the Souhegan river, near the Wilton line, before the settlement of Milford, N. H. He was a Revolutionary soldier, and was at Bunker Hill and Lexington. He removed to Greenfield, N. H., in 1814, and died there, and his gravestone in the cemetery in the centre of the town is inscribed: "Lieut. Benjamin Lewis, who died Feb. 1, 1817, aged 64 years." He married, July 18, 1775, in Billerica, Sarah, born in Billerica, Jan. 31, 1754, daughter of Samuel and Mary (Brown) Blanchard, who died Oct. 27, 1838, aged 84 years, 9 months and 27 days (Wilmington, Mass., Records).

Children of Benjamin and Sarah, born at Milford, N. H.:

464. SARAH, b. Feb. 4, 1776; m., July 25, 1793, Jacob Richardson, b. Aug. 10, 1769, in Billerica, Mass.; and d. Nov. 9, 1839, at Greenfield, N. H., æ. 70 yrs. She d. there Oct. 21, 1829. Had: (1) Jacob, b. Jan. 12, 1794; (2) Sarah, b. Feb. 25, 1797; d. unm. July 20, 1875; (3) Benjamin Lewis, b. Feb. 13, 1799; d. July 28, 1800; (4) Lewis, b. Aug. 3, 1801; (5) Albert Louis, b. Oct. 16, 1803; (6) Julia Ann, b. July 21, 1806; d. 1840; (7) Charles, b. July 30, 1809: (8) Cyrus, b. Aug. 23, 1812; (9) Mary Davis, b. Apr. 21, 1817; (10) Elizabeth. b. Mar. 22, 1819.
465. MARY, b. Nov. 25, 1777; m., April 20, 1804, Solomon Davis, b. July 31, 1776, in New Ipswich, N. H., son of Jonathan and Sarah (——) Davis. Lived at New Ipswich and Hancock, N. H., where she d. Jan. 4, 1809.
466. BENJAMIN, b. Sept. 21, 1779; d., unm., July 5, 1805, at Milford, N. H.
467. ASA, b. Sept. 14, 1781.
468. CYRUS, b. June 5, 1783; he taught school at Lyndeboro, N. H., in 1811, and it is stated that scholars came from other districts when he taught. He d. at Milford, Oct. 15, 1813. He was lieutenant of militia.
469. CHARLES, b. June 30, 1785.
470. HANNAH, b. July 10, 1787; m., Nov. 22, 1810, Henry Carter of Wilmington, Mass., b. July, 1785; s. of Jonathan and Lydia (Gowing) Carter of Wilmington, Mass. Resided at Wilmington, Mass.

212 Moses Lewis, born April 17, 1770, in Billerica, Mass., settled in Bridgewater, now Bristol, N. H. He was a man of wealth in 1812, with large business interests, but the war used up his means and he was imprisoned for debt. He was a selectman in 1801 and 1802, and paid taxes on a tannery in 1810. He removed to Gainesville, Ala., where he died Jan. 10, 1852. He married, Aug. 15, 1794, at Alexandria, N. H., Sally, born in Pembroke, N. H., July 21, 1776, daughter of William and Jane (McDonald) Martin of Pembroke, N. H.

Children of Moses and Sally, born in Bridgewater, N. H.:

471. MARY, b. Oct. 20, 1796 (Oct. 14, family records); d. Nov. 6, 1827, of consumption.
472. WILLIAM MARTIN, b. Aug. 29, 1798.
473. RUFUS GRAVES, b. Sept. 14, 1800.
474. HIRAM, b. Aug. 14, 1802; d. March 14, 1803 (Feb. 18, town records).
475. ELIZA WEBSTER, b. June 26, 1804; d. Oct. 1, 1843, at Kempner Springs, Miss.
476. SARAH, b. Sept. 1, 1807; m., May 28, 1835, at Springfield, Ala., Dr. Samuel Smith; d. Aug. 29, 1844, at Lowdonville, Ohio.

215 Jonathan Lewis, born March 20, 1758, in Billerica, Mass., was a Revolutionary soldier, and was at the battle of Bunker Hill and at the surrender of Gen. Burgoyne near Saratoga, N. Y. He was of Pepperrell, and removed to Harvard, Mass., where, according to his family Bible, he married, first, widow Hannah (Willard) Turner, daughter of Dr. Lemuel Willard, who died Aug. 1, 1785. (She had one child by her first marriage.) He married, second, Sept. 28, 1786, Sarah Warren, who died July 2, 1795, at Concord, Vt. He married, third, March 22, 1796, at Royalston, Mass., Lucy Stockwell, who died Jan. 1, 1841. He removed from Harvard, Mass., to Concord, Vt., March 20, 1788, and from thence to Kirby, Vt., March 20, 1806, where he was the first town clerk and an influential man. He died at Kirby, Vt., Aug. 1, 1841.

Children of Jonathan and Sarah:

477. JONATHAN, b. July 6, 1787, at Harvard, Mass.
478. SALLY, b. Aug. 1, 1789 (first female child born at Concord, Vt.); m. John Bates, and d. at Mooers, Clinton Co., N. Y.
479. CALVIN, b. June 8, 1791, at Concord, Vt., where he d., unm., Nov. 23, 1872.
480. LUTHER, b. July 27, 1793; m. Elethea Streeter; d. Feb. 12, 1843, at Burke, Vt.

(*To be continued.*)

Children of Jonathan and Lucy:

481. STILLMAN, b. Dec. 20, 1796; m. Nancy Chapin of Waterford, Vt.
482. TRUMAN, b. Jan. 1, 1799; never married.
483. ISAAC, b. June 5, 1801; m. Betsey Chase of Concord, Vt.
484. LUCY, b. Mar. 24, 1803; m. Seth Burroughs of Kirby, Vt.
485. POLLY, b. Jan. 31, 1806; unm.
486. RHODA, b. Feb. 21, 1808; m. Benjamin Nutter of Kirby, Vt.

218 Isaac Lewis, born Feb. 4, 1766, and was brought up in the family of Benjamin Lewis (205), at Milford, N. H. He removed from Roxbury, Vt., to Williamstown, Vt., where he died July 27, 1824. He married, Oct. 14, 1789, Elizabeth Cram, born at Lyndeboro, N. H. Jan. 2, 1764, daughter of David and Mary (Badger) Cram, who died Feb. 26, 1845.

Children of Isaac and Elizabeth, born at Roxbury, Vt.:

487. BETSEY, b. Sept. 27, 1791; d. Dec. 3, 1838; m. James Hatch, b. Apr. 27, 1787; s. of Asa and Roxanna (Delano) Hatch.
488. JONATHAN, b. July 2, 1793; d. June 14, 1870, at Williamstown, Vt.
489. CYNTHIA, b. Apr. 15, 1795; m. Elam Clark.
490. MOSES, b. May 19, 1797.
491. SOPHIA, b. Aug. 10, 1799; m. Sanford Hatch.
492. DAVID CROSBY, b. Aug. 4, 1808.

222 James Lewis, born in Billerica, Mass., Jan. 26, 1761, was a major in the militia. He removed to Groton, May 24, 1796, and was a deputy sheriff from 1809 to 1813. He was a justice of the peace from Feb. 25, 1811, until his death; postmaster at Groton from Sept. 9, 1815, until July 1, 1826, and also appointed postmaster for Pepperell in 1818. He was appointed coroner for life on July 4, 1803. He was a democrat. He bequeathed to his sons James, Aaron, Levi, Andrew, Frederick A. and William C., one dollar each; to his son Merric all the rest and remainder of both real and personal estate, he to support and maintain his (James) beloved wife Lucy in his present mansion house. He was married at Billerica by Rev. Henry Cummings on Dec. 19, 1782, to Lucy Crosby, born Nov. 10, 1765, daughter of Hezekiah and Lucy (Kittredge) Crosby of Billerica. He died in Groton, Dec. 24, 1828, and his wife followed him six days later.

Children of James and Lucy, six born in Billerica, and the last two in Groton:

493. JAMES, b. Feb. 1, 1785.
494. AARON, b. Dec. 11, 1786.
495. LEVI, b. Nov. 28, 1788.
496. ANDREW, b. Oct. 19, 1790.
497. LUCY, b. June 15, 1792; d. Dec. 31, 1794.
498. MERRIC, b. July 25, 1795.
499. FREDERICK AUGUSTUS, b. Sept. 10, 1798.
500. WILLIAM CROSBY, b. Sept. 15, 1800, m. 3 times and had son, Winslow R., who lives in New Haven, Conn.

226 Seth Lewis, born in Billerica, Mass., Sept. 22, 1766, family record (May 6, 1766, town record). He lived in Townsend, Mass., and late in life moved to Lunenburg, where he died June 23, 1833. He married, Sally Marshall, who died in Lunenburg, Nov. 17, 1834, aged 67 years.

Children of Seth and Sally Lewis:

501. MARSHALL, b. Oct. 16, 1794.
502. ERI, b. July 29, 1796.
503. SALLY, b. June 24, 1798; d. July 11, 1802.
504. ITHRA, b. Jan. 14, 1801.
505. NANCY, b. Feb. 8, 1803; d. Sept. 11, 1825, unm., in Lunenburg.
506. HAMOR, b. Aug. 20, 1805.

243 Asa Shedd Lewis, born in Groton Mass., June 25, 1790. He was a farmer in Groton until about 1830, when he removed his family to Weston, Vt., and after living there several years, moved back to the same place in Groton where he first lived, and where Asa, Abi and Reuben died. His will, dated Dec. 4, 1862, was filed Jan. 6, 1863. He married, first, Elizabeth Marble, born in

Somerset, Mass., April 1, 1794, who died in Groton Aug. 16, 1818. He married, second, Jan. 19, 1820, Mindwell H. Shattuck, b. Feb. 27, 1800, who died in Groton Dec. 31, 1854. She was the daughter of Moses and Abigail (Wood) Shattuck of Pepperell, Mass. He married, third, Harriet P., who survived him.

Children of Asa Shedd and Elizabeth, born in Groton:

507. REUBEN, b. Sept. 13, 1816.
508. ELIZA ANN, b. July 13, 1818; d. in Nashua, N. H., Dec. 29, 1866; m. John Gardner Wright, b. in Dighton, Mass., July 11, 1815, a farmer at Somerset, Swansea and Groton, Mass., and Concord, N. H., where he died. They had 11 children.

244a Samuel Lewis, born Aug. 24, 1779; married Hannah M. Bradley, born June 20, 1782. He lived at Claremont, N. H., Cabot, Vt., and later at Northfield, Vt., where he died Oct. 28, 1846. His widow died at Moretown, Vt., Nov. 21, 1854.

Children of Samuel and Hannah:

509. SILAS, b. April 4, 1810, at Claremont, N. H.
510. CYNTHIA, b. July 31, 1811; m. David Perigo; lived at St. Johnsbury, Vt.
511. ALVIRA, b. Nov. 8, 1812; d. Sept. 29, 1841.
512. FANNY, b. Nov. 6, 1814; m. Ephraim French Bailey; d. April 28, 1856, at Moretown, Vt.
513. SUSAN, b. April 24, 1817; m. Alvin Smith; d. Jan. 25, 1854, at Roxbury, Vt.
514. HANNAH M., b. Aug. 11, 1819; m. Andrew Bailey; d. Jan. 18, 1893, at Cornish, N. H.
515. GEORGE R.
516. WILLIAM H.
517. EMILY B.
} All b. June 20, 1821, and d. within four weeks after.

244b John Lewis, born in Washington, N. H., in 1781. He married, July 27, 1806, Rhoda Baldwin, born in Billerica, Mass., in 1785, and died in Townsend, Mass., Nov. 3, 1860. He lived in Townsend, Mass., and died there on or about Feb. 7, 1866.

Children of John and Rhoda:

518. ANN MARIA, b. Nov. 13, or 15, 1806 (two records); d. Nov. 29, 1806, in Billerica.
519. CHARLES HENRY, b. April 10, 1808.

520. BENJAMIN FRANKLIN, b. Feb. 12, 1810; d. Nov. 7, 1814, in Townsend.
521. ANN MARIA, b. Jan. 23, 1812; d. Nov. 6, 1887, in Shirley, Mass.; m., first, Nov. 29, 1832, Silas Shattuck, b. in Townsend; d. in Shirley, June 1, 1846, son of Silas and Sally (Bailey) Shattuck of Shirley. He lived in Mason, N. H., and Shirley, Mass. She m., 2d, Feb. 27, 1849, Joel Adams. Lived in Shirley. Five children.
522. HARRIET ELIZABETH, b. Feb. 26, 1814; d. Feb. 4, 1894; m. Feb. 6, 1838, Walter Fessenden of Townsend, Mass., b. in Groton, Mass.; d. Jan. 28, 1884; son of Benjamin and Lavinia (Stevens) Fessenden of Townsend. Lived in Townsend. Three children.
523. BENJAMIN FRANKLIN, b. July 26, 1816.
524. SARAH JANE, b. Oct. 18, 1818; m. Nov. 12, 1845, Elijah Tracy, b. in Cornish, N. H., who d. Oct. 31, 1873. They both were deaf mutes. No issue.
525. MARY, b. July 27, 1821; d. July 10, 1825.
526. ALBERT, b. May 11, 1824.
527. MARY AUGUSTA, b. Mar. 23, 1826; d. Feb. 20, 1832.
528. NANCY CATHARINE, b. Oct. 6, 1828; m. Apr. 29, 1849, George Robinson of Townsend, Mass., who d. Dec. 21, 1893. One child.

244c Isaac Lewis, married Mary, or Polly, Holt, born in Townsend, Mass., Sept. 14, 1786; died Sept. 8, 1851. He left his wife and family, and nothing is known of him.

Children of Isaac and Mary:

529. WALTER, was in trade in the West Village of Townsend, Mass.; d. unm.
530. ALEXANDER.
531. JULIA.

247 Asa Lewis, born July 19, 1778, in Groton, Mass., and lived there during his life. He was a wheelwright by occupation, and died June 10, 1846. He married, first, Lucy Fletcher, born April 28, 1777, who died in Groton Sept. 29, 1835, daughter of Lieut. Ezekiel and Bridget (Parker) Fletcher. He married, second, Martha, sister of his first wife, who died Feb. 4, 1856, æ. 70 years.

Children of Asa and Lucy, born in Groton:

532. LUCY, b. Feb. 4, 1803; d. Feb., 1849; m. Levi Burgess of Concord, Mass. Three children.
533. WILLIAM, b. June 18, 1804; m. Jane Bond Wadleigh.
534. HARRIET, b. Apr. 13, 1806; m. Josephus Morton (2d wife).
535. MARY, b. Mar. 25, 1808; m. Josiah Cushman of Kingston, Mass.
536. SARAH, b. June 15, 1810; m. Josephus Morton.
537. ASA, b. Nov. 5, 1812; d. 1863; m. Maria Pollard of Boston; was a book publisher in Boston.
538. LUTHER, b. June 26, 1815; m. Achsah Cole of Belfast, Me.
539. LOUISA, b. Sept. 6, 1818; m. J. Perkins Tyler, or Taylor, of Woburn, Mass.
540. BENJAMIN, b. Mar. 16, 1820; m. Lucy Horton in 1846; lived at Worcester, Mass.

251 Henry Lewis, born in Groton, Mass., July 5, 1788, and died June 18, 1832. He was a truckman, and lived in Boston. He married, June 16, 1811, Hannah S. Allen, born March 20, 1793, and died Oct. 3, 1835, daughter of Samuel and Martha (Trask) Allen.

Children of Henry and Hannah S., born in Boston:

541. GEORGE HENRY, b. Dec. 16, 1811; died in U. S. naval service during the civil war.
542. EDWARD, b. July 14, 1813; was in the U. S. naval service during the civil war, and never heard from.
543. MARTHA ANN, b. Aug. 5, 1815; d. Feb. 8, 1897; m. William Hall; lived in Boston. Five children.
544. LORENZO TURNER, b. Feb. 7, 1817.
545. BERNARD (M.), b. March 12, 1819.
546. LOTHROP, b. Aug. 19, 1822; d. June 7, 1841, unm., in New York.
547. JOHN WILLIAM, b. Mar., 1825; d. 1852, at sea.
548. MARY ANN, b. June 9, 1828; m. in Boston, Aug. 31, 1851, John Briard Brimblecom, b. in Marblehead Aug. 16, 1828, son of Nathaniel and Elizabeth (Briard) Brimblecom. Four children.
549. WILLIAM HENRY, b. Aug. 5, 1830.

252 Ebenezer Lewis, born in Groton, July 25, 1790, was a blacksmith, and lived in Boston until 1819, when he removed to Windham, N. H., and was employed in the blacksmith shop at the mills. In 1828 he built a house in the centre of the town, in which he lived until his death, Nov. 12, 1869. He formed a partnership with Silas Dinsmore, and carried on blacksmithing in a shop which stood where the Presbyterian church now is. He married, Oct. 13, 1812, Mary, daughter of Jonathan Hamblett of Dracut, Mass. She was born Feb. 3, 1791, and died Feb. 10, 1875.

Children of Ebenezer and Mary, three born in Boston, Mass., five born in Windham, N. H.:

550. JULIA ANN, b. Mar. 7, 1813 (Bible record); d. Oct. 31, 1897; m. Stephen Brown; lived at Barnstead, N. H. Two children.
551. EBEN AUGUSTUS, b. April 3, 1815.
552. ANDREW, b. June 1, 1817.
553. MARY E., b. Oct. 9, 1819; d. May 3, 1855; m. John Hartwell Tower of Saxonville, Mass. Three children.
554. JOHN B., b. Mar. 2, 1821; m. Catherine ——; lives at South Bangor, Franklin Co., N. Y.
555. CHARLES, b. Sept. 2, 1828; m. 1st, Ellen E. Taylor; m. 2d, Oct. 19, 1881, Mary A. (Estes) Gloyd, dau. of D. and Maria Estes of Lynn.
556. CORNELIUS COOLIDGE, b. Mar. 2, 1831; m. Sept. 14, 1859, Cordelia M. Studley. No issue.
557. LUCINDA F., b. Sept. 29, 1833; m. John G. Bradford, b. in Pelham, N. H., Jan. 8, 1830. They reside in the old homestead of her father, in Windham, N. H.

254 Luther Lewis, born in Groton, Mass., Nov. 12, 1795; lived in Groton, Charlestown and Boston, where he died Oct. 27, 1842. He married in Boston, May 20, 1824, Susanna Wallis Curtis, born in Charlestown, Aug. 7, 1807, and died there June 9, 1844, daughter of Lebbeus and Susanna Wallis (Frothingham) Curtis.

Children of Luther and Susanna W. born in Boston:

558. SUSAN, b. Dec. 21, 1825; d. Mar. 21, 1901, in Chelsea, m. at Ashburnham, Mass., April 1850, Walter Searle of Chelsea, 4 children.
559. CHARLES BENJAMIN, b. Aug. 13, 1827.
560. HENRY FROTHINGHAM, b. Oct. 21, 1829.
561. LUTHER, b. Nov. 2, 1832.
562. Frederick Thomas, b. Nov. 2, 1839.
563. William Henry Huggaford, d. young.

258 Robert Lewis, born in Lynn, April 3, 1774 or 1775 (recorded in both years), and died Dec. 28, 1854 æ: 79 y. 8 m. 24 d. His will made Dec. 27, 1854 gives to wife Hannah all estate of every description wherever, after her decease; to go to his children, Sally Rich: Mary Stone: Robert: Abigail Fowler: Asa: Benjamin H: Otis: Warren: Jacob M. and to his wife's daughter Hannah, wife of Nathaniel Boynton.

He married, first, Aug. 13, 1797, Abigail Phillips, probably the daughter of William and Sarah (Bartlett) Phillips of Marblehead, who died Aug. 23, 1810. He married, second, Mar. 31, 1812 Hannah, widow of Benjamin Humphreys who was lost at sea in 1802. She was born in Marblehead, Mar. 16, 1778, and was the daughter of Benjamin and Jemima (Gale) Humphreys of Marblehead. She died Feb. 12, 1855. All the sons worked at shoemaking in winter and went fishing in the summer.

Children of Robert and Abigail, born in Lynn:

564. SALLY, b. Mar. 29, 1797; d. Dec. 4, 1872; m. in Lynn Aug. 4, 1816, Stephen Rich, b. in Berlin, Mass., Jan. 4, 1792; d. in Lynn, Mar. 23, 1870, son of James and Hannah (Baker) Rich of Nantucket. He was a shoemaker and grocer in Lynn, and had born in Lynn: (1) Abigail Phillips, b. Nov. 30, 1816; m. Oct. 5, 1836, Edwin Breed. (2) Mary Etta, b. Apr. 6, 1819, d. young. (3) William Allen, b. Oct. 26, 1821; m. Caroline G. Stone. (4) Sally Maria, b. Sept. 15, 1823; m. 1st Dunshuttle; m. 2d George Arrington. (5) Martha Ellen, b. Sept. 15, 1823; m. John Hamilton Brown. (6) Stephen Sumner, b. July 7, 1826. (7) Elbridge Everett, b. May 25, 1832. (8) Eliza Jane, b. Jan. 13, 1834; m. Henry M. Batchelder. (9) Otis, b. Oct. 24, 1838; d. June 30, 1856.

565. MARY, b. 1801; d. in infancy.

566. MARY HODGES, b. Dec. 3, 1804; d. June 4, 1878, m. in Lynn, Oct. 1, 1820, Williams Stone, b. Apr. 26, 1796, d. in Lynn, Feb. 28, 1865, son of Caleb and Anna (Williams) Stone of Lynn. He was a wholesale fish dealer. His father Caleb Stone was a Frenchman who came ashore at Nahant on a bunch of sea weed from a whaling vessel that was wrecked off Nahant. Children born in Lynn: (1) Emeline, b. Apr. 4, 1821. (2) William, b. Apr. 10, 1823. (3) Mary Abigail, b. July 26, 1826. (4) Anna Williams, b. Feb. 5, 1829. (5) Harriet Ellen, b. 1836. (6) Lucinda Priscilla.

567. WILLIAM, b. Mar. 25, 1806; removed to Cape Cod, and when about to be married he went to Boston to buy furniture. He reached there and nothing was ever heard of him after. A case of mysterious disappearance.
568. ROBERT, b. June 16, 1808.
569. ABIGAIL, b. Aug. 6, 1810 (Nabby in Lynn Record), d. Oct. 13, 1873, m. in Lynn, Dec. 10, 1826, Samuel Fowler Jr. b. in Lynn Apr. 19, 1803, d. there Dec. 28, 1887, son of Samuel and Elizabeth (?) Fowler of Lynn. He was a shoemaker and lived in what is now Swampscott. Children born in Lynn: (1) William, b. June 2, 1827. (2) Elizabeth, d. in Salem. (3) Ann Boynton, b. Aug. 21, 1836; d. July 1878; m. I. A. Trask (gs). (4) Rebecca Newhall, b. May 21, 1840; d. Feb. 17, 1883 (gs); m. James P. M. S. Pitman. (5) Robert Lewls, b. Jan. 17, 1843.

Children of Robert and Hannah, born in Lynn:

570. ASA, b. May 28, 1814.
571. BENJAMIN HUMPHREYS, b. Sept. 18, 1816.
572. OTIS, b. Oct. 2, 1818.
573. WARREN, b. Dec. 8, 1820.
574. JACOB MEEK, b. Oct. 13, 1823; d. Jan. 4, 1905; m. Oct. 13, 1845, Roxanna Wilkins Stone, b. in Lynn Jan. 12, 1826, and d. Aug. 14, 1905, daughter of Joshua and Sally Stone. No issue. They celebrated their golden wedding in 1895. He was engaged in shoemaking, fishing, a grocer, a shoe manufacturer for 25 years, and his last years in the real estate and insurance business. He was elected to public office more times than any other man in Lynn. He was a member of the Water Board for eight years; Common Council in 1852-3, Alderman for 9 terms in succession from 1859 to 1871, and Mayor of Lynn from 1873 to 1887. He was of great influence in conducting negotiations in the settlement of the great strike in 1860, and he was founder and organizer of the Lynn Mutual Aid Association. He was one of the oldest and most respected citizens at the time of his death. He was greatly interested in the genealogy of his family and while Mayor he examined all the records of the city. From what he gathered and knew personally and his brother Warren, now living, has confirmed, I have obtained much that is given in this publication. He was a genial, whole-souled gentlemen of quiet thoughtful habits, his tendencies always being apart from a love of display.

260 John Lewis, called 3rd, born in Lynn Feb. 13-15, 1779 : married June 13, 1799, in Lynn, Martha Porter, b. Oct. 15, 1779 at Salem and died in Lynn Sept. 30, 1814, daughter of Thomas and Martha Porter of Salem. He died in 1805 and his widow married again.

Children of John and Martha, born in Lynn :

575. HENRY, b. Oct. 10, 1799.
576. JOHN, b. Oct. 9, 1802.
577. ROBERT, b. Mar. 15, 1805: d. ae. 5 or 6 years.

261 Blaney Lewis, born in Lynn Oct. 7, 1780, was a cordwainer, and lived in Lynn. He married in Lynn Nov. 13, 1800 Elizabeth Humphrey of Marblehead, and died July 8, 1821. His widow died Jan. 7, 1828.

Children of Blaney and Elizabeth, born in Lynn :

578. MARY, b. Jan. 14, 1801; d. 1868; m. in Lynn John Gibson, b. May 1800, and d. Oct. 5, 1862 (gs). Children: (1) James, b. July 27, 1820, moved to Reading. (2) Joseph, b. Nov. 26, 1822, d. Oct. 1826. (3) Martha Lavinia, b. Apr. 5, 1825. (4) Mary Elizabeth, b. Nov. 21, 1827. (5) Caroline Augusta, b. Jan. 19, 1830, m. Dow. (6) John. (7) Sarah, m. S. Heatley.
579. MARTHA, b. Oct. 14, 1802; m. in Lynn Apr. 3, 1823, Hiram Williams, a carpenter. Children born in Lynn. (1) Mary Jane, b. Dec. 20, 1823. (2) Sarah Ann, b. Jan. 22, 1826. (3) Sidney Ingalls, b. Nov. 27, 1827, d. Aug. 12, 1848. (4) Rebecca Maria, b. Sept. 3, 1834. (5) Blaney. (6)Adaline (twin). (7) Blaney (twin).
580. BLANEY, b. Aug. 15, 1804; m. and removed to Cape Cod.
581. LEVINA, b. Mar. 7, 1807; m. Oct. 12, 1823 in Lynn, Joseph Batcheller.
582. BETSEY, b. June 30, 1809; d. Apr. 18, 1810.
583. RUTH, b. July 2, 1811; d. Dec. 20, 1812.
584. ELIZABETH, b. Dec. 8, 1813; d. Dec. 30, 1846; m. Aug. 19, 1832; Henry Washington Alley. Children born in Lynn. (1) John H. (2) William. (3) Mary Adelaide, b. Mar. 28, 1841, d. Aug. 13, 1842. (4) Blaney Otis, b. June 11, 1844; d. Sept. 18, 1844. (gs)
585. REBECCA MATILDA, b. Dec. 10, 1816; m. Mar. 5, 1834, in Lynn, John J. Foster, d. June 2, 1852 (ae. 38 years gs), from Salem. Children born in Lynn: (1) Lydia Ellen, b. Apr. 28, 1836. (2) John Henry, b. Apr. 30, 1839. (3) Joseph Franklin, b. Aug. 31, 1841. (4) James Marsh, b. Sept. 19, 1843. (5) Phebe Ann Elizabeth, b. Oct. 23, 1847.

586. ALFRED, b. abt. 1820; d. Apr. 7, 1892 (ae. 72 y. Lynn Rec.); m. in Lynn, June 6, 1850 Lydia Maria, daughter of Allen Smith Rich of Lynn, and had a daughter Dora B.

263 Nathaniel Lewis, called Nathan, born in Lynn Jan. 22, 1783, was a cordwainer and lived in Lynn where he died in 1832. His widow was appointed administratrix of his estate July 3, 1833, and on Aug. 20, was allowed $150 for care of two small children. He married first, in Lynn Nabby Floyd, born in Lynn Feb. 10, 1789 and died Oct. 9, 1828, daughter of Hugh and Abigail Floyd of Lynn. He married, second, in Lynn (published Nov. 15, 1829) Elizabeth Curtin.

Children of Nathaniel and Nabby, born in Lynn:

587. ELBRIDGE GERRY, b. Aug. 10, 1807.
588. LEONARD, b. Dec. 7, 1810.
589. BICKFORD, b. June 10, 1813.
590. ADLINE, b. Nov. 28, 1815; d. June 1, 1886; m. Nov. 13, 1834, Amos E. Mower, b. Aug. 30, 1810, d. Apr. 4, 1880, son of John jr. and Sarah Mower of Lynn. Children born in Lynn; (1) Maria, m. ——— Mellen. (2) James E. B. (3) Charles F. b. July 10, 1845. (4) Earl A. b. Oct. 11, 1846, m. Emmeline Page.
591. AARON LUMMUS, b. July 16, 1818.
592. MARIA, b. Sept. 20, 1820, m. in Lynn, June 13, 1841, James Chase, b. in Weare, N. H., Mar. 17, 1819, and d. in Lynn Oct. 14, 1889, son of John Chase of Weare, N. H. Children born in Lynn. (1) Charles E. b. Oct. 20, 1842. (2) Addie, b. Nov. 25, 1847.

264 Henry Lewis, born in Lynn, Jan. 20, 1785; was a shoemaker and lived in Lynn. He married, first, in Lynn, Nov. 15, 1807, Huldah Ingalls, born in Lynn, July 25, 1788, who died there Sept. 19, 1813, daughter of Edmund and Huldah (Batcheler) Ingalls of Lynn. He married, second, in Lynn, June 29, 1817, Eunice Foster, born in Groveland, Jan. 2, 1791, who died May 17, 1884, at the great age of 93 y., 4 m., 15 dys., daughter of Reynolds and Elizabeth Foster.

Children of Henry and Huldah, born in Lynn:

593. HARRIET, b. Jan. 28, 1808; m. in Lynn, June 6, 1844, Blaney Graves, b. Jan. 27, 1811; son of Mark and ——— Graves; no issue.

594. HENRY, b. Sept. 26, 1809. Went to California in 1849; remained until a short time before his death, when he returned to Lynn and died unm. on July 30, 1875.

Children of Henry and Eunice, born in Lynn:

595. GEORGE WASHINGTON, b. Apr. 12, 1818.
596. HULDAH, b. Oct. 15, 1819; m. in Lynn, June 1, 1843, Benjamin Lovett of Beverly. Children: (1) Ellen; (2) Lewis; (3) William H.; (4) Frank E.; (5) Israel; (6) Martha F.
597. EUNICE ELLEN, b. Oct. 3, 1821; m. in Lynn, June 18, 1851, C. Warren Johnson, b. June 2, 1823, son of Caleb Johnson of Lynn.
598. ELIZABETH CONANT, b. Jan. 1, 1823; m. in Lynn, Nov. 5, 1850, Charles H. Gamage, b. in Bristol, Me., in 1822; son of Joseph Gamage.
599. IVERS FOSTER, b. May 3, 1826.
600. AROLINE AUGUSTA, b. Nov. 28, 1828; d. Nov. 25, 1885.
601. ABBY JANE, b. July 31, 1831; d. —— 1890; m. in Lynn, Feb. 18, 1857, Augustus A. Oliver, b. in Malden, in 1832; son of Henry Oliver. Children: (1) Anna; (2) Grace; (3) Fred.

268 Amos Lewis, born in Lynn Oct. 17, 1794; was a shoemaker in Lynn, where he died May 20, 1869. He married in Marblehead, Nov. 22, 1819, Ruth Brown, born in Danvers and died in Lynn May 4, 1867, aged 75 y., 21 days, daughter of Ebenezer (of Reading) and Ruth (of Marblehead) Brown.

Children of Amos and Ruth, born in Lynn:

602. AMOS NELSON, b. Dec. 23, 1820; d. in Lynn, Oct. 25, 1868; m. Apr. 22, 1842, Ruth M. Barker of Marblehead; no issue.
603. BETSEY PREBLE, b. Mar. 28, 1823; m. in Lynn, May 31, 1842, Enos Hoyt Gordon, b. in Henniker, N. H. Children b. in Lynn: (1) Adrian Frank, b. April 10, 1845; (2) Charles Edwin Lewis; (3) Mary Eliza; (4) William Hoyt; (5) Abby Isabel.
604. ABIGAIL FIELDING, b. July 30, 1824; m. in Lynn, Sept. 27, 1846, Joseph H. Valpey. Lived in Detroit, Mich. Children: (1) Eliza Ellen, b. in Lynn, Aug. 9, 1847; (2) Abba Frances, b. Sept. 13, 1849; (3) Lewis Nelson, b. July 6, 1854; (4) Celia Louise, b. Dec. 7, 1858.
605. CHARLES EDWIN.
606. SARAH PREBLE, b. 1842; d. Oct. 13, 1848.

269 George Lewis, born in Lynn, May 31, 1800, was a stone mason and lived in Lynn, where he died intestate, May 12, 1880. He married in Lynn, Jan. 19, 1826, Mary Felton of Marblehead, born May 20, 1801, and died in Lynn Nov. 25, 1885, daughter of Joseph and Mary Felton of Marblehead.

Child of George and Mary, born in Lynn:

607. MARY JANE, b. July 14, 1826; pub. in Lynn, Nov. 26, 1848, with John H. Bradshaw, b. Oct. 12, 1823, and d. Nov. 9, 1859. Children: (1) Edward Cook; (2) George Lewis; (3) Margaret S.; (4) Caroline.

275 Benjamin Lewis, born in Lynn, Nov. 3, 1796, and died there Oct. 18, 1868. He married in Lynn, Oct. 7, 1819, Betsey Farrow, born in Bristol, Me., Sept. 15, 1799 (gs), and died May 5, 1877, daughter of John and Betsey Farrow.

Children of Benjamin and Betsey, born in Lynn:

608. LYDIA, b. Feb. 7, 1822; m. in Lynn, July 8, 1841, John Richards Parrott, b. in Lynn, Dec. 25, 1818; son of Nathaniel and Catherine Parrott of Lynn. (Mrs. Catherine Parrott became the third wife of Joseph Lewis, No. 281.)
609. BENJAMIN WILSON, b. April 12, 1824; d. May 12, 1824.
610. MARTHA, b. Jan. 29, 1826; d. in infancy.
611. FRANCES ELLEN, b. 1828; m. Apr. 19, 1853, Lemuel Lord, b. Apr. 29, 1826; son of Brackett Lord of Lynn.
612. MARTHA ELIZABETH, b. Aug. 16, 1830; d. Dec. 30, 1849.
613. NATHAN, b. Aug. 16, 1830; d. Sept. 25, 1832.
614. JAMES WARREN, b. Oct. 15, 1833; m. 1st, in Lynn, July 25, 1858, Lydia O. Salter, b. in Sullivan, Me., dau. of William and Hannah Salter. He m. 2d, in Lynn, Nov. 14, 1865, Annie Mackintosh, b. in New Brunswick.
615. RUTH ANN, b. 1836; m. in Lynn, Jan. 1, 1857, Algernon S. Fisher, son of Moses S. Fisher.
616. BENJAMIN ADDISON, b. 1838; m. in Lynn, April 21, 1861, Susan M. Kendrick, b. at South Orleans, daughter of Zebedee and Augusta (Small) Kendrick.
617. CATHERINE AUGUSTA, b. Mar. 22, 1840; m. in Lynn, Aug. 1, 1867, Richard J. Nichols, b. June 15, 1839, son of Nathan and Harriet H. Nichols of Lynn.

279 John Richards Lewis, born in Lynn, June 20, 1804, and died there Feby. 17, 1843. He lived in Lynn and was a teamster. He married in Lynn, May 22, 1825, Martha G. Knapp, born in Marblehead, May 14, 1804, and died in Lynn, Feb. 17, 1889, daughter of Samuel and Grace Knapp of Marblehead.

Children of John Richards and Martha G., born in Lynn:

618. SAMUEL AUGUSTUS, b. Nov. 15, 1825.
619. CLARISSA ANN, b. Jan. 5, 1829; d. Feb. 12, 1843.
620. JOHN WESLEY, b. May 20, 1830.
621. RICHARD EVERETT, b. Sept., 1835; d. June 18, 1852.
622. HANNAH R., b. July 21, 1838; d. Aug. 20, 1864.
623. MARGARETT ANN, b. Feb. 17, 1843; the same day her father died. She m. Mar. 9, 1872, Edward Henry Knight, b. in Salem, son of William and Lydia Knight.

281 Joseph Lewis, born in Lynn, Oct. 6, 1790, was brought up by his uncle Benjamin (144), whom his mother married, and was often called his son. He married, first, in Lynn, Oct. 10, 1813, Rebecca Lummus. He married, second, in Lynn, Dec. 23, 1819, Fanny Ashbee. He married, third, in Lynn, Dec. 25, 1831, Mrs. Catherine Parrott, widow of Nathaniel Parrott (see No. 608).

Children of Joseph and Rebecca, born in Lynn:

624. ELIZA ANN, b. Jan. 9, 1814; m. Feb. 26, 1835, George W. Watts, b. Apr. 12, 1809, son of Daniel and Betsey Watts of Lynn.
625. SALLY JANE, b. Sept. 15, 1817.

Children of Joseph and Fanny, born in Lynn:

626. CAROLINE AUGUSTA, b. Aug. 16, 1825.
627. JOSEPH WARREN, b. Nov. 22, 1827.
628. JOSEPH WARREN, b. June 23, 1828; d. Apr. 19, 1829.

283 Benjamin Richard Lewis, born in Lynn, May 26, 1793; removed to Northampton, Mass., and later to Westfield, Mass., where he died Mar. 31, 1868. He married in Lynn, Oct. 29, 1815, Hannah, daughter of Samuel and Grace (Guiller) Knapp of Marblehead. Grace Guiller was a friend and playmate of General Lafayette, who, on his last visit to this country in 1824, went to Marblehead to call upon her. At this interview Hannah and her son were present. She died at Westfield, Mar. 14, 1869.

Children of Benjamin R. and Hannah, first 3 born in Lynn, rest in Northampton:

629. HANNAH KNAPP, b. Aug. 26, 1816; m. at Northampton, Jan. 23, 1839, Addison Bryant, son of Ashael and Eunice Bryant of Chesterfield, Mass. Lives in Janesville, Wis. Children: (1) Helen, b. Dec. 18, 1839, in Montague, Mass.; m. Nov. 24, 1863, Lewis B. Lathrop of Lockport, N. Y., in Chicago, Ill.; (2) Frances, b. Dec. 8, 1841, in Westfield; (3) Addison Lewis, b. Aug. 5, 1848, in Westfield; (4) Willis C., b. June 5, 1852, in Great Bend, Pa.; d. in Westfield.
630. BENJAMIN FRANKLIN, b. Oct. 22, 1820.
631. ALBION WESLEY, b. Aug. 4, 1823; d. Oct. 12, 1826, in Lynn.
632. ALBION WESLEY, b. May 8, 1828.
633. MARTHA ELLEN, b. May 8, 1828; d. in infancy.
634. MARTHA ELLEN, b. Nov. 28, 1830; d. Apr. 1, 1835, at Northampton.
635. MARY GRACE, b. June 8, 1834; m. Charles Henry Stebbins, son of Edy and Rebecca (Wetherbee) Stebbins of Westfield, Mass. She died at Northampton, Mar. 30, 1907.
636. EDWARD TALBOTT, b. July 25, 1837; unm.; lives in Milwaukee, Wis.

287 Thomas Lewis, born in Lynn, Jan. 7, 1801, was a cordwainer and lived in Lynn, where he died Jan. 25, 1839. He married, first, in Lynn, July 6, 1819, Mary Harris of Marblehead, born in 1800 and died in Lynn, Jan. 20, 1829. He married, second, Oct. 18, 1829, Nancy Briant.

Children of Thomas and Mary, born in Lynn:

637. ELIZABETH ANN, b. Nov. 17, 1819; m. in Lynn, Jan. 28, 1841, John B. Twisden, b. Nov. 3, 1816; d. Apr. 13, 1886; son of Samuel Twisden. Children: (1) Mary Elizabeth, b. Feb. 14, 1842; d. Nov. 24, 1844; (2) Sarah Jane, b. Aug. 24, 1845; (3) Nancy Ellen, b. Mar. 20, 1848; (4) John Henry, b. May 27, 1854; d. May 29, 1894.
638. BURRILL TURNER, b. Sept. 19, 1825.
639. THOMAS HARRIS, b. Jan. 6, 1829.

Children of Thomas and Nancy, born in Lynn:

640. CHARLES WARREN, b. Nov. 28, 1832.
641. MARY ELLEN, b. May 10, 1835; m. 1st, Nov. 19, 1856, Charles A. Johnson, b. in Lynn, Dec. 17, 1833; d. Jan. 10, 1884; son of Jacob I. and Mary Johnson. She m. 2d, Dec. 15, 1886, Eben H. Downing, b. in Lynn, Aug. 14, 1839, son of Eben P. and Sarah Downing of Lynn.

288 Richard Lewis, born in Lynn, Nov. 6, 1802, was a shoemaker and lived on Summer St., Malden, Mass., during his married life and died there Jan. 18, 1878. He married, Nov. 16, 1825, Hannah Farnham, born in Andover, Mass., Sept. 30, 1804, who died at Malden, May 25, 1886, daughter of Timothy and Sarah (Berry) Farnham of Andover, Mass. In 1832 they adopted a daughter of her brother, Lydia Ann Farnham, born Aug. 28, 1830, and died Nov. 30, 1855, who married July 20, 1850, William Coffin Peabody and had two children: (1) Elizabeth Frances; (2) George. All are now dead.

Child of Richard and Hannah, born in Malden:

642. HENRIETTA FARNHAM, b. Sept. 8, 1840; m. May 3, 1871, James Scales, b. Aug. 8, 1830, in Rotherhithe, London, Eng.; son of James Boughton and Caroline Maria (Bisley) Scales. Child: (1) Josie Gertrude, b. Sept. 5, 1872; m. Nov. 12, 1894, Henry Austin Dunshee. Live on the homestead of Richard in Malden, Mass.

294 Stephen Lewis, born in Lynn, Jan. 4, 1794, was a silk dyer and finisher, employed at the Malden Dye House for many years, and later moved to Lynn, where he died Mar. 10, 1855. He married at Malden, April 8, 1821, Dolly Wood, born in Bradford, Mass., Apr. 28, 1793, who died April 26, 1861, daughter of Lieut. Thomas and Dolly (Carleton) Wood of Bradford.

Children of Stephen and Dolly, first 3 born in Malden, last in Lynn:

643. GEORGE, b. Apr. 7, 1823; d. Sept. 9, 1848; unm.
644. JANE, b. Oct. 2, 1825; m. at Woburn, Mass., Nov. 16, 1848, Henry Symonds, b. Jan. 17, 1819; d. Jan. 27, 1873; son of Zebadee and Amittia (Webber) Symonds, of Lincoln, Mass. Children: (1) Clara Josephine, b. Nov. 2, 1849; m. May 8, 1872, Dwight M. Clapp, b. June 5, 1846, son of Moses and Almira (Russell) Clapp of Southampton, Mass.; (2) Emma Frances, b. July 30, 1852; m. Charles B. Dennis, son of Willard and Hannah Dennis of Fitchburg, Mass.
645. ALMIRA, b. Oct. 1, 1829; m. —— Heath.
646. CHARLES WINSLOW, b. Jan. 7, 1832. His birth record and his father's will call him Winslow. In the record of his marriage he is Charles Winslow and in the record of his death he is Charles W., a soldier.

302 Nathaniel Lewis, born in Lynn, Feb. 28, 1799, is called junior in the birth records of his children, his father being then alive.

No. 147. Nathaniel, born in 1768, married Rebecca (Richards) and died Jan. 24, 1824, and had a son Nathaniel (286), born (May 29), 1799, who d. Dec. 30, 1822.

No. 150. Nathaniel, also born in 1768, was called junior, also married a Rebecca (Clark) and had a son Nathaniel (302), also born in 1799. (Feb. 28.) This continued similarity in names and births has led to confusion and the descent has been carefully investigated. This explanation is made to correct an error made by Alonzo Lewis in Lynn Records—where he copied them, and it is verified by Ex-Mayor Jacob M. Lewis, who knew the families.

He was a shoemaker and lived in Lynn. He married, first, Nov. 11, 1824, Abigail A. Perkins, who died Nov. 28, 1829. He married, second, Sept. 16, 1830, his first wife's sister, Louise Perkins. They were daughters of Jonathan and Margaret Perkins. He died Nov. 2, 1867.

Children of Nathaniel and Abigail, born in Lynn:

647. Allen Webster, b. June 17, 1825.
648. John Conway, b. Nov. 28, 1827.

Children of Nathaniel and Louisa, born in Lynn:

649. Mary Abigail, b. Oct. 9, 1831; d. young.
650. William Prescott, b. Aug. 17, 1833; d. May 9, 1860.
651. Emeline Augusta, b. Oct. 24, 1835; m. Aug. 27, 1856, in Lynn, Francis Henry Broad.
652. Adelaide V., b. ——; m. Joseph Parsons at Northwood; d. in Lynn.
653. Laura E., b. ——, 1843; m. in Lynn, Jan. 13, 1863, Henry Merrill, son of Samuel B. and Lucretia Merrill.
654. Chester Percival, b. Nov. 18, 1844; was in Co. M, First Heavy Artillery and taken a prisoner and died at Florence, S. C.
655. Clara Jane, b. Jan. 28, 1847; m. in Salem.
656. Horace Peck, b. Feb. 28, 1850; m. 2d, July 29, 1889, Annie B. Swainamer, in Lynn.
657. Oliver Perry, b. April 9, 1852; m. and d. in Northboro, N. H.

307 Joseph Lewis, born in Lynn, Mar. 21, 1796, was a teamster and fish dealer. He lived in Lynn and was called "junior," No. 281 being "senior." He died in Lynn, Sept. 14, 1873. He married, first, Dec. 11, 1823, Lydia R. Lewis (276), born April 9, 1798, who died Nov. 29, 1828. He married, second, Sept. 30, 1830, Lydia Goldsmith, born Feb. 12, 1798, who died May 1, 1848, daughter of Joseph and Lydia (Ireson) Goldsmith of Lynn. He married, third, in Lynn, Jan. 1, 1857, widow Irene Hastings, aged 50 years, born in Uniontown, Me., daughter of Thomas Jones, who survived him.

Children of Joseph and Lydia R., born in Lynn:

658. JOSEPH WARREN, b. Feb. 28, 1824; d. young.
659. EVERETT EUSTIS, b. Dec. 23, 1824; d. Oct. 28, 1853; m. July 28, 1847, Jane B. Hammond, dau. of John and Hannah Hammond.
660. LYDIA MARIA, b. May 18, 1826.
661. ELIZABETH ANN, b. Nov. 4, 1828; m. in Lynn, Nov. 15, 1849, Benjamin Spear, son of William Henry Spear of Boston.

Children of Joseph and Lydia, born in Lynn:

662. HARRIET, b. Feb. 19, 1832; m. July 3, 1851, Robinson L. Weeks, son of Ninphus Weeks.
663. JOSEPH WARREN, b. Oct. 3, 1834; d. Aug. 10, 1852.

311 Jonathan Blaney Lewis, born in Lynn, Nov. 22, 1799, recorded as Blaney and recorded as Jonathan Blaney in deed of his father's heirs (Essex Co. Deeds, v. 261, f. 212), Oct. 8, 1831. He married, Nov. 13, 1823, Abigail A. Marshall, born in Salem in 1805; died in Lynn, Oct. 29, 1882. He died Oct. 17, 1876.

Children of Jonathan Blaney and Abigail A.:

664. EDWARD, b. Feb. 2, 1825; d. Oct. 26, 1856.
665. CHANDLER, b. July 26, 1827; moved to Rockport, Me.
666. ANGELINA, b. Feb. 11, 1834; d. Oct. 19, 1850.
667. WARREN A., b. ——, 1838; d. Sept. 6, 1882, of a fractured spine, æ. 44 yrs.

313 Joseph Felt Lewis, born in Lynn, Sept. 2, 1804, was a fish dealer and was found drowned on the Chelsea marshes on Dec. 10, 1872. He married in Lynn,

Oct. 27, 1834, Almira Davis, who died March 23, 1857, æ. 52 years.

Children of Joseph Felt and Almira:

668. JOHN EDWIN, b. Oct. 14, 1835; d. Oct. 9, 1836.
669. JOSEPH EDWIN, b. Feb. 11, 1838.
670. MARY EMILY, b. Aug. 22, 1840; d. July 27, 1842.
671. EMILY ADELAIDE, b. Jan. 2, 1846; m. in Lynn, May 22, 1864, Gustavus Hall of Lynn.

318 James Lewis, born in Lynn, Feb. 11, 1802, was a shoemaker and lived in Lynn where he died Oct. 25, 1877. He married, first, in Lynn Oct. 13, 1825, Malinda Short, born in West Newbury, May 3, 1804, who died Dec. 7, 1842. He married, second, Martha Stone of Marblehead, who was born Jan. 2, 1816 and died Mar. 26, 1897, daughter of Benjamin and Hannah Stone.

Children of James and Malinda, born in Lynn:

672. THEODORE AUGUSTUS, b. Feb. 9, 1827.
673. JAMES HERMON, b. Feb. 13, 1831; d. May 17, 1896: m. 1st, Jane Burrill, b. in Lynn; m. 2d, May 19, 1881, Fanny Brown at Hamilton; m. 3d, widow Mary (Raymond) Ellis, b. in Danvers, dau. of Robbins and Elizabeth Raymond. No issue.
674. WILLIAM, b. Jan. 25, 1835; d. July 28, 1856; unm.

Children of James and Martha, born in Lynn:

675. BENJAMIN FULLER, b. Oct. 12, 1845; m. 1st, at Plymouth, Mass., Apr. 24, 1871, Sarah Elizabeth Pierce, b. in Plymouth, Dec. 27, 1849, and d. Sept. 14, 1893, dau. of Benj. and Lydia Pierce. Children: (1) Frank Burton, b. in Lynn, May 30, 1875, d. June 26, 1898. He m. 2d, Apr. 19, 1897, widow Mary (Hodge) Healey, b. Sept. 12, 1858, dau. of Freeman O. and Olive Hodge.

326 Thomas Vickary Lewis, born in Lynn, Sept. 3, 1820, and died Mar. 25, 1899. He married in Lynn, Oct. 2, 1842, Lydia Maria Ireson, born in Lynn, Feb. 20, 1823, daughter of Benjamin and Martha (Putnam) Ireson of Lynn. His widow survives him.

Children of Thomas Vickary and Lydia Maria, born in Lynn:

676. MARTHA ELLEN, b. Oct. 31, 1846; d. Apr. 13, 1849.
677. ANNIE MARIA, b. Sept. 10, 1854.
678. THOMAS HERBERT, b. Apr. 12, 1861; d. Apr. 5, 1887.

341 Thomas Lewis,* born in Boston, May 24, 1808, removed from Boston, Sept. 21, 1829 and located himself as a merchant and general storekeeper at Shelbyville, Ill., where he died April 28, 1838. He married in 1833, near Vincennes, Ind., Jane Armstrong, born in Kentucky, Nov. 7, 1812, daughter of William and Mary Armstrong. After his death she married, second, Dr. William Keller of Shelbyville. They moved to Sullivan, Ill., in 1844, where she died July 18, 1855, of cholera as did her husband three days after.

Children of Thomas and Jane:

679. THOMAS, b. and d. in infancy.
680. THOMAS, b. and d. in infancy.
681. THOMAS, b. Feb. 20, 1837 in Shelbyville, Ill.

344 Abiel Smith Lewis, born in Boston, July 15, 1814. He and his brother William Gustavus, were shipping and commission merchants in the West India and African trade with a store on Long wharf, Boston, for many years trading under the name of A. S. & W. G. Lewis. He removed to Framingham, Mass., in 1851 where he died Mar. 2, 1895. He was a state senator in 1856. He married, first, in Roxbury, Apr. 17, 1842, Elsie E. Davis, born in Roxbury, Aug. 12, 1822, and died in Framingham, Mar. 25, 1853, daughter of Charles and Harriet (Fellows) Davis of Roxbury. He married, second, in Framingham, Nov. 16, 1854, Eliza D. Upham, born in Boston, Sept. 30, 1830, who died in Framingham, Dec. 8, 1861, daughter of Charles and Elizabeth (Curtis) Upham of Boston. He married, third, Dec. 6, 1865, Harriet Phipps Richardson, born in Medway, June 9, 1841, who died on Long Island, Boston Harbor, July 16, 1871, daughter of George and Harriet N. (Phipps) Richardson of Framingham. He married, fourth, Dec. 30, 1874, Mary Blake Humphreys, born in Dorchester, Feb. 28, 1841, daughter of Henry and Sarah Blake (Clapp) Humphreys of Dorchester.

Child:

682. ELSIE SUSAN (adopted), b. in New Orleans, La., Jan. 20, 1849; m. April 21, 1870, Paymaster George E. Hendee U. S. Navy.

*Thomas Lewis had a brother Joseph who m. and lived in St. Louis, Mo., and had (1) William F.; (2) Herbert; (3) Sarah L., m. —— Bradley; (4) Josephine.

Children of Abiel Smith and Eliza D. born in Framingham:

683. MARION, b. Dec. 11, 1855.
684. EVA, b. June 27-28, 1857; m. June 21, 1888, Frederick H. Ellis.

Child of Abiel Smith and Harriet P. born in Framingham:

685. GEORGINA, b. July 4, 1868; m. Dec. 28, 1891, J. P. Carl Weis of Providence, R. I.

345 William Gustavus Lewis, born in Boston, Aug. 21, 1816, was in business with his brother Abiel S. (344). He removed to Framingham in 1856, where he bought the Capt. R. Fiske farm at Salem End, and later acquired several estates in the vicinity, and entered quite extensively into agriculture. In 1881-2 he was president of the Middlesex South Agricultural Society. A selectman in 1890. He died in Framingham, Feb. 25, 1901 (gs). He married, in Roxbury, Oct. 13, 1841, Mary Ann Davis Dudley, born in Boston, Aug. 9, 1821, daughter of David and Hannah (Davis) Dudley of Roxbury, Mass.

Children of William G. and Mary Ann:

686. MARY AUGUSTA, b. in Boston, Aug. 22, 1842; m. Dec. 2, 1868, Frederick Waterston Clapp, b. Feb. 25, 1843; d. Nov., 1879 (Thanksgiving day), son of Nathaniel B. and Mary B. (Clapp) Clapp. Children: (1) Fanny Lewis, b. Sept. 25, 1869; (2) Frank Nathaniel, b. Oct. 2, 1870; (3) Gustavus, b. Oct. 28, 1871; (4) John Wilson, b. Mar. 10, 1873; (5) Amy Dudley.
687. CHARLES DUDLEY, b. Sept. 26, 1844, in Roxbury.
688. WILLIAM GUSTAVUS, b. Nov. 24, 1846; d. Aug. 26, 1847, in Roxbury.
689. FRANCES WILSON, b. Mar. 7, 1851 in Roxbury; m. June 15, 1875, James Henry Humphreys, b. Mar. 6, 1850, son of Henry and Sarah Blake (Clapp) Humphreys. Lives in Dorchester. Child: (1) Bertha.
690. ELSIE ELIZABETH, b. Dec. 21, 1852, in Framingham; d. July 25, 1858.
691. HELEN GERTRUDE, b. Sept. 28, 1857, in Framingham; m. June 6, 1883, George Evans Whitney, lives in Cambridge.

351 John Lewis, born in Boston, Jan. 21, 1819, died in Malden, June 27, 1892. He married in Malden, Sept. 24, 1843, Eliza Tufts, born in Malden, Jan. 17, 1824, daughter of Joseph Warren and Eliza Tufts of Malden.

Children of John and Eliza, born in Malden:

692. JULIA ELIZA, now living in Malden.
693. GEORGIANA ATWOOD, b. Feb. 11, 1848; d. Nov. 19, 1849.
694. GEORGIANA ATWOOD, m. —— Foljambe.

357 Nathaniel Lewis, born in Malden, Sept. 21, 1827, was a farmer removed to Minnesota in 1857, thence to Indiana in 1859, and in 1870 to Otisfield, Me. He died in Everett, Mass., July 10, 1899. He married in Boston, in 1857, Lydia Farnham b. in Pittsfield, Me., Nov. 3, 1836, daughter of Joseph and Kessia Farnham of St. Albans, Me.

Children of Nathaniel and Lydia:

695. AUGUSTA H., b. in Louisville, Ky., in 1859; m. Ernest B. Eldredge. Lives in Leicester, Mass.
696. EMMA BELLE, b. in Otisfield, Me., in 1860; m. William Taylor. Lives in Westboro, Mass.
697. GEORGE ATWOOD, b. in Otisfield, Me., in 1869; unm. in 1901; a hotel clerk in Boston.

358 Thomas Lewis, born in Boston, July 21, 1829; married, Oct. 17, 1850, in Boston, Elizabeth Ann Scadding, born in Boston, April 1, 1830, who died in Medford, Jan. 7, 1897, daughter of John and Phebe (Pierce) Scadding of Woburn, Mass. Lives in Medford, Mass.

Children of Thomas and Elizabeth Ann:

698. HANNAH PIERCE, b. in Boston, Oct. 14, 1852; m. in Everett, Mass., Jan. 15, 1872, Augustus Baldwin, b. in Malden, June 24, 1845, son of Charles and Sarah (Ward) Baldwin of Malden. He was a mill overseer, and lived in South Walpole, Mass., Lebanon, and now in Manchester, N. H. Children: (1) Mary Elizabeth, b. Nov. 14, 1874, in Everett, Mass.; m. W. E. Blakeley, Sept. 11, 1897. (2) Thomas Lewis, b. Mar. 23, 1876; d. in Everett, April 5, 1876. (3) William Augustus, b. Feb. 14, 1878, in Everett. (4) Grace Marion, b. Dec. 22, 1881, in Everett. (5) Irene Beatrice, b. May 25, 1892, in Lebanon, N. H.

699. SARAH LIZZIE, b. in Malden, June 22, 1855. Lives in Medford, Mass.
700. MARY FRANCES, b. in Malden, May 12, 1864. Lives in Medford, Mass.

362 Franklin Henshaw Lewis, born in Boston, July 20, 1825; merchant in Boston, where he died, Aug. 28, 1871. His widow lives in Brookline, Mass. He married, in Fall River, Dec. 27, 1848, Sarah Borden Durfee, born in Fall River, Dec. 14, 1829, daughter of Matthew Challenor and Fidelia (Borden) Durfee of Fall River.

Children of Franklin H. and Sarah B.:

701. FRANKLIN HENSHAW, b. Nov. 27, 1849; d. unm., Apr. 25, 1891.
702. SARAH BORDEN DURFEE, b. Nov. 28, 1851; unm.; lives in Boston.
703. LUCY SHAW, b. Jan. 7, 1854; m. June 20, 1881, Louis Robeson, b. Aug. 24, 1844, son of Thomas and Sibyl (Washburn) Robeson. Child: Sibyl, b. May 11, 1892. Lives in Brookline.
704. WALTER SHANNON, b. July 5, 1856; d. Apr. 15, 1859.
705. JOSEPHINE, b. Jan. 28, 1859; unm.; lives in Boston.
706. JAMES DANFORTH, b. Aug. 3, 1861; m. in Newburyport, Sept. 14, 1894, Mrs. Anna Cora Hale. Child: Ann Cora, b. Feb. 24, 1897, in Newburyport. Lives in Los Angeles, Cal.

379 Thomas Lewis, born in Lynn, Sept. 29, 1776; was a sea captain, and was lost at sea Jan. 2, 1804. He married, in Lynn, April 30, 1797, Polly Alley.

Children of Thomas and Polly, born in Lynn:

707. THOMAS, b. Oct. 29, 1797; died Nov. 27, 1800.
708. SALLY, b. Jan. 10, 1800; d. Oct. 11, 1800.
709. SALLY, b. Jan. 10, 1802; m. April 1, 1822, James Gaven.
710. MARY (twin), b. June 23, 1804; d. Sept. 7, 1805.
711. SUSANNAH (twin), b. June 23, 1804.

381 Isaac Lewis, born in Lynn, April 12, 1785, and died there Feb. 7, 1814. He married in Lynn, Nov. 15, 1807, Jane Tufts, born Aug. 19, 1789, daughter of David and Jane Tufts of Lynn. After his death she married, second, July 3, 1817, Richard Mansfield of Saugus, and after his death she married, third, John Putnam of Saugus.

Children of Isaac and Jane, born in Lynn:

712. MARY JANE, b. Feb. 15, 1808; d. Sept. 18, 1825.
713. SUSAN, b. Apr. 6, 1810; d. Mar. 2, 1811.
714. SUSAN, b. Feb. 12, 1812.

384 Jesse L. Lewis, born in Lynn, April 16, 1792; married, first in Lynn, Jan. 1, 1819, Nancy Barry, born Mar. 4, 1799, daughter of James and Sally Barry, who died April 2, 1837. He married, second, in Lynn, Nov. 30, 1843, Elizabeth Townsend, widow of Daniel Townsend. She died Feb. 28, 1860. He died in Lynn, Sept. 19, 1874.

Children of Jesse L. and Nancy:

715. NANCY JANE, b. Jan. 21, 1819; d. July 18, 1849.
716. SUSAN HENRY, b. Nov. 10, 1821, in Portsmouth, N. H.
717. ISAAC HENRY, b. Mar. 23, 1824, in Portsmouth, N. H.
718. MARY ELIZA, b. Mar. 15, 1826; d. Dec. 26, 1834, in Lynn.
719. SAMUEL BARRY, b. Mar. 7, 1828; d. unm., June 7, 1849.
720. SARAH BRIMBLECOM, b. Jan. 26, 1830; m. June 13, 1850, Benjamin A. Homan, b. May 7, 1829.
721. JOHN T., d. Mar. 1, 1855, æ. 23 y.
722. HENRY G., d. Oct. 16, 1857, æ. 23 y.
723. MARY ELIZA, b. Mar. 31, 1837.

395 John Lewis, born in 1780; married Ann Jencks Voce.

Children of John and Ann Jencks:

724. SAMUEL.
725. JESSE.
726. ALFRED; m. Martha Colt.
727. JOHN N., m. Jan. 20, 1839, Betsey Oxx.
728. SARAH ANN, m. Washington Ling.
729. CAROLINE, m. Jonathan D. Waldron.
730. MARY MASON, b. 1814; m. James Nichols Palmer.
731. ELEANOR, d. in infancy.
732. ELEANOR, m. Alexander Manchester.

399 Benjamin Lewis, born in Dighton, Mass., Feb. 14, 1785; died in Providence, R. I., June 11, 1848. He married, first, Mary Sprague, who died Oct. 25, 1823, æ. 38 years. He married, second, in Providence, Aug. 15, 1824, Mary Hopkins Mann, born Dec. 2, 1805, and died Dec. 5, 1874, daughter of David E. and Amy (Hopkins) Mann. He was a mason by occupation, and lived in Providence, R. I.

Children of Benjamin and Mary:

733. LYDIA GARDNER, b. July, 1815; d. June 17, 1885; m. George W. Briggs, b. Feb. 25, 1811; d. April 1, 1839. Children: (1) George D., b. in Swansey, Aug. 20, 1836; m. Celestinia L. Jencks. (2) Mary E., b. June 1, 1838; m., Aug. 11, 1868, Charles H. Bliss, b. Aug. 22, 1837, who was drowned off Watch Hill from the steamer Metis, which was burnt Aug. 30, 1872. After jumping overboard, he was struck by a trunk on the head, which so stunned him he was unable to swim, otherwise he might have been saved. (3) Albert L., b. Feb. 13, 1845; m. Mary Cobb of Dighton, Mass. (4) Clara, b. Sept. 24, 1855; d. April 10, 1856. (5) Walter B., b. Oct. 15, 1858; unm.

734. MARY S., b. Dec. 2, 1817; d. Dec. 24, 1817.

735. DEXTER BOSWORTH, b. Sept. 20, 1820.

Children of Benjamin and Amy:

736. SARAH HOLBROOK, b. Aug. 1, 1825; d. May 23, 1826.

737. HENRY HOPKINS, b. Mar. 10, 1827.

738. MARTHA LANKSFORD, b. Feb. 7, 1829; d. April 13, 1845.

400 James Lewis, born in Dighton, Sept. 10, 1787; died in Providence, R. I., Feb. 7, 1872; married, first, May 26, 1816, Celia Chace, born Nov. 17, 1795, and died Oct. 6, 1836, daughter of Caleb and Rosamond (Bullock) Chase. He married, second, May 18, 1837, Nancy Whittaker, born May 13, 1812, and died July 21, 1858. He married, third, Nov. 7, 1859, widow Mary A. Talbot, who died Feb. 10, 1888, æ. 81 years. He was for many years a mason, and built some of the most substantial buildings in Providence, including the Arcade. He amassed considerable wealth, and was highly esteemed by his fellow-citizens.

Children of James and Celia:

739. JAMES CHACE, b. April 16, 1817; d. July 21, 1818.
740. ALFRED BOSWORTH, b. June 7, 1819.
741. CELIA CHACE, b. Jan. 29, 1821; d. Mar. 2, 1822.
742. CAROLINE, b. Mar. 2, 1823; d. Mar. 16, 1891; m. Oct. 9, 1843, Nicholas B. Gardner, son of Peleg W. and Rhoda (Brown) Gardner. Children: (1) James Lewis, b. July 12, 1844; m. Aug., 1867, Mary E. Brown. (2) Walter, b. Dec. 4, 1846; m. June 9, 1887, Abbie Austin Dean; no issue. (3) Esther, b. Mar. 21, 1850; d. May 5, 1850. (4) Lawrence, b. May 10, 1851; d. Aug. 22, 1852. (5) Laura Isabel, b. May 10, 1854; d. Nov. 21, 1885. (6) Frederick Bowen, b. May 24, 1856.
743. CORDELIA ANGELINE, b. Oct. 3, 1824; d. June 11, 1885; m., 1st, Aug. 12, 1845, Thomas Gladding Dana, who d. Aug. 6, 1852, son of George and Mary Ann (Gladding) Dana; m., 2d, Thomas E. Roper, and separated.
744. MARY CHACE, b. April 3, 1829; m. June 9, 1873 (2d wife), Dr. Charles W. Fabyan of Providence, who d. July 23, 1886.
745. CELIA JANE, b. Feb. 25, 1831; d. unm., Oct. 17, 1875. Teacher in the public schools of Providence for 20 years.

Children of James and Nancy:

746. ANNA HARRIET, b. Nov. 26, 1842; d. Aug. 14, 1843.
747. JAMES, b. Nov. 30, 1847; d. April 4, 1849.

405 Chace Lewis, born in Dighton, Mass., Nov. 1, 1798; died in Providence, R. I., April 30, 1883. He married, first, Nancy West, who died July 21, 1834, daughter of Capt. Joseph West. He married, second, Sarah J. Gordon, who died Dec. 30, 1895, æ. 87 years.

Child of Chace and Nancy:

748. JOSEPH WEST, b. Dec. 17, 1831.

406 Bowers Lewis, born in Dighton, Mass., Mar. 13, 1801; died in Providence, R. I., Dec. 24, 1865. He was a carpenter, and later in life a grocer. He married, first, June 1, 1823, Catharine Thurber, born April 24, 1801, and died in Providence, R. I., Aug. 4, 1858, daughter of William and Elizabeth Thurber. He married, second, April 3, 1859, Mary E. Springer, who died Sept. 24, 1865, æ. 28 years, daughter of William Springer.

Children of Bowers and Catharine:

749. KINGSLEY THURBER, b. in Johnstone, R. I. Feb. 24, 1824.
750. GEORGE WASHINGTON, b. July 16, 1825.
751. CATHARINE ELIZA, b. April 27, 1827; d. Mar. 2, 1830.
752. CAROLINE MASON, b. Dec. 12, 1828; d. June 12, 1881; m. Aug. 20, 1845, Tristram Harris Angell, who d. Dec. 24, 1893, son of Daniel and Sarah (Kelton) Angell. Children, b. in Providence, R. I.: (1) Edward Lewis, b. Mar. 11, 1847. (2) George Bowers, b. July 25, 1848. (3) a son, b. and d. Nov. 23, 1852. (4) Henry Herbert, b. Sept. 23, 1853. (5) William Harris, b. Mar. 17, 1858. (6) Carrie Crawford, b. Feb. 4, 1864; d. Sept. 14, 1865.
753. CATHARINE ROUNDS, b. Jan. 4, 1840; d. Dec. 3, 1875; m., 1st, Oct. 17, 1860, Henry A. White, who d. Oct. 20, 1869. She m., second, Jan. 19, 1871, Azro A. Hillman, son of Justin and Abigail Hillman of Conway, Mass. Child by 1st m., Grace A., b. May 31, 1862. Children by 2d m., Frederick (twin), b. Feb. 2, 1873; Frances (twin), b. Feb. 2, 1873.

407 Levi Lewis, born in Dighton, Mass., May 24, 1803; died in Providence, R. I., Mar. 31, 1884. He married, first, Sept. 30, 1827, Joanna M. Thurber, born Mar. 31, 1807, and died Dec. 9, 1863, daughter of William and Elizabeth Thurber. He married, second, Nov. 2, 1864, widow Harriet A. Macreading, born April 15, 1821, daughter of Nicholas and Harriet (Brown) Briggs. He was a mason in Providence, where he was well to do and highly esteemed.

Children of Levi and Joanna M., born in Providence:

754. LEVI JASON, b. July 27, 1828.
755. WILLIAM T., b. Mar. 26, 1831.
756. J. ELIZA, b. Aug. 25, 1836; d. in Norristown, Pa., Aug. 3, 1865; m. Jan. 8, 1857, Eaton W. Maxey, jr., D. D., rector of Christ's Church, Troy, N.Y. Child: Carroll, b. May 28, 1865.

757. HARRIET I., b. Mar. 24, 1842; d. Oct. 7, 1893; m., 1st, Nov. 25, 1863, Edward K. Godfrey; m., 2d, May 8, 1879, Erastus L. Walcott, who d. Oct. 7, 1893.

409 Jeremiah Lewis, born in Dighton, Mass., Dec. 2, 1806; died Nov. 15, 1882. He was a mason and built the water works at New Bedford, Mass., and many fine buildings in New York city and Brooklyn, N. Y. He married in Thompson, Conn., Dec. 29, 1835, Luetta L. Carpenter born at Woodstock, Conn., Feb. 2, 1812, daughter of Elijah and Phebe (Wilson) Carpenter.

Children of Jeremiah and Luetta L.:

758. MARIA ALMIRA, b. in Thompson, Conn., Oct. 1, 1836; m. Mar. 26, 1861, Isaac C. Manchester of Tiverton, R. I. They were school teachers. She began to teach at the age of 16, and taught at Cohasset and Taunton, Mass. She has been engaged in philanthropic work along several lines, including the W. C. T. U., and was National President of the Loyal Women of American Liberty. They lived in Providence, R. I. Children: (1) Hattie Lewis, b. Dec. 14, 1864; m. Mar. 5, 1891, Frank N. Pidge; (2) Annie Maria, b. June 6, 1866; m. Sept. 1, 1887, Arthur E. Hill of Andover, Mass.

759. ELIJAH C., b. in Brooklyn, N. Y., Jan. 13, 1839.

760. LYDIA JOSEHHINE, b. in Brooklyn, N. Y., Mar. 13, 1842; d. June 28, 1846.

761. PHEBE LAVINIA, b. in Brooklyn, N. Y., July 20, 1844; d. Aug. 15, 1882, in Providence, R. I.; m. Nov. 15, 1866, at Dighton, Nathan H. Chase of New Bedford, Mass.

762. JANE FRANCES, b. in Dighton, Mass., Feb. 21, 1850; m. Nov. 22, 1868, Simeon M. Moulton of Standish, Me. Now in business at Somerset, Mass. Children: (1) Lewis E., b. Feb. 26, 1872. (2) Lavinia Gertrude, b. Nov. 5, 1876. (3) Willard Conkling, b. May 31, 1882.

411 Alfred Lewis, born Feb. 28, 1810 in Dighton, Mass. He was a mason by trade but in 1836 removed to Providence, R. I., where he successfully engaged in the jewelry and hardware business, for 18 years. In 1856 he removed to Wheaton, Ill., and became a Trustee of Wheaton College. He died in Chicago, Ill., June 10, 1876. He married in Providence, R. I., Nov. 16, 1836, Hannah Farnham, b. Nov. 16, 1807, daughter of Stephen and Olive (Leffingwell) Farnham of Plainfield, Conn.

Children of Alfred and Hannah, born in Providence:

763. HANNAH ANGELINE, b. Nov. 22, 1837; m. Feb. 12, 1870, Guy Wellesley Acheson.
764. HARRIET ADELE, b. Mar. 7, 1840; d. Aug. 10, 1841.
765. CLARA ADELAIDE, b. Dec. 19, 1842; m. June 3, 1864, George Howard Beecher, a nephew of Rev. Henry Ward Beecher, son of Rev. Edward Beecher. Children: (1) Isabella Anna, b. Apr. 13, 1865, in El Paso, Ill.; m. Nov. 17, 1888, Wans Albert of Wurzburg, Ger.,(2) Esther Harriet, b. in Galesburg, Ill., Sept. 9. 1867; d. Aug. 27, 1868. (3) Jessie Colton, b. in Galesburg, Oct. 7, 1869; d. Sept. 18, 1870.
766. EMMA ARABELLA, b. Aug. 27, 1845; d. Mar. 29, 1852.
767. DORA ELLA, b. Feb. 23, 1847; d. Mar. 14, 1852.
768. JOSEPHINE, b. Dec. 25, 1849; d. Mar. 25, 1852.
769. HELEN AMELIA, b. Nov. 5, 1853, a pastel crayon artist in Chicago, Ill.

412 Sylvester Lewis, born in Dighton, Mass., May 2, 1812, was a mason and lived in Providence, R. I., where he died May 22, 1878. He married, first, in Providence, R. I., July 8, 1833, Elizabeth Winslow, b. in Providence, Jan. 25, 1817; and died there June 6, 1859, daughter of Henry Bowers and Elizabeth (French) Winslow. He married, second, Oct. 19, 1859, Frances (Shepard) Hopkins, widow of Russell Hopkins. She died Oct. 26, 1886.

Children of Sylvester and Elizabeth, born in Providence:

770. ELIZABETH, b. Sept. 3, 1834; d. Sept. 14, 1836.
771. SYLVESTER, b. Oct. 16, 1836; died Oct. 18, 1836.
772. HENRY BOWERS, b. Nov. 10, 1837.
773. BENJAMIN, b. Mar.13, 1843, unm., lives in Providence, a veteran of the Civil War.

427 Reuben Lewis, born about 1797, married in Providence, R. I., Sarah Borden of Fall River, Mass. He died by suicide in Providence May 4, 1858, aged 61 years.

Children of Reuben and Sarah:

774. WILLIAM BROWN, b. Oct. 5, 1821, in Bristol, R. I.
775. JACOB BORDEN, b. 1824?
776. GEORGE WASHINGTON, b. abt. 1827.

435 Edward Simmons Lewis, born Nov. 26, 1794 in Philadelphia, Pa., was possessed of rare literary and musical gifts, and contributed to Philadelphia periodicals. He lived at Washington, D. C., where he died Sept. 22, 1829. He married Dec. 3, 1815, Susan Jean Washington, born Apr. 30, 1795, and died July 2, 1829, daughter of Lund and Susanna (Greyson) Washington.

Children of Edward S. and Susan J.:

777. SUSAN ELIZABETH, b. Oct. 8, 1816; d. 1845.
778. LUND WASHINGTON, b. Apr. 11, 1818; d. 1819.
779. EDWARD AUGUSTUS, b. Feb. 22, 1820, in Washington, D. C.
780. VIRGINIA BEVERLY, b. Mar. 27, 1822; d. 1823.

445 Augustus Lewis, born in Hinsdale, N. Y., Jan. 30, 1832; married Dec. 17, 1879, Sarah Reed at Fontanelle, Neb.

Children of Augustus and Sarah, born in Fontanelle:

781. ROBERT J., b. Jan. 14, 1881.
782. SADIE AUGUSTA, b. July 20, 1882.
783. OSCAR D., b. Nov. 25, 1883.

447 John Conrad Lewis, born in Portville, N. Y., April 29, 1834; married May 14, 1879, Henrietta Fennell, at Fontanelle, Neb. He lived at Albion, Neb., in 1895.

Children of John Conrad and Henrietta, born in Albion, Neb.:

784. LAURA KATE, b. May 24, 1879; d. Feb. 27, 1882.
785. LOIS, b. Nov. 14, 1881.
786. EMILY, b. Jan. 28, 1884.
787. AUGUSTUS DAN, b. June 17, 1886.

449 Oscar Lewis, born in Portville, N. Y., Oct. 25, 1840, married Laura H. Jones at Burlington, Iowa. He resided at Arlington, Neb., in 1896.

Children of Oscar and Laura H.:

788. ANNA KATE, b. July 22, 1872; d. Oct. 4, 1872.
789. MARY LOIS, b. June 2, 1874, at Middletown, Iowa; m. Fred Webber.
790. WHITFIELD DAN, b. Apr. 15, 1877, at Fontanelle, Neb.

450 Osmar Lewis, born in Portville, N. Y., Oct. 25, 1840, married Oct. 9, 1868, Jane Gibson at Fontanelle,

Neb., and lives at Los Gatos, Cal., where he is engaged in the hardware business with his eldest son.

Children of Osmar and Jane, first born at Burlington, rest at Fontanelle, Neb.:

791. GEORGE R., b. August 23, 1869.
792. ALLIE MAY, b. Jan. 30, 1871; d. May 5, 1879.
793. GERTRUDE HELEN, b. Jan. 25, 1877.
794. FRANK, b. Oct. 25, 1881; d. Oct. 12, 1883.
795. BESSIE, b. Jan. 6, 1886.

458 James Richards Lewis, born in Lockport, N. Y., June 28 or July 5, 1855 (2 family records); married at Stanton, Mich., Mar. 24, 1888, Miriam Springsteen Compton, born in Muscatine, Iowa, June 23, 1863, daughter of Henry Springsteen and Adelaide Eliza (Bishop) Compton.

Children of James Richards and Miriam S. born in Minneapolis, Minn.:

796. HARRIET ADELAIDE, b. Apr. 13, 1889.
797. GERTRUDE MIRRIAM, b. Apr. 9, 1891.
798. RUTH HAWLEY, b. July 14, 1893.

467 Asa Lewis, born in Milford, N. H., Sept. 14, 1781, lived at Concord, Mass. for a time, but returned to Milford, N. H., where he died Mar. 1, 1810. He married Rebecca Davis, b. Aug. 30, 1784, who died Nov. 23, 1870.

Children of Asa and Rebecca born in his father's house in Milford, N. H.:

799. BENJAMIN, b. May 23, 1808.
800. ASA, b. Mar. 3, 1810, on the day his father's corpse was buried.

469 Charles Lewis, born in Milford, N. H., June 30, 1785; was a lawyer, and removed to Malden, Mass., where he was a Justice of the Peace for many years. He was over six feet in height. He married, first, Jan. 24, 1818, Elizabeth Hall of Charlestown, Mass., born April 11, 1787, and died in Malden, Dec. 31, 1837. He married, second, at Littleton, Mass., Sept. 23, 1841, Sabra Jacques Warren, born Mar. 31, 1810, and died in Malden, Nov. 20, 1890. She was a member of the Malden School Committee for several years. He died in Malden, Aug. 7, 1865.

Children of Charles and Elizabeth:

801. CHARLES OLIVER, b. Aug. 17, 1817; m. Ophelia Conklin, and lived in New York city.
802. SARAH BLANCHARD, b. Nov. 18, 1821; m. in Malden, July 6, 1844, Thomas William Claggett of Upper Marlborough. Prince George Co., Md., and later lived at Keokuk, Iowa.
803. MARY ELIZABETH, b. Sept. 1, 1824, lived at Malden.
804. EMILY AUGUSTA, b. Nov. 15, 1827; lived at Keokuk, Ia.

Children of Charles and Sabra J. W., born in Malden:

805. ELLA FRANCES, b. June 29, 1842; d. May 17, 1859.
806. MARION WARREN, b. April 21, 1844; d. Feb. 27, 1845.
807. WILLIAM CLAGGETT, b. May 9, 1847; d. Dec. 9, 1868.
808. CARRIE BLANCHARD, b. Dec. 10, 1849; d. May 11, 1857.

472 William Martin Lewis, born in Bridgewater, N. H., Aug. 29, 1798. Was the founder of Gainesville, Ala., to which he donated a church and a seminary. He was a merchant and dealer in real estate, an elder of the Presbyterian church, and a man of wealth up to the time of the Civil War, which greatly depreciated the value of his property in the South. He died at Gainesville, Ala., Feb. 13, 1881. He married, first, Sept. 25, 1828, Mary Bartlett, born at Bristol, N.H., in 1802, and died at Springfield, Ala., May 28, 1831, daughter of Ichabod and Ann Bartlett. He married, second, May 2, 1836, at Columbus, Miss., Aurelia Hiley Axtell, born at Windsor, Mass., Oct. 6, 1811, and died at Gainesville, Ala., July 15, 1865, daughter of Sylvester and Hiley Axtell of Windsor, Mass.

Child of William M. and Mary, born in Gainesville, Ala.:

809. WILLIAM FREDERICK, b. May 2, 1831.

Children of William M. and Aurelia H., born in Gainesville, Ala.:

810. ELIZA JANE, b. Aug. 10, 1837; called "Lida"; m., at Gainesville, Ala, Jan. 14, 1858, Charles Crozat Converse, b. Oct. 7, 1832, at Warren, Mass., son of Maxey Manning and Anne (Guthrie) Converse. He lives at Highwood, N. J. Children; (1) Charles William, born in New York City, Aug. 10, 1864; d. July 29, 1865. (2) Clarence Conyers, b. in Brooklyn, N. Y., Feb. 12, 1867. An author and humorous writer.

811. SYLVESTER CRESWELL, b. Aug. 8, 1839.
812. MOSES BOARDMAN, b. Aug. 6, 1842; d. Jan; 15, 1844.
813. LAURA AURELIA, b. April 6, 1844; d. April 16, 1845.
814. MARTHA CRESWELL, b. May 14, 1846; d. Oct. 29, 1862.
815. MARY RUSSELL, b. Oct. 30, 1848; d. Aug. 16, 1850.
816. CHARLES CARRINGTON, b. Sept. 26, 1850; d. in Brooklyn, N.Y., Feb. 11, 1873.
817. SALLY MARTIN, b. Mar. 27, 1854; d. 1887, at Tuscaloosa, Ala.

473 Rufus Graves Lewis, born in Bridgewater, N. H., Sept. 14, 1800, was a merchant in New Hampton, N. H., and dealer in real estate in Alabama and Mississippi, a leading man in the town, and a patron of the New Hampton Institute. He married at Concord, N. H., Oct. 9, 1828, Sally Smith, born April 4, 1806, and died Oct. 15, 1878, daughter of Daniel Smith. He died Sept. 27, 1869.

Children of Rufus G. and Sally, born in New Hampton, N. H.:

818. An infant son.
819. RUFUS SMITH, b. June 14, 1833.
820. EDWIN CRESWELL, b. Nov. 28, 1836; grad. of Harvard College, 1859; editor and proprietor of the Laconia, N. H., Democrat; member of the Governor's Council; served on the School Board and the Executive Committee of the New Hampton Institute. Lives in Laconia, N. H. He married Mrs. Eliza B. (Hilton) Lewis, widow of his brother, Rufus Smith Lewis (823). No issue.
821. SARAH ELIZA, b. Sept. 4, 1839; m. at New Hampton, N. H., June 12, 1866, Frank Cutter Gordon, b. at Biddeford, Me., Mar. 20, 1834, son of Cyrus and Ellen M. (Cutter) Gordon of Biddeford, Me. Children: (1) Ellen Belle, b. April 18, 1867, at New Hampton, N. H. (2) Cyrus Lewis, b. July 9, 1869; d. Oct. 31, 1874, at Biddeford. (3) Benjamin Lewis, b. Oct. 21, 1871, at Biddeford. (4) Sally Lewis, b. Feb. 22, 1873, at Biddeford.
822. JAMES PICKERING, b. Feb. 10, 1842.

477 Jonathan Lewis, born in Harvard, Mass., July 6, 1787, was taken to Concord, Vt., Mar. 20, 1788, when less than one year old, and lived there until his death, Aug. 6, 1877. He married there, Jan. 5, 1819, Lucretia McCarty Willard, born April 13, 1794, at Hartland, Vt. She died in Concord, Vt., in 1880.

Children of Jonathan and Lucretia M., born in Concord, Vt.:

823. MARY MELVINA, b. Nov. 11, 1819; d. Feb. 15, 1833.
824. WARREN CLARK, b. Aug. 18, 1821; m., 1st, at Concord, Vt., Aug. 18, 1849, Mehitabel Brown Frye, b. March 11, 1835, at Concord, Vt., and d. there March 25, 1877, dau. of Hon. Harvey G. and Lucy (Hill) Frye of Concord, Vt. He m., 2d, at Lyndon, Vt., Oct. 29, 1878, Annette Augusta (Frye) Burroughs, a widow, and cousin of his first wife, b. in Lyndon, Vt., June 5, 1842, dau. of Henry B. and Rebecca (Hovey) Frye of Concord, Vt. He lived at West Concord until June 30, 1882, when he removed to St. Johnsbury, Vt., where he is a land surveyor and insurance agent.
825. JOHN WILLARD, b. Aug. 26, 1823.
826. ETHAN NICHOLS, b. July 25, 1825.
827. ALMA ELIZA, b. July 28, 1827; d., unm., March 30, 1854.
828. SUMNER WEST, b. April 6, 1829.
829. NANCY C., b. April 11, 1831; d. April 19, 1834.
830. ADELINE M., b. Feb. 21, 1834; d., unm., July 29, 1859.
831. MORRILL C., b. Nov. 20, 1835; d., unm., Feb. 22, 1857.

488 Jonathan Lewis, born in Roxbury, Vt., July 2, 1793, and died at Williamstown, Vt., June 14, 1870. He married, first, at Williamstown, April 3, 1817, Sally Smith of that place, who died June 12, 1833. He married, second, Mrs. Amanda (Wiggin) Lamphere. He married, third, in 1854, at Chelsea, Vt., Mrs. Eunice (Waldo) Davis, b. in Williamstown, Dec. 9, 1798, where she died, June 15, 1883, daughter of Anson and Mehitabel (Burroughs) Waldo. She married, first, Feb. 18, 1844, at Chelsea, Vt., Nathan Davis, who died in 1847.

Children of Jonathan and Sally:

832. MARIA SALLY, m. Herbert P. Martin of Williamstown, Vt., and had Lewis D., an osteopathic physician at Barre, Vt.
833. LUCINDA MARIA, b. April 22, 1819; d., unm., Sept. 10, 1844. She was a school teacher.
834. CARLOS SMITH, b. Feb. 22, 1824; d. 1854. He was a teacher of vocal music and a boatman on the great lakes. He married Jane M. Danley. No issue.
835. ELAM CLARKE, b. March 16, 1826; attended public district school, Newbury Seminary, and Black River Academy. At the age of 23 he began the study of medicine, but disliking

the thought of medical practice, he engaged in the business of drugs, medicines, paints, oils, glass, etc., which he continued for forty years. He removed to Rutland, Vt., in 1853, and held responsible offices in both city and county of Rutland, Vt.; was president of the Marble Savings Bank 13 years, and trustee-director in the Rutland County National Bank for over 20 years. He m., 1st, Mar. 13, 1848, Emily Williams Allen of Wallingford, Vt., b. Sept. 25, 1826, and d. June 14, 1894. He m., 2d, Mar. 4, 1896, Eliza Johnson White of South Hadley Falls, Mass., b. Aug. 5, 1835; d. Nov. 13, 1902. No issue.

490 Moses Lewis, born in Roxbury, Vt., May 19, 1797, was a Methodist minister connected with the N. H. and Vt. conferences, from 1831 until his death, Sept. 26, 1869. He married Apr. 8, 1819, Satira Davenport, born May 3, 1799, who died Jan. 8, 1863.

Children of Moses and Satira:

836. LUCIA, b. Jan. 21, 1820; d. Feb. 6, 1820.
837. FANNY SATIRA, b. Jan. 20, 1821; d. Sept. 5, 1823.
838. JULIA ANN, b. Dec. 29, 1823; m. May 4, 1841, Aaron Gurdon Martin. Children: (1) Gurdon, b. July 3, 1848; (2) Satira Lewis, b. Jan. 25, 1863.
839. ISAAC, b. July 5, 1825; d. Oct. 4, 1844.
840. FANNY SATIRA, b. Jan. 10, 1829; m. Mar. 1, 1848, Luther H. J. Merrill. Children: (1) Matilda F., b. Sept. 19, 1851, who m. Jan. 11, 1881, Lucius B. Wright, and had 2 children.
841. MOSES, b. Mar. 25, 1832; d. Sept. 3, 1839.
842. EMILY ELIZABETH, b. May 26, 1837; d. July 11, 1869.

493 James Lewis, born in Billerica, Mass., Feb. 1, 1785, removed with his parents to Groton, Mass., in 1796. He graduated at Dartmouth College in 1807, read law with Judge Dana of Groton and practised in Marlboro in 1810, removing to Pepperrell, Mass., May 12, 1812. He was a member of the State legislature and senate, and died in Boston, Feb. 6, 1845. He married Jan. 17, 1819, Harriet Parker, born Jan. 15, 1798, and died Mar. 26, 1875, in Newburyport, Mass., daughter of Samuel and Submit (Gilson) Parker of Pepperrell.

Children of James and Harriet, born in Pepperrell:

843. CAROLINE CROSBY, b. Dec. 25, 1819; d. in Boston, Mar. 5, 1880; m. Aug. 21, 1844, William Frederick Freeman of Boston.

844. HARRIET LUCRETIA, b. July 13, 1822; d. in Boston, Dec. 29, 1860; m. Feb. 14, 1844, Charles M. Ellis of Boston.

845. SAMUEL PARKER, b. Nov. 16, 1824; d. Nov. 26, 1882 in Pepperrell; m. in Boston, Oct. 4, 1870, Catherine, dau. of Jonas Haskins and Catherine (Marshall) Titus, a native of Detroit, Mich. He was a lawyer. Children: (1) Madaline; (2) James.

846. MARY FRANCES, b. Mar. 31, 1830; m. June 10, 1857, Francis Augustine Howe, b. in Pepperrell, Apr. 20, 1827, son of James and Harriet (Nason) Howe. Children: (1) James Lewis, b. Aug. 4, 1859; (2) Francis Freeman, b. 1864; d. Dec. 16, 1868; (3) Edith March, b. Jan. 21, 1870.

494 Aaron Lewis, born in Billerica, Mass., Dec. 11, 1786, kept a hotel in Groton, Mass., on the great road, so-called, leading from Boston to Vermont. He was a lieutenant in the 9th regiment of Groton during the war of 1812-15, resigned and was released Sept. 1, 1814, and died in Groton, Oct. 9, 1849. He married Dec. 28, 1814, Sarah Spaulding, born in Groton, Oct. 25, 1790, and died there Apr. 19, 1832, daughter of Oliver and Abigail (Hall) Spaulding of Groton, Mass.

Children of Aaron and Sarah, born in Groton:

847. GEORGE COURTLAND, b. June 30, 1815; d. Jan. 16, 1820.

848. WILLIAM ANDREW, b. Nov. 3, 1818; d. unm., July 30, 1893.

849. ELLEN AUGUSTA, b. Nov. 9, 1821; m. in New York, Sept. 13, 1845?, Joseph Augustus Tucker of Pepperrell, Mass., and d. in Roxbury, Mass., July 29, 1883; no issue.

850. GEORGE COURTLAND, b. Jan. 29, 1825.

851. ELIZABETH JAMES, b. Mar. 28, 1828; school teacher; d. unm. at Hollis, N. H., Sept. 11, 1883.

495 Levi Lewis, born in Billerica, Mass., Nov. 28, 1788, lived in Groton until 1815, when he removed to Lancaster, Mass., where he kept the store in the North Village until his death, June 28, 1839. He dealt quite extensively in lands. He was a Justice of the Peace in 1823, a member of the legislature in 1833. He left 10 children under 21 years of age at his death. He married

Sept. 17, 1817, Abigail Ballard, born in Lancaster, Aug. 15, 1800, and died there Sept. 18, 1867, daughter of Thomas and Abigail (Richardson) Ballard of Leominster, Mass.

Children of Levi and Abigail, born in Lancaster:

852. LEVI, b. Dec. 21, 1818.
853. ABIGAIL, b. June 13, 1820; d. Jan. 28, 1898; m. Solomon Carter; lived in Boston, Mass.
854. JACKSON, b. Feb. 1, 1822; d. Oct.27, 1887, at San Jose, California.
855. MARTHA, b. Feb. 9, 1824; d. Jan. 15, 1825.
856. CROSBY, b. Apr. 24, 1825.
857. AUGUSTUS, b. Jan. 12, 1827; d. Nov. 24, 1831.
858. FRANCIS, b. Sept. 15, 1828; d. June 18, 1876, at San Jose, Calif.
859. MARTHA JANE, b. Oct. 15, 1830; m. at Westminster, Mass., June 21, 1859, Joseph Balcom Sawyer, b. in Templeton, Mass., Oct. 21, 1819; d. Oct. 10, 1883; son of John and Lucy (Balcom) Sawyer of Templeton, Mass. He was a manufacturer of chairs and inventor and patentee of machinery for weaving rattan chair seating. Children b. in Templeton: (1) Warren Francis, b. Mar. 25, 1860; d. June 30, 1860; (2) Burnside Ellsworth, b. Oct. 10, 1861; (3) Louis Joseph, b. June 10, 1863; pastor of a church at Seattle, Wash.; (4) Albert Harris, b. June 23, 1868; (5) Frank Hastings, b. Sept. 28, 1869.
860. SUSAN AUGUSTA, b. June 28, 1832; d. Feb. 12, 1852.
861. LUCY ELIZABETH, b. Feb. 1, 1834; d. Nov. 4, 1890, in Seattle; m. Amos Holbrook Harris.
862. WILLIAM AUGUSTUS, b. Feb. 1, 1834; d. July 1, 1892, at Capitola, Calif.
863. JAMES BALLARD, b. Aug. 21, 1836; d. Nov. 19, 1887, at San Jose, Calif.

496 Andrew Lewis, born in Billerica, Mass., Oct. 19, 1790, was a captain in the U. S. Army and died at Fort Brooke, Tampa Bay, Fla., Nov. 30, 1840. He married at Newport, Ky., Oct. 1, 1829, Mary Aurelia Mayo, b. at Newport, Aug. 11, 1803, and died there May 4, 1844, daughter of Daniel and Mary (Putnam) Mayo of Belpre Station, Ky.

Children of Andrew and Mary A.:

864. AUGUSTA MAYO, b. in Newport, Ky., July 2, 1830; m. Sept. 10, 1851, Henry K. Lindsey, b. in Newport, Ky., Nov. 3,

1825, son of John B. and Maria (Noble) Lindsey of Newport, Ky. She died at Covington, Ky., Feb. 26, 1886. Children; (1) Aurelia, b. Oct. 1, 1852, in Newport, Ky.; (2) Lizzie Maria, b. July 21, 1854, in Newport, Ky.; (3) Henry Augustus, b. Aug. 29, 1856, in Covington, Ky.; (4) Louisa, b. May 12, 1862; d. Aug. 23, 1862, in Walnut Hills, Ohio; (5) Augusta Lewis, b. June 4, 1868, in Covington, Ky.; d. Apr. 12, 1872.

865. MARY CROSBY, b. Apr. 11, 1833; d. at Newport, Ky., Feb. 23, 1845.

866. ANDREW, b. July 30, 1835; d. at Pepperrell, Mass., Aug. 27, 1855, of typhoid fever, while on a visit to his cousin, Mrs. E. Augusta Tucker.

499 Frederick Augustus Lewis, born in Groton, Mass., Sept. 10, 1798, removed to Lancaster, Mass., in 1816, and thence to Belfast, Me., in 1823, where he built a brick house on the corner of Church and Pine streets in 1825, and engaged in various industries until 1848, when he was admitted to the bar. He died there Dec. 23, 1867. He married in Lancaster, Mass., Aug. 3 or 6, 1824 (3, Fisher Record; 6, Family Record), Sally Fisher, born July 16, 1800, and died in Belfast, Oct. 25, 1878, daughter of Jacob and Nancy Carter of Lancaster, Mass.

Children of Frederick A. and Sally Lewis, born in Belfast, Me.:

867. HENRIETTA, b. July 11, 1825; m., Sept. 8, 1868, Nathan Walker of Ellsworth, Me., son of Abel and Sally (Bowley) Walker of South Hope, Me. He was a surveyor and sheriff, and d. June 1, 1877; when his widow removed to Belfast. No issue.

868. AUGUSTUS, b. May 16, 1827. He went to California July 9, 1849; made one voyage to Oregon as mate of a ship, after which he was in government employ, boating on the bay and river as pilot. Said to be living in San Francisco or San Jose in 1898, unm.

869. JAMES, b. Feb. 24, 1829. He learned the printer's trade in Belfast, Me., and went into business in Boston, March, 1880, and removed to New Hampton, N. H., in 1887, where he still resides. He m. in Quincy, Mass., Nov. 26, 1860, Martha Hoyt Sanborn, b. in New Hampton, N. H., April 18, 1821, and d. in Boston, Apr. 22, 1887, daughter of John and Nancy (Sanborn) Sanborn of New Hampton, N. H. No issue.

870. FREDERICK, b. Sept. 10, 1835.

500 William Crosby Lewis, born in Groton, Mass., Sept. 15, 1800, where he died Sept. 13, 1861. He married in Westboro, Mass., Oct. 2, 1835, Emeline Augusta Bellows, daughter of Asahel and Hannah (Valentine) Bellows. Lived in Groton, where he was sheriff.

Child of William Crosby and Emeline Augusta, born in Groton:

871. WILLIAM HENRY HARRISON, b. Nov. 30, 1840. He received his early education at Lawrence Academy, and graduated at Bellevue Hospital Medical College, New York City, in 1864, and practiced at Bergen Point and Newark, N. J. In 1861 he dropped the name of Harrison. He m., 1st, Dec. 24, 1861, Serene, daughter of Jonathan and Maria Ann (Churchill) Buffington of Roxbury, Mass., who, on Sept. 10, 1870, obtained a divorce. He m., 2d, in Newark, N. J., Oct. 4, 1890, Olivia Prescott Woodford, b. in New York City, Oct. 22, 1852, daughter of Oliver Prescott and Elizabeth (Burnell) Woodford, of Irvington on the Hudson, N. Y. He died suddenly of heart disease, at Santa Barbara, Calif., April 24, 1905, where he had resided for several years. He was a genial, whole-souled gentleman, highly esteemed in the community in which he lived.

501 Marshall Lewis, born in Townsend, Mass., Oct. 16, 1794, died Sept. 11, 1825, of fever caused by running after a runaway yoke of oxen. Sept. 27, 1825, administration was granted on his estate, his widow Sally and *only child*, Marshall A., being named as heirs (Middlesex County Probate Records, file 9980). He married, May 30, 1822, Sally Adams, born in Townsend, Dec. 4, 1799, daughter of Capt. Joseph and Mary (Brooks) Adams of Townsend, Mass. After his death she married, second, Samuel Warner, who died May 24, 1880, by whom she had four children. She died May 13, 1880.

Child of Marshall and Sally, born in Townsend:

872. MARSHALL ADAMS, b. April 15, 1823; m., May 23, 1865, a daughter of Amos and Martha (Choate) Carter of Blue Hill, Me., b. May 3, 1837. He was engaged in the notion business on Washington street, near Cornhill, Boston, and was found dead in his office, with the door fastened, on May 23, 1883. He lived in Newton, Mass.

502 Eri Lewis, born in Townsend, Mass., July 29, 1796, lived at Mason, N. H., and afterwards removed to Townsend, Mass., and bought a farm, upon which he and his wife died. He married, Nov. 23, 1820, Roxie Going of Mason, N. H. He died July 29, 1871.

Children of Eri and Roxie, born in Mason, N. H.:

873. ROXANA, b. June 24, 1822; m., June 13, 1844, Thomas Farrar, at Townsend. Child: (1) Flora C., b. Sept. 2, 1855; a music teacher at Woonsocket, R. I.
874. SALLY MARSHALL, b. July 20, 1824; m. George Brackett, son of Nathan and Betsey Brackett of Hillsboro, N. H.; school teacher.
875. NANCY, b. July 20, 1827; d. March 21, 1876; m. Oct. 22, 1848, Harry Williams, b. in Ireland, d. in Townsend, March 17, 1877. Children, b. in Townsend, except 1st: (1) Sarah A., b. Dec. 17, 1849, in Va.; d. May 20, 1875. (2) Eliza R., b. Dec. 30, 1851; m., Sept. 4, 1773, Bowman C. Nickerson; d. April 19, 1897. (3) James H., b. Oct. 20, 1853; d. Sept. 3, 1854. (4) John T., b. July 25, 1856; d. Aug. 30, 1856. (5) Alice M., b. Aug. 21, 1858; d. Aug. 13, 1864. (6) Harry A., b. Nov., 1867; d. Aug. 5, 1868.
876. ERI BRAINARD, b. June 6, 1829; died at Amherst College while studying for the ministry.

504 Ithra Lewis, born in Townsend, Mass., Jan. 14, 1801, was a selectman in Lunenburg, Mass., eleven years, and a member of the legislature in 1845. He died Mar. 27, 1884, when it was written of him, "A grand old Hero is fallen." He married, first, Nov. 2, 1826, Mary Howard, born Feb. 15, 1804, and died Oct. 16, 1847, daughter of Deacon Timothy and Sarah (Scripture) Howard of Lunenburg. He married, second, May 2, 1848, Charlotte Brown, who died in Lunenburg, May 8, 1882, daughter of Peter and Theodosia (Ashley) Brown of Lunenburg.

Children of Ithra and Mary, born in Lunenburg:

877. JAMES, b. July 25, 1827; d. Apr. 10, 1853.
878. MARTHA, b. Aug. 4, 1831; m., June 4, 1851, George Harrington, b. in Concord, Mass., April 6, 1826, son of Isaac and Relief (Watkins) Harrington of Walpole, N. H. Child: (1) James Lewis, b. Oct. 17, 1854.
879. MARY, b. Apr. 28, 1838; d. July 2, 1838.
880. MARY, b. Jan. 7, 1840; d. Oct. 10, 1847.

Children of Ithra and Charlotte, born in Lunenburg:

881. MARY, b. May 8, 1850; m., Jan. 22, 1879, Isaac Frederick Duran, b. in Carlisle, Mass., Oct. 31, 1844, son of George Frederick and Lucy A. F. Duran of Carlisle, Mass. Child: (1) Arthur F., b. in Lunenburg, Sept. 7, 1885; d. in Acton, Mar. 10, 1887.

882. CHARLOTTE, b. Nov. 25, 1854; m., April 16, 1879, Herman Leslie Duran, b. in Carlisle, Mass., Jan. 30, 1852, son of George Frederick and Lucy A. F. Duran of Carlisle, Mass. Children: (1) Roy Leslie, b. in Lunenburg, Oct. 26, 1881; (2) Ethel Marrian, b. in Acton, Mar. 12, 1891.

506 Hamor Lewis, born in Lunenburg, Mass., Aug. 20, 1805, lived in Townsend, Mass., and was one of the first trustees of the Methodist Church. He died there, Oct. 19, 1886. He married, first, in Lunenburg, Mass., Nov. 22, 1832, Olive Marshall, born in Lunenburg, Oct. 11, 1811, and died in Townsend, April 8, 1841, daughter of Jacob and Polly (Harrington) Marshall. He married, second, Sept. 30, 1841, Lucy Stevens, born in Peterboro, N. H., Dec. 8, 1812.

Children of Hamor and Olive, born in Townsend:

883. ELLEN, b. Jan. 22, 1837; d. in infancy.

884. HANNAH AUGUSTA, b. Sept. 15, 1840; d., unm., Feb. 2, 1890.

Children of Hamor and Lucy, born in Townsend:

885. SELINA, b. Feb. 14, 1845; m., in Townsend, Sept. 23, 1869, Albert H. Fessenden of Townsend. Children, b. at Port Huron, Mich.: (1) Willie Pitt, b. Feb. 7, 1871. (2) Nora Belle, b. Jan. 7, 1894. (3) Ernest Garfield, b. Aug. 20, 1882. (4) Roy Alfred, b. Dec. 15, 1887.

886. PORTER JAMES, b. Oct. 23, 1846.

887. ORA ANN, b. Sept. 27, 1848; school teacher; d., unm., Sept. 21, 1873.

888. WILBUR, b. Mar. 28, 1852; m. Dec. 12, 1894, Alice Newcomb. Had (1) Beatrice Linda, b. Oct. 20, 1896.

888a. CHARLES HENRY, b. Feb. 19, 1846; m. June 10, 1873, Lucy Moors, b. in Groton, Feb. 28, 1849, dau. of Joseph and Mary (Hubbard) Moors. Had (1) Joseph Danforth, b. in Sterling, Mass., Aug. 29, 1877.

888b. FRANCIS DANFORTH, b. Sept. 22, 1867; m. in West Groton, Nov. 10, 1898, Mary Abby Hill, b. in Charlestown, Mass., Sept. 29, 1867, dau. of Charles Henry and Mary Susan (McIntyre) Hill. Had (1) Lawrence Hill, b. Nov. 23, 1899, in Groton.

507 Reuben Lewis, born in Groton, Mass., Sept. 13, 1816; a farmer, and resided at Groton, where he died Jan. 29, 1897, on the place his father owned. He married, first, July 3, 1842, Eliza Ann Danforth, born in Hillsboro, N. H., Dec. 21, 1818, daughter of Jonathan and Catherine (Duncklee) Danforth of Hillsboro, N. H. She died in Groton, Dec. 12, 1865. He married, second, Nov. 8, 1866, Susan Frances Lawrence, born in Groton, Nov. 30, 1828, daughter of Curtis and Lucy (Merriam) Lawrence of Groton, who survives him.

Child of Reuben and Eliza Ann, born in Groton:

889. CHARLES HENRY, b. Feb. 19, 1846; m. June 10, 1873, Lucy Moors, b. in Groton, Feb. 28, 1849, dau. of Joseph and Mary (Hubbard) Moors. Had (1) Joseph Danforth, b. in Sterling, Mass., Aug. 29, 1877.*

Children of Reuben and Susan F., born in Groton:

890. FRANCIS DANFORTH, b. Sept. 22, 1867; m. in West Groton, Nov. 10, 1898, Mary Abby Hill, b. in Charlestown, Mass., Sept. 29, 1867, dau. of Charles Henry and Mary Susan (McIntire) Hill. Had (1) Lawrence Hill, b. Nov. 23, 1899, in Groton.*

891. SUSAN ELIZA, b. Nov. 9, 1868; m. April 21, 1891, George Samuel Knapp, b. in Dummerstown, Vt., Nov. 29, 1857, son of George Washington and Meriel (Mansfield) Knapp of Dummerstown, Vt. Children, b. in Groton: (1) Hazel Louise, b. Oct. 1, 1892; d. Jan. 21, 1893. (2) Lewis Mansfield, b. Mar. 4, 1894. (3) Lillian Elizabeth, b. June 25, 1897.

*This record through an error was included in the previous family.

509 Silas Lewis, born in Claremont, N. H., April 4 1810, lived at Concord, N. H., and at Northfield, Vt., where he died Sept. 23, 1869. He married, at Concord, N. H., Nov. 2, 1836, Lois Colby, b. in Goshen, N. H., May 3, 1812, who died his widow, at Lebanon, N. H., July 20, 1896. She was the daughter of Abner and Deborah (Gunnison) Colby of Auburn, N. H.

Children of Silas and Lois, first two born at Concord, N. H., the others at Northfield, Vt.:

892. AUGUSTA ANN, b. June 14, 1837; d. Oct. 13, 1838.
893. JOHN GUNNISON, b. April 29, 1839.
894. EDWIN COLBY, b. Jan. 5, 1842.
895. CHARLES EVERETT, b. Jan. 25, 1844.
896. MARY AUGUSTA, b. April 15, 1846; m. in Northfield, Vt., Jan. 2, 1868, Joseph Waldo Atwood, b. in Ripton, Aug. 8, 1844, s. of Arnon Adams and Olive Almira (Royce) Atwood of New Haven, Vt. She d. in Randolph, Vt., Feb. 13, 1878. Had, b. in Randolph, Vt.: (1) Louis Arnon, b. Mar. 12, 1869; (2) Henry Joseph, b. Nov. 13, 1874; d. Oct. 4, 1881.
897. CAROLINE ELIZABETH, b. Nov. 14, 1848; m. at Northfield, Vt., Feb. 16, 1871, Marcus M. Rice, b. in Northfield, Vt., Aug. 21, 1840; son of Titus and Louisa (Jones) Rice of Northfield, Vt. Lives at St. Albans, Vt., and had born there: (1) Maud Louise, b. June 25, 1873; (2) Bessie Lois, b. Oct. 27, 1875; (3) Carrie Ellen, b. July 24, 1877; d. Oct. 2, 1882.

519 Charles Henry Lewis,, born in Townsend, Mass., April 10, 1808, lived in Concord, Townsend, and later in Holden, Mass., where he died Oct. 10, 1892. He married, first, Mrs. Sarah Wales, and, second, May 6, 1845, Mary Elizabeth Gleason, born in Weston, Mass., April 1, 1824, daughter of Amos and Mary (Nutting) Gleason.

Children of Charles Henry and Sarah:

898. GEORGE HENRY, b. 1834; d. April 1, 1855.
899. MARY AUGUSTA, b. 1836; d. Oct. 19, 1854.

Children of Charles Henry and Mary Elizabeth, 3 born in Concord and 3 born in Townsend:

900. MARTHA E., b. Mar. 20, 1846; m. April 15, 1869, George Sumner Graham, b. Nov. 8, 1840, son of Samuel and Aseneth (Adams) Graham. Resides in Holden, and had born there: (1) Charles Sumner, b. May 5, 1870; (2) Maud Elima, b. Nov. 4, 1871; (3) Edith Mabel, b. Jan. 25, 1874; d. July 9, 1887; (4) Bertha Amanda, b. April 14, 1876; (5) Agnes May, b. Nov. 27, 1879; d. Jan. 3, 1880; (6) Florence Ethel, b. April 17, 1882; (7) Albert Arthur, b. Jan. 6, 1884.

901. FAUSTINA DELUCIE, b. Feb. 8, 1848; unm.

902. HARRIET ADELINE, b. June 25, 1853; m. Dec. 24, 1868, Asaph Evans, b. in Townsend, s. of Hosea and Hannah Evans. Had: (1) Everett Lewis, b. Oct. 12, 1871, in Townsend; (2) Forest Leon, b. Dec. 31, 1882, in South Merrimac, N. H.

903. EMMA LOUISE, b. May 30, 1858; m. Dec. 21, 1881, Freeman George Smith, b. in Centre Sandwich, N. H., May 4, 1857, son of George and Mary (Clifford) Smith. Resides at Gilford, N. H.

904. RHODA JANE, b. Dec. 14, 1861; m. May 8, 1884, John Dana Graham, s. of Eliakim and Mary (Fleming) Graham. Resides at Groveton, N. H., and have (1) Clyde Lewis, b. June 20, 1892.

905. MAUD GERTRUDE, b. Oct. 19, 1865; d. Aug. 1, 1867.

523 Benjamin Franklin Lewis, born in Townsend, Mass., July 26, 1816, was a cooper by trade and lived in Taunton previous to 1842 when he moved to Fall River, and in 1844 moved to Townsend where he owned a farm. He worked at his trade the first part of his life, and later in the office of A. M. Adams, a lumber dealer in Townsend. He was town assessor for several years; a member of the State legislature in 1871; a deputy-sheriff for Middlesex County for 36 years; and for many years a licensed auctioneer. He died in Townsend, Mar. 15, 1890. He married, Sept. 20, 1841, Elizabeth Lamson, b. Jan. 31, 1820; d. Dec. 15, 1897, daughter of Daniel and Abigail (Prentice) Lamson of Townsend.

Children of Benjamin Franklin and Elizabeth, born in Townsend:

906. ABBIE ELIZABETH, b. Nov. 26, 1843; m. Nov. 26, 1865, Oren Leonard Bruce, b. in Townsend, s. of Leonard and Mary (Jenkins) Bruce. Resides at Ashby, Mass. Had, b. in Townsend: (1) Berton Lovell, b. Mar. 6, 1873; (2) Wilbur Lamson, b. Oct. 30 1875.

907. ELDORA ADELINE, b. Oct. 22, 1846; m. Jan. 12, 1871, Charles Brooks Hart, b. in Townsend, June 9, 1845, s. of Samuel and Lefy (Brooks) Hart. Resides in Brookline, Mass.

908. NANCY JANE, b. April 14, 1851; m. Charles Jefferson Towne, b. Dec. 30, 1840, at Stoddard, N. H., s. of Isaac and Lucretia (Taylor) Towne. Resides at Essex, Mass.

909. CHARLES FRANCIS, b. Feb. 21, 1864; d. April 28, 1877.

526 Albert Lewis, born in Townsend, Mass., May 11, 1824, is a farmer living at Creston, Ill. He married at Rockford, Ill., June 23, 1856, Louisa Marsh Lewis, born at Enfield Center, N. Y., Jan. 24, 1836, daughter of Huron and Elizabeth (Mettler) Lewis of Enfield Center, N. Y.

Children of Albert and Louise M., born in Creston, Ill.:

910. JOHN FRANKLIN, b. Oct. 4, 1857; m. at Creston, Ill., Feb. 17, 1881, Caroline Belle Swingley, who d. at Omaha, Neb., Oct. 21, 1896, dau. of Upton and Frances (Potter) Swingley of Creston, Ill. Had: (1) Frank Swingley, b. Aug. 9, 1884, in Creston, Ill. Mr. Lewis resided at Omaha, Neb., in 1899.

911. ALBERT EDWARD, b. Feb. 5, 1861; resides at Pittsburgh, Pa.

912. NELLIE LOUISE, b. April 13, 1864; resides at Pittsburgh, Pa.

913. GRACE ELIZABETH, b. Jan. 15, 1867; m. at Creston, Ill., Sept. 12, 1888, Charles Pratt Whitney, s. of John Brooks and Katharine (Pratt) Whitney of Mass. Resides at Edgewater, Ill. Had b. in Chicago, Ill.: (1) Lewis Husted, b. Feb. 8, 1892; (2) Charles Pratt, b. Dec. 12, 1893; (3) Katharine Fay, b. Apr. 23. 1896.

914. EDNA MABELLE, b. April 23, 1875; resides at Creston, Ill.

530 Alexander Lewis, born in Townsend, Sept. 10, 1806, married, 1827, Abigail Robinson of Lunenburg, Mass. Lived in Peabody, Mass., where he died about 1882. She died Jan. 4, 1841.

Children of Alexander and Abigail:

915. CHARLES, b. 1828; m. Lydia Phippen of Salem, Mass., and d. May 10, 1854. Had: (1) Charles A.; engineer; lives in Salem.

916. GEORGE ALEXANDER, b. Jan. 7, 1832; m. June 1, 1854, Harriet Trofatter, who d. Aug. 12, 1890; morocco dresser; no issue; resides in Salem, Mass.

917. JULIA ANN, b. July 4, 1840; m., Dec. 16, 1860, Ambrose Davis, who d. Jan. 27, 1864. Resides in Salem, Mass.

533 William Lewis, born in Groton, Mass., June 18, 1804, was a merchant in Bangor, Me. He died June 8, 1876. He married Jane Bond Wadleigh, who married, second, —— White.

Children of William and Jane B.:

918. WILLIAM DEXTER, b. Apr. 5, 1831, in Boston, Mass.; m., Nov. 27, 1856, at Bangor, Me., Annie F. Lyon.
919. ABBY?
920. CHARLES HILDRETH, b. Aug. 5, 1836-7; a graduate of Norwich, Vt., University; m., Oct., 1863, Oriana Pendleton, at Watertown, Mass.
921. EMMA JANE, b. Sept. 27, 18—; m. Jan. 18, 1872, Henry E. Call, at Bangor, Me.

544 Lorenzo Turner Lewis, born in Boston, Mass., Feb. 7, 1817, died Feb. 5, 1855. He married at Havre, France, Mar. 15, 1851, Clemence Clarissa Cormedesz, who died in 1888.

Children of Lorenzo Turner and Clemence Clarissa, born in Boston:

922. EMMA MAY, b. 1852; m. F. H. Melendy in 1876. Had (1) Ruth Clarence, b. April 25, 1882, in Malden, Mass.
923. FRANK T., b. 1854; m. Annie E. Draffin in 1875. Had: (1) John Franklin, b. Aug., 1876, in Reading, Mass.; (2) William Malcolm, b. Sept., 1879, in Plymouth, N. H. He and his two sons are bookkeepers in the offices of the West End R. R. Co., Boston.

545 Bernard M. Lewis, born in Boston, Mar. 12, 1819; died Sept. 13, 18—. He was wounded in the Civil War, received a pension, and was employed in the supply department of the Boston Post-office. He married June 6, 1843, Arvilla Clapp, b. Feb. 2, 1820, daughter of Isaac and Vesta (Reynolds) Clapp of South Weymouth, Mass.

hild of Bernard M. and Arvilla:

924. JAMES TRASK ALLEN, b. Sept. 16, 1844; m. Jan. 4, 1871, Josephine Bolndell.

549 William Henry Lewis, born in Boston, Aug. 5, 1830, was injured in the Civil War, and held a position in the quartermaster's department at Washington, D. C. until his death, July 6, 1891. He married Elizabeth A. Sanford, widow of a comrade killed in the Civil War.

Children of William Henry and Elizabeth A., born in Washington, D. C. :

925. Charles R., b. Feb. 1, 1863.
926. Edward H., b. Sept. 3, 1864; d. Sept. 7, 1866.
927. William Edgar, b. Nov. 10, 1867.
928. James H., b. June 17, 1873; d. May 23, 1875.
929. Joseph Warren, b. Sept. 21, 1875.
930. George Brimblecom, b. Apr. 8, 1880.

551 Eben Augustus Lewis, born in Boston, April 3, 1815, was a brass finisher, and resided in Boston, from which he removed to Dedham. He married Matilda Hanscom, born at Eliot, Me., May 5, 1822, who died June 24, 1898, daughter of Samuel and Ann Maria (Paul) Hanscom of Eliot, Me.

Children of Eben Augustus and Matilda:

931. Ann Maria, b. Jan. 14, 1846; m. John J. Hilton; resides in Malden, Mass.
932. Warren A., b. Mar. 7, 1847; d. April 9, 1868; lived in Boston; m., 1st, Mary Homer; m., 2d, Lucy Davis.
933. Mary Emma, b. June 12, 1848; m. Charles R. Griggs; resides in Dedham, Mass.
934. Susan Frances Gates, b. Sept. 23, 1849; m. William F. Bacon; resides in Malden, Mass.
935. Edna Matilda, b. Oct. 5, 1854; d. Feb. 19, 1889; m. Benjamin R. Chase.
936. Walter Clifford, b. and d. in infancy.
937. Willie Samuel, b. Sept. 16, 1861; d. in South Boston, Mar. 20, 1876.
938. George Eward, b. Jan. 20, 1863; m. Emily Warren of Roslindale, Mass. Had: (1) George; (2) Clarence.
939. Etta, b. and d. young.

552 Andrew Lewis, born in Boston, June 1, 1817 and died Feb. 8, 1897. He married May 7, 1840, Mary Ann Kittredge, b. Nov. 18, 1819, of Mt. Vernon, N. H., and lived in Haverhill, Mass.

Children of Andrew and Mary Ann:

940. HATTIE A., b. Mar. 13, 1841, in Dracut, Mass.
941. CHARLES A., b. May 19, 1842.
942. J. OTIS, b. June 21, 1844.
943. IRVING, b. Mar. 18, 1852.
944. ELLEN M., b. Oct. 30, 1855.

559 Charles Benjamin Lewis, born in Boston, Aug. 13, 1827, and died Mar. 4, 1885, at Medford, Mass. He married, first, at Charlestown, Sept. 25, 1849, Sarah Newhall, aged 21, daughter of John and Sarah Newhall. He married, second, Nov. 8, 1854, Hannah Maria Sisson, aged 20, daughter of William Bates and Mary Farnsworth (Curtis) Sisson. He married, third, Jan. 3, 1877, at Chelsea, Harriet N. Reed, aged 33, of Boston, daughter of Thomas and Martha Reed of Gardner, Me. He served on board the U. S. Frigates Macedonian and Potomac during the Mexican war. He was freight agent for the Boston and Lowell R. R. for many years, and lived in Boston and West Medford, Mass.

Children of Charles Benjamin and Hannah Maria:

945. WILLIE WALLACE, b. Dec. 17, 1855, at Charlestown; changed his name to Lunt.
946. ANNIE HAVEN (twin), b. Oct. 5, 1867, in Boston.
947. A child (twin), b. Oct. 5, 1867; d. same day.

560 Henry Frothingham Lewis, born in Boston, Oct. 21, 1829, married in South Boston, Dec. 7, 1851, Mary Adaline Hopkins, born in Eastham, daughter of John and Diana (Cole) Hopkins of Eastham, Mass. He resided in Chelsea and Revere, but is now living with his daughter in Hyde Park, Mass.

Children of Henry Frothingham and Mary Adaline:

948. MARY SUSIE, b. Oct. 10, 1852, in Eastham; m. in Chelsea, June 23, 1874, George H. Norris of Chelsea; now living at Hyde Park.
949. CHARLES BENJAMIN, b. July 17, 1854, in Charlestown; now living at 87 Sixth Ave., New York City.
950. HENRY F., b. May 13, 1856, in Charlestown; d. Aug. 6, 1856.

561 Luther Lewis, born in Boston, Nov. 2, 1832; died Dec. 15, 1898, at the Boston City Hospital. He married in Boston in July, 1852, Almira H, Smith, born at Eastham, Sept. 16, 1833, daughter of Freeman and Phebe (Gill) Smith of Eastham, Mass. Resided in Boston, Charlestown and Stoneham, Mass.

Children of Luther and Almira H.:

951. LUTHER EDWARD, b. Mar. 28, 1854, in Boston; m. Abby Harding of Charlestown.
952. ELSIE S., b. Mar. 17, 1856, in Boston; m. Lyman Harding of Charlestown. Now is Mrs. Elsie S. Peterson of Eastham, Mass.
953. PHILIP F., b. July 16, 1862, in Chelsea.
954. JONATHAN SNOW, b. Nov. 14, 1864, in Boston; lives in Stoneham, Mass.
955. ALMIRA E., b. Oct. 16, 1873; d. May 9, 1876, in Charlestown.
956. WALTER N., b. Dec. 25, 1875, in Charlestown.

562 Frederick Thomas Lewis, born in Boston, Nov. 2, 1839; died Dec. 25, 1900, in Chelsea. He married, first, Mary Crocker Baker, daughter of Seymour and Annie Bangs of Eastham, Mass. He married, second, Jan. 18, 1893, Lilla C. Freedley. Lived in Chelsea.

Children:

957. FREDERICK E., employed by Swift Bros., Chicago, Ill.
958. GEORGE, with John Hancock Insurance Co., Chelsea, Mass.

568 Robert Lewis, born in Lynn, June 16, 1808, was a fisherman, and lived at Magnolia, a part of Gloucester, where his children were born, except the third, who was born in Lynn. He died in New Orleans, La., Nov. 20, 1864. He married in Gloucester, Dec. 28, 1846, Susan Maria, born in Gloucester, May 9, 1827, daughter of Winthrop and Charlotte (Merchant) Sargent of Gloucester. After his death she married, second, at Watertown, Mass., John Barnard, who resided in Boston, and died in 1899.

Children of Robert and Susan M.:

959. GEORGE.
960. ROBERT FRANKLIN, b. Nov. 2, 1848; d. May 7, 1849.

961. ROBERT FRANKLIN, b. April 6, 1850, in Lynn.
962. ANNA AUGUSTA, b. July 2, 1853.
963. MARY MARSH, b. Mar. 26, 1855.
964. JACOB MEEK, b. Feb. 12, 1857.
965. CLARENCE HERBERT, b. Aug. 28, 1860.

570 Asa Lewis, born in Lynn, May 28, 1814, was a shoemaker in early life, but a fisherman for more than 50 years, and captain of a vessel for more than half that time. He died in Lynn, Aug. 3, 1888. He married, first, in Lynn, Nov. 6, 1834, Dorcas Davis, born in Lynn, Mar. 5, 1815, and died there, Feb. 26, 1855, daughter of Joseph and Susan (Boynton) Davis of Lynn. He married, second, in Lynn, April 14, 1858, his wife's sister, Mrs. Mary Ann (Davis) Allen, widow of Amos Allen, who was born in Lynn, Oct. 20, 1812, and died Aug. 1, 1881.

Children of Asa and Dorcas, born in Lynn:

966. HANNAH MARIA, b. Jan. 27, 1835; m. in Lynn, Oct. 26, 1862, Jonas Ball Goodwin, b. in Lynn, June 20. 1833, son of Jonas B. and Elizabeth (Graves) Goodwin of Marblehead. Had: (1) William Otis, b. Dec. 11, 1870.
967. AMOS EDWIN, b. Jan. 19, 1837; d. young.
968. WILLIAM OTIS, b. Aug. 13, 1839; was killed Feb. 11, 1862, by the falling of a mast on the U. S. Gunboat Huron.
969. SUSAN ADELAIDE, b. June 14, 1841; d. Sept. 24, 1842.
970. LUCY ELLEN, b. Nov. 15, 1843; m. Nov. 23, 1864, Edwin Thompson Dorman, b. in 1842, son of Amos and Sarah Richards (Hallowell) Dorman of Lynn. Had: (1) Jennie Maria, b. Oct. 15, 1865; (2) Josie Emily, b. July 29, 1869; (3) Lewis Asa, b. Sept. 25, 1875; (4) Arthur Warren, b. Oct. 18, 1878.
971. EDWIN DAVIS, b. Dec. 14, 1849; m. in Lynn, Jan. 25, 1871, Eliza Ellen Collyer, b. in Lynn, Jan. 6, 1839, dau. of Thomas and Eliza J. Collyer of Lynn. Had: (1) Edwin Collyer, b. in Lynn, Aug. 13, 1872.
972. DORCAS EMILY, b. Feb. 9, 1855; m. at Danvers, Sept. 9, 1886, William Edward Standley, son of Benj. F. and Sarah E. (Withey) Standley. Lived in Danvers, and had: (1) Earl Lewis, b. Feb. 3, 1887; d. Mar. 25, 1887; (2) Lewis Elmer, b. June 19, 1889; (3) Ruth Withey, b. Mar. 22, 1893; (4) Amos Linwood, b. Mar. 7, 1899.

571 Benjamin Humphreys Lewis, born in Lynn, Sept. 18, 1816, was a shoemaker, and lived in Lynn, where he died, July 6, 1876. He married in Lynn, Sept. 9, 1853, Hannah Chase, born in Henniker, N. H., April 11, 1824, who died in Lynn, June 9, 1899. She was the daughter of Jonathan and Patience (Peaslee) Chase of Henniker, N. H.

Children of Benjamin Humphreys and Hannah, born in Lynn:

973. FRED CHASE, b. June 29, 1854.
974. FRANK HERBERT, b. June 6, 1858; m. in Lynn, April 21, 1887, Clara Ida Millan, b. June 6, 1860, in Pittsfield, Vt., dau. of George Henry and Jane Elizabeth (Cadwell) Millan of Lynn. Had: (1) Henry Benjamin, b. July 23, 1896; d. Oct. 26, 1896.
975. ASA WARREN, b. April 7, 1863; m. June 19, 1901, Sarah Achsah Clark of Henniker, N. H. Had: (1) Lester Clark, b. in Lynn, June 4, 1902.

These three brothers are engaged in the grocery business on Lewis street, Lynn.

572 Otis Lewis, born in Lynn, Oct. 2, 1818, was a fisherman, and associated in business with his brother Asa. He lived in Lynn, where he died Jan. 12, 1893. He married in Lynn, Mar. 7, 1847, Harriet Osgood Straw, born in Hopkinton, N. H., April 23, 1815, and died in Lynn, Dec. 4, 1878 (suicide). She was the daughter of William and Hannah (Huse, of Weare, N. H.) Straw of Hopkinton, N. H.

Children of Otis and Harriet O.:

976. A child, b. in Weare, N. H.; d. Oct. 2, 1848.
977. WILLIAM PAGE, b. Oct. 6, 1858, in Lynn; m. in Lynn, Mar. 26, 1873, Rebecca Frances Howes, b. in Chatham, Mass., July 11, 1850, dau. of Ephraim Owen and Priscilla (Doane) Howes of Chatham. Had: (1) Herbert Otis, b. in Lynn, April 29, 1877; m. April 26, 1900, Florence Jessie Rhodes, dau. of Howard J. Rhodes.

573 Warren Lewis, born in Lynn, Dec. 8, 1820, is now living with his son, and is hale and hearty. He has been a shoemaker, fisherman, and farmer. He married in Swampscott, Jan. 16, 1848, Sarah Glover Standley, born in Swampscott, Dec. 2, 1828, daughter of Thomas and Sarah (Phillips) Standley of Swampscott, and granddaughter of Walter and Sarah (Glover-Lewis) Phillips. Sarah Glover was the daughter of Gen. John Glover, and married Capt. Samuel Lewis, who died Mar. 15, 1792, at St. Martin's, W. I. Gen. John Glover's Bible record, in possession of the family, says: "Feb. 3, 1771, Sally Glover, born ——, married Captain Samuel Lewis, March 22, 1791." On another leaf it says: "Betsey L. Lewis died Aug. 6, 1815, aged 23 years in June the 7th, their only child." After the death of Capt. Samuel Lewis, she married, second, Walter Phillips, and had four children, viz.: (1) John Glover, (2) Walter, (3) Sarah, (4) Content. Walter, jr., married late in life, and had no children; Content died in girlhood; Sarah married Thomas Standley of Lynn, now Swampscott, and had a large family, of whom Sarah Glover Standley above mentioned was one. Capt. Samuel Lewis was born April 1, 1769, son of Thomas and Elizabeth (Lemmon) Lewis of Marblehead, who was son of Capt. Philip and Lydia (Barrett) Lewis of Boston, who was son of Capt. Philip and Martha (Burrill) Lewis of Boston.

Child of Warren and Sarah G., born in Salem:

978. WILLARD FRANCIS, b. Nov. 17, 1848; m. 1st, in Lynn, Feb. 5, 1872, Abbie Jane Phillips, b. in Lynn, Feb. 5, 1849, and d. Sept. 5, 1873, dau. of James B. and Augusta (Hanaford) Phillips of Lynn. He m. 2d, in Lynn, Oct. 3, 1877, Salome A. Ward, b. in Orange, Mass., June 10, 1850, dau. of Asa Albee and Jane Chatman (Sawyer) Ward of Lynn. He is a dealer in real estate and lives in Swampscott.

575 Henry Lewis, born in Lynn, Oct. 10, 1799, was called "junior" in the birth record of his children, his uncle Henry (264) being "senior." He was a shoemaker and lived in Lynn, and was buried July 25, 1840. He married in Lynn, Jan. 8, 1820, Susan Pickett, born in Marblehead, Sept. 21, 1802, and died in Lynn Aug. 21, 1888, aged 85 y. 11 m. 21 d. (Lynn Rds.)

Children of Henry and Susan, the first seven born in Lynn:

979. SUSAN, b. June 4, 1820; d. Oct. 25, 1821.
980. SUSAN, b. Oct. 18, 1821, m. 1st, —— Mansfield; m. 2d, —— Lincoln.
981. JOHN, b. Feb. 16, 1823 (called John 4th); m. 1st, Feb. 5, 1846, Mary A. Merrow, b. in Eaton, N. H., 1820; d. Dec. 1, 1850. He m. 2d, Sept. 22, 1851, Lucenia Buck, b. in Corinth, Me., 1821, dau. of James Buck, and had (1) George Martin, b. June 28, 1852.
982. HANNAH RUSSELL, b. Nov. 4, 1824; m. April 11, 1843, John N. Berry of Salem, Mass.
983. OLIVER QUESTRAM, b. Aug. 6, 1826.
984. MARTHA, b. April 17, 1828; m. Nov. 5, 1843, Benj. Proctor.
985. HENRY, b. Jan. 15, 1830; d. Sept. 11, 1830.
986. MARY ANN, b. 1834; m. Nov. 11, 1852, James O. Newhall.
987. CHARLES H., d. Apr. 28, 1873, æ. 38 y. 10 m. (Lynn Rds.)
988. ELIZABETH P., b. 1836; m. May 19, 1853, Geo. F. Newhall, Jr.
989. IANTHA, b. May 9, 1840; m. 1st, Sept. 21, 1862, George W. Foster, s. of Nehemiah and Susan M. Foster of Lynn; m. 2d, Feb. 10, 1879, Jonathan Gerry Lewis (993), and d. Aug. 30, 1904.

576 John Lewis, born in Lynn, Oct. 9, 1802, was a shoemaker and lived in Lynn where he died Feb. 15, 1880. He married Dec. 12, 1824 (Lynn Rds.), Mary Babson Griffin, born April 26, 1806, and died May 25, 1895, daughter of Capt. Nathaniel and Priscilla (Lane) Griffin of Gloucester, Mass.

Children of John and Mary B., born in Lynn:

990. LUCINDA PRISCILLA, b. Sept. 15, 1825; d. Jan. 30, 1903; m. Jan. 1, 1857, Robert Phillips Mansfield, b. Aug. 1, 1827, d. July 15, 1864, son of Epes and Elizabeth (Bucknam) Mansfield. Had: (1) Ernest Lane Lewis, b. Mar. 6, 1858; (2) Mary Ellen, b. June 15, 1859; d. Sept. 3, 1859; (3) Addie A., b. Oct. 24, 1860.
991. FITZWILLIAM GRIFFIN, b. July 7, 1834.

587 Elbridge Gerry Lewis, born in Lynn, Aug. 10, 1807, and died April 25, 1861. He married, Aug. 7, 1834, Nancy Stone, born Feb. 6, 1813, daughter of Jonathan and Nancy (Batchelor) Stone of Lynn.

Children of Elbridge Gerry and Nancy, born in Lynn:

992. NATHAN BICKFORD, b. Sept. 20, 1836.
993. JONATHAN GERRY, b. Mar. 15, 1840; m. Feb. 10, 1879, Iantha (Lewis) Foster (989).

588 Leonard Lewis, born in Lynn, Dec. 7, 1810, and died July 10, 1857. He was a shoemaker and lived in Lynn. He married, first, in Lynn, May 21, 1835, Susan Fowler, born in Lynn, Feb. 19, 1807, and died Sept. 21, 1849, daughter of Samuel and Elizabeth (?) Fowler of Lynn. He married, second, in Lynn, Aug. 13, 1851, Nancy Brown, born 1821, in Marblehead, daughter of Simeon Stone.

Children of Leonard and Susan:

994. SARAH ELIZABETH, b. Feb. 22, 1836; m. 1st, John B. Harris, s. of John and Emma (Leavitt) Harris of Marblehead, who died in 1864 and she m. 2d, Jeremiah Lord Horton, son of George and Elizabeth (Sutton) Horton of Marblehead.
995. CHARLES STEWART, b. Aug. 16, 1838; unm. Station agent on B. & M. R. R. at Phillips Beach since 1874.
996. LEONARD PERCIVAL, b. June 7, 1846, in Lynn; m. June 10, 1866, Josephine, dau. of Benjamin and Mehitabel Green.
997. SUSAN LUCENA, b. Mar. 24, 1849; d. Sept. 18, 1849.

589 Bickford Lewis, born in Lynn, June 10, 1813, and died April 21, 1880. He was a shoemaker and lived in Lynn. He married, in Lynn, Nov., 1840, Mary Ann Stone, born in Lynn, Jan. 24, 1818, and died July 27, 1870, daughter of Joshua and Sarah (Wilkins) Stone of Lynn.

Children of Bickford and Mary Ann, born in Lynn:

998. CHARLES FREEMAN, b. April 7, 1841; d. Sept. 27, 1885; m. Feb. 24, 1880, Mrs. Mary (Whitman) Nickerson; dau. of Jacob and Susan Whitman of Liverpool, N. S.
999. WILLIS GAYLORD, b. Feb. 21, 1845; d. Sept. 19, 1846.
1000. MARY ANN, b. Dec. 18, 1848; d. in infancy.

591 Aaron Lummus Lewis, born in Lynn, July 16, 1818, removed to Kenduskeag, Me., near Bangor, where he married Rachael T. Tilton of Lowell and is said to have had the following children:

1001. James.
1002. William.
1003. Levi.
1004. Nathaniel.
1005. Fanny.
1006. Edwin.
1007. Hannah.

595 George Washington Lewis, born in Lynn, April 12, 1818, was a shoemaker and lived in Lynn where he died Nov. 15, 1903. He married Nov. 25, 1841, Catherine E. Whippen, daughter of Joseph and Patience (Ivins) Whippen of Marblehead.

Children of George W. and Catherine E.:

1008. Sarah Frances. For many years was principal of the Lewis Grammar School at Glenmere (Lynn), formerly called Gravesend, and d. unm.
1009. Catherine Washington, b. Sept. 27, 1848 in Philadelphia; d. Aug. 3, 1850 (Lynn Rds.).

599 Ivers Foster Lewis, born in Lynn, May 3, 1826, a shoemaker by trade and lives in Lynn. He married, in Lynn, Sept. 4, 1854, Harriet Augusta P. H. Collins, born Nov. 26, 1829 (Nov. 30, 1828, family record), daughter of John D. Collins.

Children of Ivers F. and Harriet A. P. H., born in Lynn:

1010. Frank Collins, b. Dec. 6, 1854; m. May 26, 1880, in Lynn, Eliza M., dau. of George and Mary A. Kelland.
1011. Mary Caroline, b. Nov. 2, 1857; m. Aug. 26, 1885, in Lynn, Joshua R. Johnson, s. of George and Sarah Johnson.
1012. Elizabeth, b. Aug. 11, 1859; d. June 21, 1865.
1013. Henry W., b. Mar. 27, 1863 (Lynn Rds.); m. April 16, 1882, in Lynn, Lottie M., dau. of George F. and Sarah A. Pevear.

618 Samuel Augustus Lewis, was born in Lynn, Nov. 15, 1825, and died Dec. 13, 1893. He married, June 16, 1852, Mary Fuller Delano, born in Attleboro,

Mass., in 1830 (g.s), and died in Lynn, Aug. 16, 1895, daughter of Rufus and Deborah Delano, whose remains are interred in the same lot in Swampscott cemetery.

Children of Samuel A. and Mary F.:

1014. JOSEPHINE LUTHER, b. May 9, 1856; m. James Hammond.
1015. A son, d. in infancy.

620 John Wesley Lewis, born in Lynn, May 20, 1830, was a shoemaker and lived in Lynn where he died Oct. 13, 1873. He married, Oct. 2, 1860, Sophia Stetson Johnson, daughter of Albert and Deborah (Lindsay) Johnson of Lynn, who died in 1904, aged 66 y. 4 m. 7 d. (Lynn Rds.)

Children of John W. and Sophia S., born in Lynn:

1016. WILLIAM JOHNSON, b. Mar. 1, 1861; d. Apr. 13, 1861.
1017. LUCY MARIA, b. Nov. 1, 1863; m. Oct. 13, 1881, at Swampscott, Augustus Tower Meacom, b. in Peabody, in 1860, s. of George E. and Maria A. Meacom.
1018. HERBERT STETSON, b. Feb. 7, 1867; d. Feb. 9, 1868.
1019. WILLIAM JOHNSON, b. May 17, 1872; m. April 18, 1900, in Lynn, Blanche Percy Hannaford, b. 1875; dau. of Charles T. and Delia A. (Spinney) Hannaford of Lynn. Had: (1) Percy Johnson, b. Aug. 2, 1902.

630 Benjamin Franklin Lewis, born in Lynn, Oct. 22, 1820, lived in Westfield, Mass., where he was engaged in the shoe business for more than 60 years. He was a member of the M. E. Church which he joined when 18 years old. He died at the house of Dr. C. W. Strang, Bridgeport, Conn., on Jan. 12, 1905. He married in Westfield, Sept. 14, 1842, Jane E. Johnson, daughter of William and Eliza (Allen) Johnson of Westfield.

Children of Benjamin F. and Jane E.:

1020. ELLA J., b. Oct. 21, 1845; m. Oct. 21, 1868, in Westfield, Dr. Clinton W. Strang, s. of Nelson and Julia (Wright) Strang. Had: (1) Louis Clinton, b. Dec. 4, 1869; (2) Marion Ella, b. Dec. 28, 1874; (3) Robert Hallock Wright, b. Feb. 22, 1881.
1021. MARION E., b. Oct. 18, 1846, in Bridgeport, Ct.

1022. FRANK ROCKWELL, b. Sept. 6, 1856; m. Oct. 2, 1883, in Westfield, Mary Felton, dau. of Dr. Charles and Mary (Barker-Johnson) Germaine. Had, b. in Westfield: (1) Ella Germaine, b. July 12, 1884; (2) Richard Viets, b. Dec. 13, 1885; (3) Catherine De Millie, b. June 24, 1888; (4) Elizabeth Allen, b. July 27, 1890.

632 Albion Wesley Lewis, born in Northampton, Mass., May 8, 1828, lived in Westfield, Mass., most of his life where he was well known and highly respected. He went to California around Cape Horn in 1850, where he remained several years. He learned the cabinetmaker's trade and was an expert workman. He was in the whip business for a while with Samuel Tryon, and also sold whips upon the road. At one time he was in the clothing firm of Loomis, Lewis & Co. He was a member of the 46th regiment Mass. Volunteers, and in the 30th Company Unattached Artillery during the Civil War. Later he went South and engaged in the cotton business. He was a Knight Templar and 32 degree Mason. He died Mar. 28, 1903. He married, Oct. 23, 1855, in Westfield, Mass., Caroline H., daughter of Timothy H. and Caroline B. Loomis.

Children of Albion W. and Caroline H., born in Westfield:

1023. FREDERICK ALBION, b. June 19, 1859; d. Sept. 13, 1875.

1024. GRACE HOLLAND, b. April 1, 1869; m. May 12, 1891, at Westfield, Raymond Wesley Richards, s. of Rodolphus Palford and Sarah (Burt) Richards. Had, b. in Westfield: (1) Donald Lewis, b. Jan. 20, 1893; (2) Dorothy Pomeroy, b. Aug. 28, 1894; (3) James Loomis, b. May 2, 1901.

638 Burrill Turner Lewis, was born in Lynn, Sept. 19, 1825, and died in Marblehead Nov. 24, 1846. He married in Marblehead, Nov. 19, 1844, Maria Jane Mailey, b. Aug. 23, 1826, and died Mar. 1, 1894, daughter of Thomas and Hannah Mailey of Marblehead.

Children of Burrill T. and Maria Jane, born in Marblehead:

1025. THOMAS B., b. Jan. 6, 1845; m. Dec. 23, 1869, Mary A. Brown. Had: (1) Josephine J., b. Jan. 10, 1871; (2) Caroline A., b. Feb. 10, 1874; (3) Anna M., b. Mar. 23, 1877.

1026. HANNAH, b. Jan. 17, 1846.

639 Thomas Harris Lewis, was born in Lynn, Jan. 6, 1829, and died Dec. 22, 1886. He married, Sept., 1849, Elizabeth A. Valentine, who died Oct. 10, 1898.

Children of Thomas H. and Elizabeth A.:

1027. THOMAS A. D., b. Aug. 24, 1851; d. April 13, 1881.
1028. ANNIE W. S., b. Mar. 28, 1857.
1029. FRANK, b. Mar. 19, 1864.
1030. LIZZIE T., b. Mar. 22, 1867.

640 Charles Warren Lewis, born in Lynn, Nov. 28, 1832, is a florist on Lewis St., Lynn. He married, first, Sept. 6, 1857, in Lynn, Susan Ellen Newhall, born in Saugus, July 11, 1836, and died Sept. 20, 1873, daughter of William P. and Mary Abby Newhall of Lynn. He married, second, July 13, 1875 (Lynn Rds.), Clarissa Ware Woodbury, born in Lynn, Nov. 14, 1830, daughter of Samuel E. and Clara Woodbury of Lynn.

Child of Charles W. and Susan E., born in Lynn:

1031. WILLIAM ENDICOTT, b. Mar. 29, 1866; d. Sept. 4, 1902. Mr. Lewis carried on a successful plumbing business at 17 Central Ave., Lynn. He was a member of the North Congregational Church, superintendent of its Sunday School, and charter member and President of its Christian Endeavor Society. He was one of the leaders in forming the C. E. Union of Lynn and vicinity; was its third President, and until his removal from the city was the Union's County representative. He was chairman of the Executive Committee of Mass. State C. E. Convention, held in Lynn in 1897, the success of which was largely due to the executive ability of Mr. Lewis. He m. Oct. 14, 1891, Annie E., dau. of John S. and Edna Knowles, and had: (1) Ruth Endicott, b. Aug. 11, 1896.

647 Allen Webster Lewis, born in Lynn, June 17, 1825, married in Lynn, Nov. 2, 1850, Maria Ryan, born in Neinha, County Tipperary, Ireland, daughter of Daniel Ryan.

Children of Allen W. and Maria, born in Lynn:

1032. CHARLES FRANCIS, b. Oct. 16, 1851; d. June 28, 1875.
1033. ALLEN WEBSTER, b. Dec. 3, 1852; d. Dec. 5, 1852.

1034. GEORGIANNA, b. Sept. 24, 1853; m. July 28, 1886, Fred P. Goldthwait, b. in Danvers, s. of Dennis and Adaline J. Goldthwait.

1035. ALLEN WALLACE, b. Jan. 18, 1856; d. Feb. 10, 1858.

1036. ALLEN WALLACE, b. Sept. 3, 1859; d. Apr. 18, 1886; m. Mar. 2, 1881, in Lynn, Miriam P., dau. of Benj. F. and Marion Crosscup.

648 John Conway Lewis, born in Lynn, Nov. 28, 1827, married in Lynn, July 18, 1852, Susan M. Alley, born in Lynn, Feb. 27, 1835, daughter of John 4th and Susan D. Alley.

Children of John Conway and Susan M., born in Lynn:

1037. SUSAN ABIGAIL, b. Nov. 26, 1852; m. April 12, 1871, Nicholas J. Roop, b. in Newburyport in 1846, son of John W. and Hannah Roop.

1038. CHARLES EDMUND, b. Sept. 8, 1854; d. Sept. 10, 1855.

1039. CHARLES EDMUND, b. 1856; m. Feb. 25, 1879, in Lynn, Sadie T. Anthony, b. in Lynn in 1858, dau. of William G. and Frances G. Anthony.

1040. FRANK ALLEY, b. June 21, 1860; m. Apr. 25, 1888, in Lynn, Mabel S. Southwick, b. in Peabody, 1870, dau. of Henry and Lucy Southwick. Had, b. in Lynn: (1) Emma Prescott, b. Sept. 6, 1888; (2) Henry Wilbur, b. Dec. 20, 1889; (3) Everett Delmont, b. May 3, 1891; (4) Harold Wilson, b. June 18, 1892; (5) Hazel Gladys, b. July 8, 1893; d. Sept. 9, 1893; (6) Harry Walcott, b. July 23, 1894; (7) Mahlon Prince, b. Sept. 25, 1895; (8) Helen Arlene, b. Apr. 24, 1897; (9) Susan Gertrude, b. May 29, 1898; (10) Frank Alley, b. Sept. 3, 1899; (11) Dorothy Bean, b. Oct. 13, 1900; d. May 14, 1902; (12) Ralph Morton, b. Sept. 22, 1902.

1041. EUNICE ALLEY, b. Jan. 13, 1863; m. Mar. 26, 1883, in Saugus, George A. Stacy, b. in Atkinson, N. H., in 1857, s. of Timothy A. and Harriet Stacy.

1042. JOSEPH CARLTON, b. Jan. 13, 1863; m. Nov. 28, 1889, in Lynn, A. Florence Churchill, b. in Lynn, in 1866, dau. of William and Sarah E. Churchill. Had: (1) Earl Carlton, b. Mar. 17, 1893, in Lynn.

1043. GEORGIANNA PIERCE, b. Oct. 26, 1865; d. Feb. 3, 1867.

1044. NATHANIEL ELLIS, b. Jan. 13, 1869, m. June 15, 1897, in Lynn, M. Josephine Churchill, b. in Lynn, in 1869, dau. of William and Sarah E. Churchill. Had: (1) Roy Ellis, b. Dec. 22, 1903, in Lynn.

1045. CHESTER VERJANNO, b. Mar. 30, 1872; m. June 27, 1894, in Lynn, Georgia M. Anthony, b. in Lynn in 1874, dau. of William G. and Celia Anthony. Had, b. in Lynn: (1) Robert Favin, b. Mar. 1, 1897; (2) Helen Pauline, b. Jan. 2, 1902.

1046. ELMER E., b. Dec. 16, 1873; m. Nov. 27, 1895, in Lynn, Bertha E. Gove, b. in Lynn in 1876, dau. of Enoch and Carrie S. Gove.

672 Theodore Augustus Lewis, born in Lynn, Feb. 9, 1827, married, first, Nov., 1852, Eunice E. Bradstreet, born in Topsfield, Mass., in 1827, and died Aug. 23, 1865, daughter of Cornelius and Eunice (Wright) Bradstreet. He married, second, Sept. 30, 1866, Martha A. Grant, b. in Norridgewock, Me., in Jan., 1832, daughter of Elijah and Louise (Curtis) Grant.

Children of Theodore A. and Eunice E.:

1047. CORNELIUS, b. Apr. 12, 1853; d. June, 1854.

1048. MELINDA A., b. May 30, 1855, in Topsfield; d. July, 1892; m. Aug. 1, 1881, in Wakefield, Rev. Charles A. Melden, b. in Salem, s. of George and Margaret Melden.

1049. WILLIAM HERMAN, b. Aug. 20, 1858, in Lynn; m. 1st, Sept. 15, 1880, at Middleton, Mary Ann Hall, dau. of Samuel and Fanny Hall; m. 2d, June 27, 1896, at North Andover, Lizzie F. Ingalls, dau. of S. William and Sarah Ingalls.

Child of Theodore A. and Martha A., b. in Lynn:

1050. JOSEPHINE BRADSTREET, b. Oct. 30, 1868 (Lynn Rds.), Oct. 13, 1868 (private rd.), unm.

681 Thomas Y. Lewis, born in Shelbyville, Ill., Feb. 20, 1837, adopted the Y. in his name while a medical student at Louisville, Ky., to prevent another Thomas Lewis from receiving his mail. He graduated at the Kentucky School of Medicine, Feb. 28, 1858, and practiced his profession at Sullivan, Ill., until 1881, when he removed to Dublin, Texas. He was Superintendent of Schools of Moultrie County, Ill., 1865-1869, and alderman at Sullivan, Ill., and at Dublin, Texas; also President of the Board of School Trustees and President of the National Bank of Dublin, Texas, upon its organization. He has in his possession the watch of his grandfather Thomas (164), which was made in London, Eng., in 1810, on the case of which is engraved his grandfather's obituary and the names of his family. He lives in Dublin, Texas. He married, in Sullivan, Ill., June 22, 1858, Cordelia Basha Elder, born near Sullivan, Ill., Oct. 31, 1841, daughter of James and Didama Elder, who were raised and married in Tennessee and moved to Illinois.

Children of Thomas Y. and Cordelia B.:

1051. EVA, b. Aug. 9, 1860; d. Apr. 17, 1885, in Dublin, Tex.; m. Apr. 18, 1880, F. M. Craig of Sullivan, Ill.
1052. THOMAS EDWARD, b. Dec. 2, 1862, in Sullivan, Ill.; m. Nov. 24, 1896, at Dougherty, Indian Ter., Hattie Marion Brown. Had: (1) Thomas Y., b. July 31, 1898. Lives at Fort Worth, Texas.
1053. MINNIE, b. Dec. 17, 1864; d. Oct., 1865.
1054. EDITH, b. Mar. 17, 1873; m. Mar. 28, 1889, S. S. Davis. Had: (1) Lewie, b. Dec. 18, 1891; (2) Carl Thomas, b. July 30, 1893.

687 Charles Dudley Lewis was born in Roxbury, Mass., Sept. 26, 1844, and died in Sherborn, Mass., May 4, 1905. He served in the Mass. legislature for eight years from 1888, and was a member and treasurer of the State Democratic Committee and a member of the National Democratic Committee and also was well known in banking circles and among cattle dealers about the state. He married at Framingham, Mass., April 3, 1872, Emily Johonnot Clark, born in Framingham, Dec. 15, 1846, daughter of James Wilson and Catharine Monroe (March) Clark of Framingham.

Children of Charles Dudley and Emily J.:

1055. JAMES WILSON CLARK, b. Apr. 27, 1875.
1056. WILLIAM GUSTAVUS, b. July 24, 1876.
1057. KATHERINE LEBARON, b. Sept. 26, 1877.
1058. FRANCES WILSON, b. Oct. 19, 1879.
1059. MARGARET DUDLEY, b. Apr. 21, 1882.
1060. CHARLES DUDLEY, b. Oct. 12, 1884; d. Apr. 14, 1896.
1061. EDMUND SANFORD, b. June 7, 1887.
1062. MARY ELIZABETH, b. Apr. 20, 1890.
1063. LEBARON, b. Oct. 10, 1892; d. July 1, 1893.

735 Dexter Bosworth Lewis, born in Providence, R. I., Sept. 20, 1820, was a merchant. He was a councilman in 1851-1853, 1875 and 1876, and a member of the Marine Artillery Company. He was a director in the Old Liberty Bank and the Second National Bank and also in the Board of Trade. He was a member of the firm of Burroughs & Lewis, engaged in the oil and cotton business and for many years was in partnership with Col. J. Lippitt Snow, under the firm name of Snow & Lewis, handling dye stuffs and chemicals. He married in Providence, R. I., Sept. 6, 1842, Mary Ann Leveck, born in Bristol, R. I., Mar. 29, 1822, daughter of John C. and Lucy W. (Dexter) Leveck. He died July 17, 1887.

Children of Dexter B. and Mary A., born in Providence, R. I.

1064. JOHN DEXTER, b. Mar. 19, 1846; m. Apr. 2, 1872, Sophie P. Lapham, b. Apr. 4, 1848, dau. of Hon. Benj. N. and Sophia M. (Bullock) Lapham. While fishing from a launch, Feb. 26, 1901, on Lake Worth, Fla., a storm came up suddenly and overturned the craft, and Mrs. Lewis was caught in the awning and drowned; her husband and youngest daughter narrowly escaped by clinging to the bottom of the boat. They were among the most prominent people of Providence. They had: (1) John Bosworth, b. Mar. 19, 1874; m. Miss Watson, dau. of Col. Arthur N. Watson of Providence; (2) Benjamin Lapham, b. Sept. 4, 1875; d. Sept. 9, 1876; (3) Mary Louise, b. July 31, 1877.

1065. ELLEN LEVECK, b. June 4, 1851; m. Nov. 20, 1873, Stephen M. Knowles, s. of Ex-Mayor Edward P. Knowles, and had, b. in Providence: (1) Helen Lewis, b. Jan. 30, 1875; (2 Stephen Dexter, b. May 31, 1880.

1066. DEXTER BOSWORTH, b. June 4, 1851; d. Aug. 18, 1851.

1067. FRANK EVENS, b. Oct. 3. 1859; unm.

740 Alfred Bosworth Lewis, was born in Providence, R. I., June 7, 1819, and died August, 1889. He married, first, Nov. 21, 1842, Sarah B. Fields, who was divorced. He married, second, Josephine V. Benson, born 1822, and died April 2, 1858.

Children of Alfred Bosworth and Josephine V. Lewis:

1068. GENEVIEVE, b. May 11, 1851; d. Aug. 17, 1853.

1069. PEMBERTON, b. Dec. 5, 1855; m. April 22, 1890, Maud Rist.

1070. ALFRED BOSWORTH, b. Nov. 3, 1856.

1071. JOSEPHINE, b. Mar. 18, 1858; m. April 23, 1881, Willis C. Dunn. Had: (1) Willis, b. June 9, 1882; d. April 22, 1883; (2) Lillian, b. Sept. 5, 1883; (3) Marion, b. Dec. 4, 1884; d. July 10, 1885.

748 Joseph West Lewis was born Dec. 17, 1831, and died Jan. 4, 1877. He married, first, Nov. 27, 1861, Annie E. Snow, daughter of Henry H. Snow, who died in childbirth Dec. 16, 1865. He married, second, Melissa A. (Horton) Clarke, a widow, born April 18, 1846; daughter of Comfort and Martha P. Horton. She married, third, June, 1884, Horace R. Handy.

Children of Joseph West and Melissa A.:

1072 JOSEPH WEST, b. Oct. 27, 1871; m. Nov. 18, 1896, Josephine Billings, dau. of Henry A. and Josephine (Lewis) Billings, a granddaughter of Bradford Lewis of Chicopee, Mass. Mr. Lewis is a graduate of Brown University.

1073. FRANK HORTON, b. July 20, 1873.

1074. HERBERT CHACE, b. May 18, 1876; d. June 2, 1877.

749 Kingsley Thurber Lewis born in Johnston, R. I., Feb. 24, 1824, married April 2, 1846, Susan A. Mathewson, daughter of William B. and Susan S. (Latham) Mathewson.

Children of Kingsley Thurber and Susan A., b. in Providence, R. I.:

1075. LOUISA JACKSON, b. Mar. 9, 1847; d. Sept. 7, 1876; a teacher in the Providence, R. I., public schools.

1076. WALTER JAMES, b. Sept. 8, 1851; d. Sept. 25, 1906. He learned the jeweller's trade and also was a conductor for the Union Railroad Co. for 9 years. He was appointed Sanitary Inspector of the Board of Health of Providence in 1894, and retained the office until his death. He was a member of Doric Lodge of Masons of Auburn, and was a charter member of Co. E. First Light Infantry regiment, a 2d sergt. upon organization and rose to 1st Lieutenant which he held at time of death. He married, Sept. 20, 1874, Ella Maria Rockwell, who was divorced in July, 1895. Had, born in Providence: (1) Grace Louise, b. Jan. 3, 1886; (2) Walter Irving, b. Aug. 9, 1891.

750 George Washington Lewis, born July 16, 1825, married, first, Feb. 10, 1845, Louisa Jackson, daughter of James and Hannah (Carpenter) Jackson. He married, second, May 3, 1848, Mary J. Billings, daughter of Samuel and Mary (Yates) Billings.

Child of George W. and Louisa J., b. in Providence, R. I.:

1077. GEORGE JACKSON, b. Dec. 4, 1846; married; d. Mar. 1, 1896, in Allegan, Mich., where he was engaged for many years in the coal and wood business.

Children of George W. and Mary J.:

1078. PHEBE BILLINGS, b. May 22, 1849, in Providence, R. I.; m. Jan. 21, 1874, Horatio A. Hunt. Had, b. in Providence: (1) Helen Nancie, b. Jan. 26, 1877; (2) Jesse Hosmer, b. Dec. 23, 1879; (3) Louise Wisnor, b. Aug. 6, 1880; (4) Fannie Evans, b. Nov. 2, 1886.

1079. MARY AUGUSTA, b. Dec. 1, 1851, in Barrington, R. I.; m. Mar. 9, 1876, Hon. Ellery H. Wilson, at one time speaker of the R. I. House of Representatives. Had, b. in Providence: (1) Lewis Bartlett, b. Feb. 17, 1877; (2) Mary Holbrook, b. Dec. 29, 1878; (3) Ellery Lewis, b. Jan. 1, 1882.

1080. FANNY BOWERS, b. Feb. 2, 1855, in Augusta, Ga.; m. May 10, 1876, Fred B. Evans. Had, b. in Providence: (1) Bailey Winslow, b. Sept. 23, 1877; (2) George Warren, b. May 16, 1880; (3) Marion King, b. Mar. 17, 1883; (4) Bertha Lewis, b. Feb. 12, 1888; (5) Margaret Hathaway, b. May 17, 1894.

1081. ELLEN JANE, b. June 18, 1857, in Augusta, Ga.; d. June 16, 1869.

1082. BERTHA, b. Nov. 18, 1860, in Barrington, R. I.; m. May 23, 1888, Walter Edward Fisk. Had, b. in Providence, R. I.: (1) Dwight Lewis, b. Aug. 25, 1891; (2) Katharine Bradford, b. July 12, 1893.

1083. CAROLINE ELIZABETH, b. Nov. 27, 1867, in Providence.

1084. WARREN BILLINGS, b. Apr. 10, 1870, in Providence.

754 Levi Jason Lewis was born July 27, 1828 and died Feb. 3, 1895. He married, Nov. 6, 1849, Clara R. daughter of Isaac and Clarissa (Brownell) Wilcox.

Children of Levi Jason and Clara R.:

1085. LEVI AUGUSTUS, b. Nov. 30, 1850; m. Oct. 1, 1873, Mary E., dau. of Wilson J. and Elizabeth (Barnfield) McCartney.

1086. FRANK L., b. May 9, 1853; m. 1st, Oct. 18, 1875, in Providence, Emma L., dau. of Samuel and Mary C. (Crandall) Taylor of New Bedford, Mass. Had: (1) Frank, b. Apr. 3, 1878, in Providence, R. I.; d. Oct. 8, 1878, in New Bedford; m. 2d, Nov. 27, 1884, Harriet E., dau. of Nicholas O. and Abbie M. (Bliven) Reynolds of Exeter, R. I. Had, b. in Providence: (2) Harry R., b. Oct. 14, 1885; (3) Faith, b. May 1, 1889.

1087. CHAUNCEY, b. June 16, 1855.

1088. WALTER, b. Mar. 7, 1857; d. April 10, 1857.

1089. CLARA JOSEPHINE, b. Apr. 17, 1858; m. Dec. 31, 1876, James Allen Blanchard, son of Allen and Barbara (Millard) Blanchard. Had: (1) Clara Francis, b. Nov. 13, 1877; (2) James Willard, b. Mar. 30, 1879; (3) Hattie Lewis, b. Oct. 31, 1883; d. Dec. 20, 1889; (4) Sarah Gertrude, b. Oct. 4, 1887; (5) Edgar Wilson, b. May 7, 1891; d. June 9, 1893; (6) Mary Estha, b. Mar. 26, 1894.

1090. HARRIET ELLA, b. Sept. 2, 1861; m. Oct. 25, 1882, Allison W., son of William B. and Rachel Trafford. Had: (1) Inez Perry, b. July 19, 1883; (2) Grace Barnard, b. Feb. 10, 1886; d. Feb. 23, 1894.

755 William T. Lewis born Mar. 26, 1831, married, first, Oct. 12, 1852, Eliza B., daughter of Lewis Thomas and Fanny P. (Burrows) Hoar, who died June 17, 1885. He married, second, Dec. 8, 1886, Mary Hoppin, daughter of Nicholas R. and Susan (Climer) Bradford of Philadelphia, Pa.

Children of William T. and Eliza B.:

1091. ARTHUR, b. Oct. 27, 1853; m. Jan. 5, 1877, Jennie, dau. of Capt. Joseph E. and Sarah Ann (Hubbard) Martin of Barrington, R. I. Had: (1) Howard, b. Nov. 15, 1875; (2) Marion, b. Mar. 9, 1882; (3) Hope Hubbard, b. Nov. 30, 1891.

1092. WILLIAM T., b. Mar. 27, 1857; m. Jan. 29, 1879, Elvira C., dau. of William A. and Sarah Smith (Bosworth) Cornell. Had: (1) Harold, b. Dec. 3, 1881; d. Apr. 4, 1889; (2) Clinton D., b. July 21, 1887; (3) William T., b. Oct. 29, 1894.

1093. FANNY, b. June 30, 1859; m. Jan. 10, 1883, Charles Sparks.

1094. ELLIOTT BURROWS, b. Dec. 13, 1872.

759 Elijah C. Lewis born in Brooklyn, N. Y., Jan. 13, 1839, lived in Providence, R. I., for 25 years and was employed as travelling agent by the Windsor line of steamships for 23 years. He was transportation agent of a Baltimore line of steamships when he died, suddenly, Dec. 17, 1896. He married Nov. 9, 1862, Emily Ann, daughter of Rev. Josephus W. and Anna (Remington) Horton.

Child of Elijah C. and Emily Ann:

1095. MINNIE EMILY, b. July 19, 1863; d. Jan. 20, 1886; m. Sept. 13, 1881, Dr. William D. Porter, a dentist, b. Sept., 1857, in Glastonbury, Conn.; d. Jan. 19, 1901, son of Dr. William Miller and Abby Frances Porter. Had: (1) Mabel Frances, b. July 31, 1882.

772 Henry Bowers Lewis was born in Providence, R. I., Nov. 10, 1837, and died in Brooklyn, N. Y., in June, 1878. He was a bookbinder and at the time of his death was foreman of the Methodist Book Concern of New York City. He married in Providence, R. I., July 2, 1859, Mary S. Davis, b. Dec. 14, 1836, in Liverpool, Eng., daughter of Francis and Rose (Kerrigan) Davis.

Children of Henry Bowers and Mary S., first two b. in Providence, R. I., last four in Brooklyn, N. Y.:

1096. FRANCIS HENRY, b. May 15, 1860.
1097. CHARLES SYLVESTER, b. June 8, 1862.
1098. SAMUEL CORNELL, b. Nov. 30, 1864; d. Dec. 2, 1865.
1099. WALDO STOCKTON, b. Dec. 29, 1867.
1100. HARRY WINSLOW, b. Oct. 15, 1871.
1101. IDA ELIZABETH, b. April 29, 1874.

774 William Brown Lewis was born in Bristol, R. I., Oct. 5, 1821, and died in Cranston, R. I., Dec. 7, 1882. He married in New York City, Jan. 12, 1842, Jane Brown Dempster, born in Edinburgh, Scotland, Feb. 24, 1824, and died Mar. 18, 1907, at the home of her son Charles E. Lewis, in Burlington, Vt.

Children of William B. and Jane B.:

1102. GEORGE WASHINGTON, b. Feb. 22, 1843, in New York City; m. July 2, 1873, in Providence, R. I., Maria Frances Warden, b. Dec. 31, 1848, in Smithfield, R. I, Lives in Providence, and had born there: (1) Edith Marie, b. Nov. 13, 1875; (2) George Leland, b. Jan. 27, 1878.

1103. THEODORE FRANCIS, b. June 18, 1845, in Rochester, N. Y.; is in the Creamery business at Oakland, Calif. He m. June 18, 1865, in Pawtucket, R. I., Ellen Maria Crocker, b. Sept. 19, 1845, dau. of Uriah B. and Maria C. (Harrington) Crocker, and had b. in Providence: (1) Theodore Wallace, b. June 15, 1872; d. Oct. 6, 1877.

1104. WILLIAM HENRY, b. Jan. 29, 1847, in Rochester, N. Y.; d. Oct. 21, 1864, from the effects of wounds received at the battle of Cedar Creek, Va.

1105. JAMES DEMPSTER, b. May 22, 1848, in Providence, R. I.; d. Aug. 21, 1848.

1106. CHARLES EDWIN, b. July 13, 1849, in Providence, R. I.; m. Alla Clark; lives at Burlington, Vt.

779 Edward Augustus Lewis, was born in St., Louis, Mo.,* Feb. 22, 1820, and died there Sept. 21, 1889. He was a lawyer by profession, presiding Judge of the Supreme Court of Missouri and Chief Justice of the St. Louis Court of Appeals for 12 years; also editor of the St. Louis Intelligencer. He married Sept. 9, 1845, Parthenia A. daughter of Walter L. Bransford of Kentucky.

Children of Edward Augustus and Parthenia A.:

1107. WALTER FELIX, b. Aug. 23, 1846.

1108. EDWARD SIMMONS, b. Aug. 22, 1848, in Richmond, Mo.

1109. FLORENCE ELIZABETH, b. May 18, 1850; m. Robert Atkinson.

1110. EUGENE WASHINGTON, b. July 20, 1855.

1111. PETER GRAYSON, b. Aug. 17, 1857; m. Minnie Carroll. Had: (1) Minnie Olive, b. Mar. 10, 1884; (2) Carroll Grayson, b. Aug. 7, 1885.

1112. BRANSFORD, b. Nov. 14, 1862, in St. Charles, Mo.; m. Jennie Jaynes. A physician and surgeon; editor of the Weekly Medical Review; lecturer in the Missouri Medical College; and formerly assistant-superintendent of the City Hospital of St. Louis, Mo.

799 Benjamin Lewis, was born in Milford, N. H., Mar. 23, 1808, and died Aug. 31, 1874. He married at Ashby, Mass., Oct. 12, 1835, Harriet Prescott Adams.

*Another record says he was born in Washington, D. C.

Child of Benjamin and Harriet P.:

1113. FREDERICK BENJAMIN ADAMS, b. Mar. 12, 1839; m. Mar. 12, 1866, Antoinette Grenell. Had: (1) Maud, lives at San Jose, Calif.; (2) Frederick DeLancey; (3) Agnes Adams, m. Morris Mansfield Bruce and had (1) Starr Lewis Bruce.

800 Asa Lewis, born Mar. 3, 1810, in Milford, N. H., died June 30, 1846, in New York City; married Nov. 9, 1837, at Concord, Mass., Abby H. Davis of Concord, Mass. Had: (1) Charles G., d. April 5, 1843, æ. 4 y.

809 William Frederick Lewis, born in Gainesville, Ala., May 2, 1831, lived on a farm in Sumpter Co. Ala., but held county office most of the time, and was county surveyor at the time of his death, Aug. 9, 1891. He married, first, at Eutau, Green Co., Ala., June 7, 1855, Mary Ann Ridgeway, b. Aug. 22, 1835, and died at Decatur, Miss., Dec. 15, 1883, daughter of Sephalon and Mary (Bell) Ridgeway of Springfield, Ala. He married, second, Dec. 22, 1887, Mary Ellen Bates, who died Aug. 1, 1892.

Children of William Frederick and Mary Ann:

1114. ICHABOD COLBY BARTLETT, b. June 1, 1856; m. April 12, 1886, Laura Ross.
1115. Infant son, b. June 24, 1858; d. July 7, 1858.
1116. MARGARET BELL, b. Sept. 13, 1859; d. Oct. 11, 1862.
1117. SALLIE MARTIN, b. Feb. 16, 1862; m. Feb. 2, 1887, Alexander Archable Chaney, b. in Decatur, Miss., Mar. 24, 1862, s. of Archable and Margaret (Jones) Chaney of Decatur, Miss. Had, b. at Chunky, Miss.: (1) Charles Alexander, b. Feb. 7, 1888; (2) James Frederick, b. Mar. 17, 1890; (3) Oscar Lewis, b. Dec. 24, 1892; (4) Mary Ella, b. Jan. 22, 1896.
1118. MARY ELLA, b. Dec. 24, 1865; m. Nov. 1, 1885, Thomas James Parke, b. Oct. 4, 1864, in Decatur, Miss.; s. of Thomas and Harriet (Hollingsworth) Park of Decatur, Miss. Had: (1) a daughter, b. Sept. 30, 1886; d. Oct. 24, 1886; (2) Mary Harriet, b. Nov. 19, 1887; (3) Bessie Lewis, b. Apr, 2, 1890; (4) Argus Frazier, b. Sept. 22, 1893; (5) a son, b. Oct. 28, 1897.
1119. WILLIAM SEPHALON, b. Mar. 28, 1867; d. Mar. 28, 1869.

1120. CHARLES BRADLEY, b. Aug. 9, 1870; m. Nov. 7, 1890, Sadie Winham.

1121. RUFUS GUSTAVUS, b. June 2, 1873; m. Aug. 12, 1891, Lou Ella Chaney.

1122. WALTER WEBSTER RUSSELL, b. Feb. 3, 1876; m. Nov. 24, 1896, Julia Beddowman.

1123. GERTIE ELIZA CONVERSE, b. Aug. 30, 1881.

819 Rufus Smith Lewis, born in New Hampton, N. H., June 14, 1833, was an invalid for years, but engaged in business in Lowell and Boston, Mass. He was Register of Deeds in Laconia, N. H., where he died May 22, 1887. He married Eliza Bean Hilton, daughter of David and Sally Fuller (Wallace) Hilton.

Child of Rufus Smith and Eliza B.:

1124. WINNIFREDA WALLACE, b. Feb. 3, 1858; m. Mar. 27, 1890, in Laconia, N. H., Charles Henry Turner, b. in Wentworth, N. H., May 26, 1861, s. of Charles and Elizabeth Kelley (Goodspeed) Turner. Reside in Washington, D. C.

822 James Pickering Lewis, born Feb. 10, 1842, in New Hampton, N. H., has been a clerk in the Post Office Department, Washington, D. C., since Mar. 10, 1875. He married June 30, 1880, in Washington, D. C., Mrs. Mary (Winn) Wilkey, born July 15, 1842, daughter of Bernard and Katherine (Dyer) Winn.

Child of James Pickering and Mary:

1125. JAMES PICKERING, b. April 14, 1883.

825 James Willard Lewis, born in Concord, Vt., Aug. 26, 1823, was thrown from a carriage at St. Johnsbury, Vt., and two weeks after died of apoplexy on May 11, 1879. He was Justice of the Peace at the time of his death. He married, first, Diantha Chloe Richardson, born in Salem, Vt., daughter of Francis and Chloe (Chamberlain) Richardson, of Waterford, Vt., who died in New York City, Sept. 9, 1858. He married, second, at Bradford, Vt., Dec. 25, 1863, Hattie Worthen, born Dec. 17, 1833, daughter of John A. and Mary (Runnels) Worthen of Bradford, Vt.

Children of John Willard and Diantha Chloe, born in Kirby, Vt.:

1126. MARY MIRANDA, b. Oct. 19, 1849; m. Aug. 2, 1870, in Lowell, Mass., Henry Gray Whittle, b. in Weare, N. H., Aug. 8, 1848; divorced May 5, 1893. Had: (1) Freddie Lewis, b. Mar. 13, 1872, in Lexington, Mass. Both father and son are railroad conductors.

1127. HENRY W., b. July, 1853; d. Sept. 22, 1857, at West Concord, Vt.

826 Ethan Nichols Lewis, born in Concord, Vt., July 25, 1825, was a carpenter by trade, and removed to Beloit, Wis., in the 50s, and thence to Springfield, Mass., in 1860, where he died July 5, 1887. He married June 11, 1851, Rebekah Partridge, born in Templeton, Mass., May 1, 1825, daughter of Otis and Unity (Fales) Partridge of Templeton, who died in Springfield, Mass., Aug. 4, 1881.

Children of Ethan Nichols and Rebekah:

1128. ETHAN ALLEN, b. April 16, 1852; m. Florence Jones, and died of wood alcohol poisoning, July 10, 1907, at New Haven, Ct., where he was a bookbinder; foreman for Price, Lee & Co. He left two daughters.

1129. JAMES HENRY, b. Oct. 17, 1853, in West Concord, Vt., has held public office in Springfield, Mass., since 1869. He m. July 20, 1876, in Springfield, Miss., Fannie G. Fisher, b. in Hartford, Conn., Dec. 25, 1852, daughter of Andrew Cobb and Ellen Louise (Pease) Fisher of Springfield, Mass. Had: (1) Raymond Irving, b. Dec. 25, 1879; (2) Herbert Willard, b. May 15, 1881; (3) Elwyn Fisher, b. May 28, 1884; (4) Beatrice, b. Jan. 1, 1888; (5) Harold Percy, b. Mar. 10, 1890.

1130. FLORA ESTELLE, b. and d. in 1854-5, at Beloit, Wis.

1131. EMMA CORA, b. Sept. 10, 1858; unm.; a trained nurse, and lives in Worcester, Mass.

828 Sumner West Lewis, born in Concord, Vt., April 6, 1829, was a machinist by trade, and lived in West Concord, Vt., where he died Nov. 30, 1885. He served throughout the Civil War in the 8th regiment Vermont Infantry, and rose from the ranks to a lieutenancy. He married, first, Nov. 7, 1859, Almira A. Balch, born in Concord, Vt., July 2, 1834, and died at Bath, N. H., Nov. 25, 1861, daughter of Abner and Lydia P. (Woodbury) Balch of Concord, Vt. He married, second, Aug. 8, 1872, Sabrina Smith, born in Lunenburg, Vt., June 11, 1848, and died in West Concord, Apr. 18, 1885, daughter of Asa and Mary (Powers) Smith of Lunenburg, Vt.:

Child of Sumner West and Almira A.:

1132. FRANK BALCH, b. Aug. 30, 1861; a druggist and jeweller at Whitefield, Vt.; m. Sept. 27, 1888, Lizzie Estelle Dudley, b. in Concord, Vt., April 30, 1866, dau. of Clarence H. and Lucy O. (Burroughs) Dudley of Concord, Vt.

Child of Sumner West and Sabrina:

1133. FRED A., b. July 26, 1876.

850 George Courtland Lewis, born in Groton, Mass., Jan. 29, 1825, was a farmer, and removed from Groton to Pepperrell in 1860, where he died April 12, 1883. He married in Pepperrell, Nov. 30, 1854, Harriet Augusta Pierce, born in Townsend, Mass., Oct. 1, 1833, daughter of Richard and Mary Ann (Hartwell) Pierce of Pepperrell.

Child of George Courtlandt and Harriet A., born in Groton:

1134. CHARLES ANDREW, b. Apr. 16, 1869; m. Oct. 31, 1882, in Waltham, Mass, Amy Hackett, b. June 30, 1859, on Labuan Island, off the coast of Borneo, dau. of Rev. Wm. Henry and Maria Elizabeth (Passmore) Hackett of London, Eng. Had: (1) Raymond Augustus, b. June 25, 1883, at Waltham, Mass.; (2) Charles Courtland, b. June 17, 1892, at Hollis, N. H.; (3) Frank Cyril, b. June 19, 1895, at Hollis, N. H.

852 Levi Lewis, born in Lancaster, Mass., Dec. 21, 1818, removed to Sterling, and in 1850, to Leominster, Mass., where he resides. He married in 1844, Frances Ann Johnson, born in Sterling, Mar. 2, 1820, daughter of Jonas and Nancy (Hayden) Johnson, who died in Leominster, Aug. 22, 1875.

Children of Levi and Frances Ann, first three born in Sterling, rest in Leominster:

1135. LEVI WALDO, b. Mar. 12, 1845; m. June 23, 1881, Ella Maria Gates, born in Leominster, Jan. 12, 1852, dau. of Augustus and Adelia M. (Puffer) Gates of Leominster. Had, b. in Leominster: (1) Bernard Waldo, b. May 10, 1882; (2) Frances Adelia, b. May 2, 1885; (3) Hazel Isabelle, b. July 31, 1887; (4) Clyde Gates, b. May 22, 1894.

1136. ISABELLE JANE, b. June 2, 1846; unm.

1137. FRANK JACKSON, b. Aug. 4, 1849; m. Nov. 26, 1881, Cevilla F. Piper, b. in Winchester, Mass., Mar. 2, 1850, dau. of Lysander and Rachel R. (Doane) Piper of Royalston, Mass. Lives in Leominster, and had born there: (1) Clarence F., b. Sept. 26, 1884; (2) Grace E., b. Nov. 12, 1886.

1138. ELIZABETH WEST, b. Nov. 12, 1850; m. Mar. 16, 1871, Daniel Walter Goss, b. in Temple, N. H., Aug. 19, 1842, s. of Henry and Sarah (Dexter) Goss of Leominster. Removed from Lancaster to Leominster in 1875, thence to Northboro in 1876, thence to Lancaster in 1881, thence to Clinton in 1884, where he now resides. Had: (1) Flora Belle, b. April 21, 1872; (2) Henry Walter, b. July 8, 1876; (3) Clarence William, b. Aug. 4, 1882; (4) Addie May, b. Mar. 3, 1886.

1139. WILLIAM WARREN, b. Dec. 12, 1853.

1140. CHARLES CROSBY, b. April 21, 1857.

856 Crosby Lewis, born in Lancaster, Mass., April 24, 1825, was a merchant, and lived in Pepperrell, Mass., until 1858, in Westminster until 1861, in Lancaster until 1863, in San Jose, Calif., until 1867, in Philadelphia, Pa., until 1877, and in Westminster, Mass., until his death, April 21, 1895. He married June 9, 1853, Martha Abba Marshall, born in Fitchburg, Mass., April 7, 1830, daughter of Chedorlaomer and Martha Fox (Upton) Marshall of Fitchburg.

Children of Crosby and Martha Abba:

1141. MARTHA AUGUSTA, b. Mar. 27, 1854, in Pepperell.

1142. CHARLOTTE ALLINA, b. Nov. 8, 1856; d. Sept. 7, 1875.

1143. ANNA WARE, b. Mar. 8, 1872, in Westminster.

870 Frederick Lewis, born in Belfast, Me., Sept. 10, 1835, learned the watchmaker and jeweller's trade in Belfast, went to Boston in June, 1857, and remained two years, and in 1859 went to Camden, Me., where he now resides. He married at Camden, Jan. 30, 1868, Georgianna Sophia Eaton, born in Camden, March 9, 1838, daughter of William and Harriet (Hosmer) Eaton of Camden.

Children of Frederick and Georgianna Sophia, born in Camden:

1144. FREDERICK WILLIAM, b. Feb. 13, 1870; d. Aug. 19, 1870.
1145. JESSIE FISHER, b. Oct. 30, 1871.
1146. EDWARD CUSHING, b. Aug. 7, 1876; d. Mar. 17, 1880.

886 Porter James Lewis, born in Townsend, Mass., Oct. 23, 1846, is a wholesale and retail dealer in grain. He lived in Townsend until 1877, when he moved to Lancaster, Mass. He married in Brookline, N. H., Mar. 18, 1875, Sarah Elizabeth Warren, born in Townsend, Jan. 2, 1847, and died in Lancaster Jan. 2, 1897, daughter of Samuel F. and Harriet Lucretia (Sawyer) Warren of Townsend.

Child of Porter James and Sarah Elizabeth, born in Townsend:

1147. ORA MABELLE, b. Nov. 9, 1876.

893 John Gunnison Lewis, born in Concord, N. H., April 29, 1839, served in Co. F, 12th Regt. Vermont Vols. in 1862 and 1863. He was a farmer, and later engineer of the water works at Lebanon, N. H. He married at Waitsfield, Vt., Aug. 22, 1862, Sarah J. Bates, born in Waitsfield, Dec. 22, 1839, daughter of Ira and Eliza (Jones) Bates of Waitsfield.

Children of John Gunnison and Sarah J., born in Waitsfield:

1148. GERTRUDE FRANCES, b. May 11, 1864; m. Edmund T. Huntington; lives at Randolph, Vt.
1149. FRED EVERETT, b. Oct. 7, 1865; lives at West Roxbury, Mass.
1150. GEORGE RENTON, b. Mar. 15, 1867; m. Ada Goodwin; lives at Lebanon, N. H.

1151. Ernest Leroy, b. Nov. 7, 1868; d. Aug. 12, 1875.
1152. Mary Ailene, b. Feb. 10, 1870; m. Bertram L. Joslin; lives at Waitsfield, Vt.
1153. Harriet Naomi, b. Mar. 19, 1872; lives at Lebanon, N. H.
1154. Edwin Colby, b. Aug. 5, 1873; lives at Lebanon, N. H.

894 Edwin Colby Lewis, born in Northfield, Vt., Jan. 5, 1842, was a photographer, and lived in Texas until June, 1882, when he removed to Waitsfield, Vt., and died there Feb. 27, 1883. He was a private in Co. F, 1st Regt. Vermont Vols., 2d Lieut. Co. G, 6th Regt. Vermont Vols., and was transferred and appointed Capt. of Co. H, 13th Regt. Heavy Artillery (colored), and served until the end of the Civil War. He married, first, at Northfield, Vt., Aug. 15, 1862, Jane King, who died in Northfield, daughter of Nathaniel and —— (Dole) King of Northfield, Vt. He married, second, in Galveston, Texas, in 1875, Annie Kane, who died in Jefferson, Texas, August, 1877. He married, third, in Galveston, Texas, Oct. 21, 1878, Kate, daughter of Patrick and Katherine Devine of White Sulphur Springs, Va.

Children of Edwin Colby and Annie:

1155. Robert Edwin, b. May 5, 1876, in Port Henry, N. Y.; lives at Hanover, N. H.
1156. Harry, b. May 5, 1876, in Port Henry, N. Y.; d. Aug., 1877.

Children of Edwin Colby and Kate:

1157. Edwin Colby, b. Mar. 29, 1879, in Bryan, Tex.; lives at St. Johnsbury, Vt.
1158. Kate Mae, b. Oct. 27, 1881, in Bryan, Texas; lives at St. Johnsbury, Vt.

895 Charles Everett Lewis, born in Northfield, Vt., Jan. 25, 1844, is a photographer. Lived at Northfield, Vt., until 1870, then removed to Lebanon, N. H. He married, first, at Waitsfield, Vt., Jan. 25, 1866, Jane M. Bugbee, born at Cabot, Vt., April 7, 1844, daughter of Alanson and Harriet (Chandler) Bugbee of Northfield, who died at Lebanon, N. H., April 11, 1882. He married, second, at Newton Centre, Mass., Aug. 20, 1884, Sarah C.

Ross, born Mar. 16, 1856, daughter of Edmund and Mary (Carmichael) Ross of Margaree, Cape Breton.

Children of Charles Everett and Jane M.:

1159. ARTHUR ALANSON, b. Dec. 16, 1866.
1160. FLORENCE JANE, b. Feb. 11, 1869; d. Aug. 15, 1875.
1161. MINNIE, b. Sept. 14, 1870; d. Oct. 19, 1870.
1162. ANNIE MAE, b. May 4, 1878.

Children of Charles Everett and Sarah C.:

1163. GUY CHARLES (twin), b. Nov. 11, 1889.
1164. ROY EVERETT (twin), b. Nov. 11, 1889.
1165. PERCY JOHN, b. Apr. 29, 1891.

983 Oliver Questram Lewis, born in Lynn, Aug. 6, 1826, married there, Nov. 5, 1745, Sarah Ann Johnson, born Dec. 30, 1826, and died May 11, 1899, daughter of Benjamin B. and Lydia (Bacheller) Johnson of Lynn.

Children of Oliver Questram and Sarah A.:

1166. ANNA WARREN, b. Mar. 9, 1849, in Swampscott; m. Oct. 28, 1869, in Lynn, Caleb B. Neagles, b. in Malden, s. of Ebenezer and Mary Neagles.
1167. ABBA JOHNSON, b. May 3, 1851; m. Nov. 30, 1870, in Lynn, Charles A. Dwyer, b. in Salem, s. of Edward A. and Sarah E. Dwyer.
1168. MARY ISABEL, b. 1856, in Nahant; m. Mar. 31, 1875, in Lynn, Eddie W. Stone, b. in Lynn, s. of John S. and Harriet M. Stone.
1169. ARTHUR C., b. 1859, in Nahant; m. Dec. 1, 1880, in Salem, Minnie A. Childs, b. in Melrose, dau. of Warren F. and Cynthia Childs.
1170. LUCY E., d. May 17, 1889, æ. 26 y. 6 m.
1171. HENRY A., b. in Swampscott; m. Feb. 22, 1887, in Lynn, Luna S. Graves, b. in Marblehead, dau. of Samuel C. and Mary E. Graves. Had: (1) Gladys May, b. Apr. 19, 1891.
1172. BENJAMIN H. J., b. Aug. 2, 1866; d. Sept. 18, 1866.

991 Fitzwilliam Griffin Lewis, was born in Lynn, July 7, 1834, and died Dec. 25, 1867. He married in Lynn, May 22, 1856, Mary Adelaide Ireson, born Sept. 8, 1834, daughter of Benjamin and Hannah (Choate) Ireson, jr., of Lynn.

Children of Fitzwilliam Griffin and Mary A.:

1173. WILLIAM HERBERT, b. April 14, 1857; m. July 5, 1890, Harriet Hammond, at Somersworth, N. H.
1174. LLOYD GLOVER, b. Nov. 25, 1861; m. Nov. 4, 1891, in Lynn, Carrie Florence Shillaber, b. in Danvers, Sept. 23, 1859, dau. of Daniel and Nancy (Richardson) Shillaber. Had: (1) Marion Shillaber, b. Aug. 2, 1892; (2) Philip Henry, b. July 14, 1894; (3) Benjamin Ireson, b. Sept. 4, 1895; (4) Carrie Florence, b. Feb. 19, 1900; d. Aug. 1, 1900.
1175. CARO W., b. April 30, 1866; d. Oct. 18, 1904; m., 1st, Aug. 3, 1886, in Lynn, Charles A. Howland, b. in Kenosha, Wis., Dec. 24, 1857, d. May 6, 1887, s. of Charles C. and Margaret (Ayer) Howland. Had: (1) Louise Ayer, b. May 26, 1887; m. Dec. 24, 1904, Chester Bickford, at W. Rumney, N. H. Caro W. m. 2d, Mar. 29, 1892, George Dodge of Bennington, N. H. Had: (1) George Lewis, b. May 6, 1894; (2) Gladys, b. Jan. 17, 1897.

992 Nathan Bickford Lewis born in Lynn, Sept. 20, 1836, married Mary R. Marsh.

Children of Nathan Bickford and Mary R.:

1176. EDWARD ELBRIDGE, b. April 20, 1858; m. Oct. 15, 1879, in Lynn, Eliza N. Tufts, b. in Lynn, dau. of Charles S. and Clara A. Tufts. Had: (1) Bertha M., b. May 20, 1880; d. April 6, 1886; (2) Irving E., b. April 13, 1882; (3) Robert E., b. May 13, 1884; d. May 14, 1884; (4) Lillian B., b. June 16, 1887.
1177. CHARLES AUGUSTUS, b. Jan. 30, 1860; m. Feb. 3, 1881, in Swampscott, Abbie M. Bates, b. in Marblehead, dau. of Joseph and Eliza M. Bates.
1178. ELLIOTT HERBERT, b. June 18, 1869.
1179. ANNA MABEL, b. 1871; m. Dec. 18, 1890, in Lynn, William O. Collyer, s. of John O. and Hannah M. Collyer.
1180. ARTHUR GERRY, b. June 2, 1876; d. Oct. 17, 1877.
1181. HATTIE L., b. 1879; m. Nov. 19, 1896, in Lynn, Charles A. Collins, s. of Charles H. and Jennie B. Collins.

1107 Walter Felix Lewis was born Aug. 23, 1846, and died June 27, 1903. He married Monemia Chase.

Children of Walter Felix and Monemia:

1182. Walter Howard, b. Feb. 3, 1873; d. July 29, 1873.
1183. George Chase, b. May 18, 1876; Lieutenant U. S. Army.
1184. Florence Parthenia, b. Sept. 24, 1877,
1185. Frances Ann, b. Feb. 1, 1884.
1186. Susan Elizabeth, b. Sept. 14, 1885.
1187. Walter Felix, b. July 13, 1889.
1188. Eugene Grayson, b. Feb. 8, 1896.

1108 Edward Simmons Lewis born in Richmond, Missouri, Aug. 22, 1848, is Vice-President of the Hargadine-McKittrick Dry Goods Co. of St. Louis, Mo., and President of the Central National Bank. In 1891 he was elected Vice-President of the Colonial Trust Co., and has served as an officer and director of several financial institutions in St. Louis. He has held the highest offices in the Traveller's Protective Association of Missouri and the National Wholesale Dry Goods Association. He resides in St. Louis, Mo. He married, first, Dec. 23, 1869, Julia McElheney. He married, second, April 4, 1876, Pattie Cooke.

Children of Edward Simmons and Julia:

1189. Edward McElheney, b. Jan. 15, 1871; d. Jan. 2, 1883.
1190. Julian, b. Feb. 17, 1872; d. Mar. 9, 1872.

Children of Edward Simmons and Pattie:

1191. Watson Cooke, b. Nov. 22, 1879.
1192. Augusta Bransford, b. Dec. 25, 1881; m. May 6, 1905, C. V. D. Hill.
1193. Edward McElheney, b. Jan. 25, 1884.
1194. Pattie Marian, b. June 9, 1886.

ADDENDA.

14. ABIGAIL, d. May 30, 1700.
23. THOMAS, m. Elizabeth Brooks, dau. of Timothy and Mary (Russell) Brooks of Swansey, formerly of Billerica.
32. JOSEPH, b. June 6, 1672. (Swansea Rds.)
35. HANNAH'S son (1) John (Stocker), b. Feb. 15, 1712-13.
49. JOSEPH, d. Nov. 23, 1729, æ. 30 y. 6 m. (Copp's Hill Epitaphs.)
50. EUNICE, pub. Mar. 26, 1720.
53. NATHANIEL, probably d. young.
54. ABIGAIL, b. Jan. 8, 1691-2.
66. ELIZABETH, d. Sept. 13, 1761, æ. 56 y. She m. 1st, Nov. 24, 1727, Ens. Hezekiah Shailer, b. May 9, 1706; d. Sept. 10, 1752, son of Thomas and Catherine Shailer of Haddam, Conn. She m. 2d, Lieut. David Smith.
69. DEBORAH, d. 1775, æ. 56 y. Her husband, Daniel Clark, d. 1787, æ. 67 y. (Church Rds.)
70. JOHN and wife Deborah were admitted to Haddam, Ct., Cong. Church, March, 1759, and dismissed by letter to church at Chester, Conn., in 1767. (Church Rds.)
113. JOSEPH, m. Sarah ——, and lived at Saybrook, Conn. His father (John (70) of Saybrook) deeded house, barn and 18 acres land in Chester, Apr. 4, 1780, to son Joseph. Had: (1) Deborah, b. Dec. 20, 1768. (2) Sarah, b. Aug. 27, 1770.
157. John Lewis born in Boston, May 10, 1774; married Susanna (Brown?), born Dec. 18, 1773, and died in Boston, Nov. 26, 1837.

Children of John and Susanna:

HARRIET.

AMOS LEWIS, b. Mar. 20, 1794 in Boston, enlisted in the Boston Home Guard in 1813, and was appointed master sailmaker in the U. S. Navy, Jan. 3, 1825 and served on board the frigates Constitution and Constellation (g.s.). He received his discharge Sept. 7, 1832. The Bible which he carried while in the service is now is the possession of his son Benjamin Lewis of Somers Point, Atlantic Co. N.J. It is said that all his teeth were double teeth and at the time of his death that he had lost but one. After his discharge from the naval service he followed his occupation as sailmaker which his three sons under the name of Lewis Bros., continued after his death. He lived in Boston, New York City, and Somers Point, N. J. where he d. March 20,

1875. He m. 1st, in Boston, Mass., Elizabeth Menunisoir. He m. 2d, Dec. 14, 1823, in Boston, Anna Hovey McIntyre, b. July 31, 1796, and d. Dec. 6, 1851 at Somers Point, N. J., daughter of Andrew and Rachel McIntyre. He m. 3d, July 23, 1853, widow Jane (Stillwell) Westcoat, who after his death lived in Philadelphia, Pa.

Children of Amos and Elizabeth, born in Boston:

I. John Brown, b. April 28, 1816; m. 1st, Nancy Lockett of Newbern, N. C. and had (1) William Henry; (2) Adelaide; (3) Mary Anna. Married 2d: Caroline ———, of Baltimore, Md. and had (4) Amos Edwards; (5) John Emmett.

II. Elizabeth, b. Sept. 13, 1819; m. —— Ellis of New York City.

Children of Amos and Anna Hovey:

III. Anne Maria, b. Oct. 22, 1825, in Boston; d. unm. Jan. 8, 1907.

IV. Adelaide, b. May 27, 1827, in New York City; m. Jan. 27, 1849, John I. Steelman, s. of John I. and Jemima (Steelman) Steelman, and had (1) Emily, m. James C. Fisher of Morris & Fisher, manufacturers of fish oil and fertilizer at Reedville, Va.; (2) Anna Hovey McIntyre, m. Albert Morris; (3) Addie, d. unm.; (4) Lewis, m. Eva Blackman, and had: (a) Addie, (b) Vera, (c) Stanley Lewis; (5) John Craig, m. Lillie Hickman, Mayor of Linwood, N. J., and had (1) Freda.

V. Thomas Kendall, b. July 20, 1829, in New York City; m. Mary Almira Lake, dau. of Enoch and Eliza Lake, and had: (1) Harriet Somers; m. David Westcoat, and had (a) Lewis Crosby; (2) Elmer Somers; (3) Anna Eliza, m. —— Riggins; (4) Sarah Elizabeth, d. unm.; (5) Lynden; (6) Frederick; (7) Jennie, m. —— Kelley.

VI. Benjamin Willis (twin), b. Dec. 11, 1831, in Somers Point, N. J.; m. Annie Smallwood, dau. of Abel and Naomi Smallwood, and had: (1) John G., m. Willimena Ingersoll; (2) Caroline, m. George Jeffries; (3) Anna Mary, m. Elfrey D. Gooy; (4) Emily, m. Richard J. Somers; (5) Walter; (6) Luola, m. her cousin Matthew C. Fife (see below.); (7) Lillie, m. —— Fenton; (8) Ida; (9) Benjamin.

VII. Amos (twin), b. Dec. 11, 1831, in Somers Point, N. J.; m. 1st, widow Sarah Ireland; m. 2d, Annie Risley. No issue.

VIII. Caroline Willis, b. Mar. 25, 1834, in Somers Point, N. J.; unm., resides Linwood, N. J.

IX. Mary Willis, b. July 17, 1836, in Somers Point, N. J., m. 1st, Matthew E. Fife, s. of Matthew and Margaret Fife, and had: (1) Margaret; (2) Annetta, d. young; (3) Matthew C., m. his cousin Luola Lewis (see above); (4) Luola, m. James McMullin. Mrs. Fife m. 2d, Abram J'agoe and resides in Philadelphia, Pa.

158. Lydia, b. 1775; d. July 25, 1814.

161. Asa, b. 1777.

164. Thomas, b. April 4, 1771; was in business with his father as Thomas Lewis & Son.

171. Samuel Shaw Lewis should be number 170.

193. Samuel, d. in Lancaster, Pa. Was a major on General Washington's staff and distinguished himself at the battle of Germantown.

280. Francis B.'s dau. (2) Mary Frances, m. Albert Lewis, a descendant of William Lewis of Roxbury, 1630.

339. Catherine L's son: (1) Henry Ware d. Nov. 28, 1900, in Auburn, Calif.

353. Charles Henry, m. Almira Tufts, dau. of Joseph Warren Tufts.

380. Henry, d. May 25, 1811.

439. William Gifford, was killed at the battle of the Alamo.

500. William Crosby, m. Emeline Augusta Bellows, b. in Westboro, Mass., Oct. 2, 1805.

604. Abigail Fielding, m. Joseph H. Valpey, b. Feb. 23, 1823, son of Richard and Mary Ann (Emmerton) Valpey.

722. Henry L. not Henry G.

757. Harriet I. did not die Oct. 7, 1893.

875. Nancy's dau.: (2) Eliza R. m. Sept. 4, 1873.

885. Selina's dau.: (2) Nora Belle, b. Jan. 7, 1874.

888a. and 888b. belong to the family of Reuben (507).

ADDENDA.

(Continued.)

9. Thomas married Mary, dau. of Allen, Senior, and Mary (——) Breed, whose son Allen, Jr., brother of Mary, married Elizabeth Ballard.

342. Joseph Lewis family, foot of page 91.

492. David Crosby, m. three times, and had son Winslow R., who lives in New Haven, Conn., as mentioned in error with No. 500.

500. William Crosby, whose family is correctly given on p. 110.

574. Jacob Meek, was mayor 1873-1877, not 1887, page 80.

825. John Willard, not James Willard, page 140.

888a, 888b, page 112. Error, see 889 and 890, page 113.

CHRISTIAN NAMES OF PERSONS BEARING THE NAME OF LEWIS

Where the name appears more than once it is marked (2).

The numbers in parenthesis are of individuals; the numbers following are the pages where they appear.

INDEX OF SURNAMES OF OTHERS THAN LEWIS.

Where more than one person of the name appears on the page it is marked (2).